AN INCLUSIVE-LANGUAGE LECTIONARY

Readings for Year B

Prepared for experimental and voluntary use in churches by the Inclusive-Language Lectionary Committee appointed by the Division of Education and Ministry, National Council of the Churches of Christ in the U.S.A.

Published for
The Cooperative Publication Association
by
John Knox Press, *Atlanta*
The Pilgrim Press, *New York*
The Westminster Press, *Philadelphia*

BOOK DESIGN BY ALICE DERR

PRINTED IN THE UNITED STATES OF AMERICA
9 8 7 6 5 4 3 2 1

Library of Congress Cataloging in Publication Data

Main entry under title:

An Inclusive-language lectionary. Readings for year B.

Includes bibliographical references and index.
1. Bible—Liturgical lessons, English. 2. Lectionaries—Texts. 3. Sexism in liturgical language. I. National Council of the Churches of Christ in the United States of America. Inclusive Language Lectionary Committee.
BS391.2.I522 1984   264'.34   84-7420
ISBN 0-664-24564-1 (Westminster Press : pbk. : Year B)

Preface

All persons are equally loved, judged, and accepted by God. This belief has been promoted by the church and has its roots in the origins of the Judeo-Christian tradition. Young and old, male and female, and persons of every racial, cultural, and national background are included in the faith community. Basic to a sense of equality and inclusiveness is the recognition that God by nature transcends all human categories. God is more than male or female, and is more than can be described in historically and culturally limiting terms. Words and language, though inadequate and limited, are means by which we convey God's holiness and mystery. Seeking faithful expression about God and about God's inclusive love for all people, the Division of Education and Ministry of the National Council of the Churches of Christ authorized the preparation of AN INCLUSIVE-LANGUAGE LECTIONARY.

A Task Force on Biblical Translation was appointed by the Division of Education and Ministry to investigate the way in which the language of the Bible presents the characteristics of God and of people. In 1980, after almost three years of study and discussion, the Task Force recommended to the Division the creation of an Inclusive-Language Lectionary Committee. Twelve persons were appointed, six women and six men. The Committee members bring not only their personal commitment to the Christian faith and involvement in particular congregations but also their experience as pastors, teachers, and leaders who have relied on the Bible as their source of inspiration and basis for understanding God's word for the church today. They bring expertise in Hebrew, Greek, linguistics, English, worship, Old and New Testaments, theology, and education. In addition, the members come from a variety of denominations and liturgical traditions. The Inclusive-Language Lectionary Committee consists of Robert A. Bennett, Dianne Bergant, Victor Roland Gold (Chair), Thomas Hoyt, Jr., Kellie C. Jones, Patrick D. Miller, Jr., Virginia Ramey Mollenkott, Sharon H. Ringe (Vice-Chair), Susan Thistlethwaite, Burton

3

H. Throckmorton, Jr., and Barbara A. Withers. David Ng is the National Council of Churches' liaison to the Committee.

The Inclusive-Language Lectionary Committee followed the general guidelines provided by the Division of Education and Ministry to prepare lectionary readings in inclusive language for use in services of worship. These readings are based on the Revised Standard Version of the Bible, with the text revised primarily in those places where gender-specific or otherwise inappropriately exclusive language could be modified to reflect in English an inclusiveness of all persons. The Committee worked on lectionary passages first in subcommittees. This initial study was based upon Greek and Hebrew texts, other translations, and commentaries. All subcommittee work was submitted to an Editorial Committee, which reviewed the texts for consistency of changes and agreement with guiding principles. Then the full Committee reviewed all work and made all final decisions.

Like most other lectionaries in use today, this lectionary follows the pattern of a three-year cycle beginning with the first Sunday in Advent. The readings for Series A were published in October of 1983, and followed the table of readings prepared by the Consultation on Church Union. This second volume for Series B contains the readings from the Table of Readings and Psalms prepared by the North American Committee on Calendar and Lectionary. The third volume, Series C (to be published for use beginning in Advent 1985), will also follow the latter table of readings. It is expected that Series A will be revised to conform to the readings prescribed by the North American Committee.

The Introduction which follows offers an explanation of what a lectionary is and discusses the need for inclusive language and how the Committee approached the bias discerned in the language of the Revised Standard Version. The lectionary passages, along with explanatory footnotes, form the major portion of this volume. An appendix, stating a rationale for the major alternative words and phrases, and an index of the Bible passages that appear in this lectionary complete this volume.

AN INCLUSIVE-LANGUAGE LECTIONARY is offered to the church as a provisional, experimental, and responsible attempt to proclaim the biblical message in an inclusive manner. Its use is voluntary, and responses are invited and can be addressed to the Division of Education and Ministry, National Council of the Churches of Christ, Room 704, 475 Riverside Drive, New York, New York 10115-0050. The hope is that no one will find that she or he has been excluded from hearing the words of promise and fulfillment. God loves and seeks to bring all persons into God's community. This rendering of the lectionary texts attempts to express that message.

Introduction

A lectionary is a fixed selection of readings, taken from both the Old and the New Testament, to be read and heard in the churches' services of worship. Most lectionaries are simply tables or lists of readings. They cite the biblical book from which the reading is taken, as well as the chapter and verses: for example, on Christmas Day, Luke 2:1-20. This lectionary contains the full text of each reading.

History of Lectionary Development. The International Commission on English in the Liturgy created an ecumenical group known as the Consultation on Common Texts. One of the tasks of the Consultation was to explore the possibilities of creating a lectionary that would be acceptable to most English-speaking Christians: Anglican, Protestant, and Roman Catholic. To that end, a small working group known as the North American Committee on Calendar and Lectionary was formed. Over a period of five years a revised table of lections, or readings, was developed that took into account the acknowledged critique of the Vatican II lectionary (early 1960s) and its subsequent adaptations by the major Protestant denominations. The report of the North American Committee was approved by the Consultation on Common Texts in 1982, and this "common texts" lectionary has been recommended for trial use in the churches beginning with Advent 1983. It is this Table of Readings and Psalms which this lectionary follows, using the Revised Standard Version as its text. The lectionary attempts to provide comprehensive and balanced coverage of the entire Bible. Over a three-year period about 95 percent of the New Testament is heard, as well as about 60 percent of the Old Testament.

Function of the Lectionary in Congregational Worship. In churches that use the lectionary every Sunday, congregations will hear the same scriptures. Thus the wider church, within denominations and across denominational lines, is united in its hearing and thinking and praying. A lectionary provides a way for Christians to live out the church year, which begins on the first Sunday of Advent and proceeds through Christmas, Epiphany, Ash Wednesday, Lent, Passion (Palm) Sunday, Maundy Thursday, Good Friday, Easter, Ascension, and Pentecost. At least four readings are prescribed for each Sunday and for special days such as Christmas, Easter, All Saints, and Thanksgiving.

It is apparent that any selection of scripture read in a service of worship has been lifted from its biblical context. In the study of the Bible, the context in which a biblical passage occurs is crucial to its interpretation. When passages are read in a service of worship, however, they are read in a new context and in relation to the church year. This radical change in the context of selections is one factor that differentiates a lectionary from the Bible.

A lectionary thus has a special function in the worship of the church. It does not supplant the Bible. The Bible is the church's book—created by and for the church. A lectionary is also the church's book, being a prescribed set of readings selected by the church from its scripture for its own special use in worship. The unique feature of AN INCLUSIVE-LANGUAGE LECTIONARY is that it recasts some of the wording of the Revised Standard Version in order to provide reader and hearer with a sense of belonging to a Christian faith community in which truly all are one in Christ.

Why Inclusive Language? The lectionary readings are based on the Revised Standard Version and the original Greek and Hebrew texts, with the intent of reflecting the full humanity of women and men in the light of the gospel. A growing number of people feel they have been denied full humanity by a pattern of exclusion in English usage. Consider, for example, the traditional English use of the word "man." A man is a male being, as opposed to a female being. But in common usage "man" has also meant "human being," as opposed to "animal." On the other hand, "woman" means female, but never *human being*. No word that refers to a female person identifies her with humanity. So the common English idiom has been subject to the understanding that "man" has been defined by his humanity, but "woman" by her sex, by her relationship to man. "Woman" becomes a subgroup under "human." "Man" is the human race; "woman" is man's sexual partner in traditional English usage.

These are some examples of how language *reflects* the way in which we think but also *informs* the way in which we think. The mandate to the Inclusive-Language Lectionary Committee is to seek "language which expresses inclusiveness with regard to human beings and which attempts to expand the range of images beyond the masculine to assist the church in understanding the full nature of God." In the Appendix the reader will find specific examples of how these kinds of exclusive imagery have been dealt with in this lectionary.

The RSV is highly respected by biblical scholars and is widely used in this country. However, in this lectionary the wording of the RSV has been recast to minimize the male bias and other exclusive imagery reflected in its language about human beings and the male bias reflected in language about Christ and God. Except for these changes the text of the RSV has been retained.

Male bias, however, is not unique to English translations of the Bible; it is characteristic of its original languages. Both the Old Testament and the New Testament were written in languages and in cultures that were basically patriarchal; and as the English language is also patriarchal, the patriarchal character of both Testaments has slipped easily into the great English versions of the Bible.

Language About Human Beings. In a few instances the RSV Bible committee has already avoided male bias in reference to human beings. For example, in Rom. 7:1 the RSV has used "person" ("the law is binding on a *person*") as a translation of the Greek word *anthropos* (meaning "man" or "person"). But most of the time *anthropos* is translated "man" or, in the plural, "men." For example, Matt. 5:16 in the RSV reads, "Let your light so shine before *men*" where the meaning of "men" is obviously "people," but not male people exclusively. This verse can be rendered, "Let your light so shine before *others*"—i.e., men and women, which represents the clear intention of the words.

Male bias also appears when masculine pronoun subjects are supplied with third person singular verbs when the context does not require them. Compare, for example, the RSV of John 6:35-37: "Jesus said to them, 'I am the bread of life; *he* who comes to me shall not hunger, and *he* who believes in me shall never thirst . . . ; and *him* who comes to me I will not cast out." What is the intention of this passage? It surely is not that only *men* come to Jesus and believe in Jesus. Why, then, does the RSV read "he" and "him"? It is because of the assumption that "he" also means "she," though we know that it does not.

In this lectionary all readings have been recast so that no masculine word pretends to include a woman. For example, the word "brethren" has been rendered in a variety of ways, including "sisters and brothers." Formal equivalents have been adopted for other male-specific words and phrases. For example, "kingdom" is rendered "realm" or occasionally "reign"; "king" in reference to God or a messianic figure is rendered "ruler" or "monarch."

Where appropriate, references to women have been added, for example, "Abraham [*and Sarah*]." Contemporary English usage also suggests that we refer to a "person with a disabling condition" rather than to a "cripple" or a "crippled person." So the biblical reference to "the blind and the lame" is rendered "those who are blind and those who are lame" (see Jer. 31:8). Where "darkness" is set in contrast with "light" and has a moral connotation, a substitute word for darkness is supplied—for example, "The light shines in the *deepest night*" (John 1:5).

Language About Jesus Christ. Jesus was a male human being. But when the Gospel of John says, "The Word became flesh" (John 1:14), it does not say or imply that the Word became *male* flesh, but simply *flesh*. Of course, to "become flesh," the one from God had to become male or female, but the language used in this lectionary tries to overcome the implication that in the incarnation Jesus' *maleness* is decisive—or even relevant—for the salvation of women and men who believe. From the very beginning of the church the salvation of women has been assumed to be equal to the salvation of men.

In this lectionary the fact of Jesus' maleness is taken for granted. Jesus is referred to as a man, and the pronouns "he," "his," and "him" are used when the reference is to the historical person. However, the name "Jesus," as well as other proper names, is occasionally substituted for pronouns both for the sake of clarity and to avoid pronoun repetition. The use of the proper name also deemphasizes Jesus' maleness, so that in hearing the gospel, the church may be reminded of the inclusiveness of all humanity in the incarnation. Pronoun references to the preexistent and postcrucifixion Jesus are replaced by the proper names—Jesus, Christ, or Jesus Christ. Formal equivalents adopted for "the Son of man," "Son," and "Son of God" are, respectively, "the Human One," "Child," and "Child of God." (For a discussion of these terms, see the Appendix.)

Language About God. The God worshiped by the biblical authors and worshiped in the church today cannot be regarded as having gender, race, or color. Such attributes are used metaphorically or analogically. God the Father is only one metaphor for God; other personal metaphors include God as mother, midwife, and breadmaker. Less familiar, but equally appropriate, are such impersonal images for God as Love, Rock, and Light. This lectionary tries to speak of God so that when the church hears its scripture read, it is not overwhelmed by the male metaphors but is also allowed to hear female metaphors for God.

In the RSV Old Testament, the major names for God are "God" (*elohim*), "LORD" (*Yahweh*), and "Lord" (*adonai*), and several variations of these nouns, for example, "the LORD God" and "the GOD of hosts." In this lectionary, "LORD" (*Yahweh*) is rendered "GOD" or "SOVEREIGN ONE" and "Lord" (*adonai*) is rendered "God."

In the New Testament passages in this lectionary the formal equivalent adopted for "God the Father" or "the Father" is "God the Father [*and Mother*]" or "God the [*Mother and*] Father." The words that have been added to the text and that may be omitted in reading are italicized and in brackets. If the reader chooses to omit the bracketed words, the sentence will read exactly as rendered in the RSV. Where God is called "Father" several times in a single passage, as is frequently the case in the Gospel of John, the word "Father" is rendered "God." (For an explanation of metaphor, and of specific ways in which this lectionary has recast scriptural language about God and images for God, see the Appendix.)

TOWARD THE FUTURE

AN INCLUSIVE-LANGUAGE LECTIONARY is a first attempt to rethink the language of scripture as inclusive of both men and women, and as such it is provisional and experimental. Although scripture is written in patriarchal language, it is clear that God is not a patriarch. Our mandate for affirming the inclusiveness of the scriptures is found in the scriptures themselves. The apostle Paul wrote: "There is neither male nor female, for you are all one in Christ Jesus" (Gal. 3:28).

ADVENT 1

Lesson 1 ~ Isaiah 63:16–64:8

Hear the prophet's intercessory prayer.

16For you, O God, are our Father [*and Mother**],
   though Abraham [*and Sarah***] do not know us
   and Israel does not acknowledge us;
   you, O SOVEREIGN ONE, are our Father [*and Mother**],
   our Redeemer from of old is your name.
17O SOVEREIGN ONE, why do you make us err from your ways
   and harden our heart, so that we do not fear you?
Return for the sake of your servants,
   the tribes of your heritage.
18Your holy people possessed your sanctuary a little while;
   our adversaries have trodden it down.
19We have become like those over whom you have never ruled,
   like those who are not called by your name.
64:1O that you would rend the heavens and come down,
   that the mountains might quake at your presence—
2as when fire kindles brushwood
   and the fire causes water to boil—
to make your name known to your adversaries,
   and that the nations might tremble at your presence!
3When you did terrible things which we looked not for,
   you came down, the mountains quaked at your presence.
4From of old no one has heard
   or perceived by the ear,
no eye has seen a God besides you,
   who works for those who wait for God.
5You meet the one that joyfully works righteousness,
   those that remember you in your ways.
Behold, you were angry, and we sinned;
   in our sins we have been a long time, and shall we be saved?
6We have all become like one who is unclean,
   and all our righteous deeds are like a polluted garment.
We all fade like a leaf,
   and our iniquities, like the wind, take us away.
7There is no one that calls upon your name,
   that bestirs oneself to take hold of you;

---

*Addition to the text. See "Metaphor" and "God the Father and Mother" in the Appendix.
**Addition to the text. RSV *Abraham does.* See Appendix.

10

for you have hidden your face from us,
  and have delivered us into the hand of our iniquities.
⁸Yet, O SOVEREIGN ONE, you are our Father [*and Mother**];
  we are the clay, and you are our potter;
  we are all the work of your hand.

Psalm 80:1-7

¹Give ear, O Shepherd of Israel,
  you who lead Joseph like a flock!
You who are enthroned upon the cherubim, shine forth
² before Ephraim and Benjamin and Manasseh!
Stir up your might,
  and come to save us!
³Restore us, O God;
  let your face shine, that we may be saved!
⁴O SOVEREIGN ONE, God of hosts,
  how long will you be angry with your people's prayers?
⁵You have fed them with the bread of tears,
  and given them tears to drink in full measure.
⁶You make us the scorn of our neighbors;
  and our enemies laugh among themselves.
⁷Restore us, O God of hosts;
  let your face shine, that we may be saved!

Lesson 2 ~ 1 Corinthians 1:3-9

Paul thanks the Corinthians because of the grace of God given them.

³Grace to you and peace from God our Father [*and Mother**] and from the Sovereign□ Jesus Christ.

⁴I give thanks to God always for you because of the grace of God which was given you in Christ Jesus, ⁵that in every way you were enriched in Christ with all speech and all knowledge—⁶even as the testimony to Christ was confirmed among you—⁷so that you are not lacking in any spiritual gift, as you wait for the revealing of our Sovereign□ Jesus Christ; ⁸who will sustain you to the end, guiltless in the day of our Sovereign□ Jesus Christ. ⁹God is faithful, by whom you were called to share with God's Child,◇ Jesus Christ our Sovereign.□

---

*Addition to the text. See "Metaphor" and "God the Father and Mother" in the Appendix.
□RSV *Lord.* See Appendix.
◇RSV *his Son.* See Appendix.

11

Gospel ~ Mark 13:32-37

The disciples are told they are to be on the watch, for they do not know when the Sovereign will come.

³²But of that day or that hour no one knows, not even the angels in heaven, nor the Child,° but only [*God*] the Father [*and Mother**]. ³³Take heed, watch; for you do not know when the time will come. ³⁴It is like some one going on a journey, who, upon leaving home, puts the servants in charge, each with a particular task, and commands the doorkeeper to be on the watch. ³⁵Watch therefore—for you do not know when the sovereign□ will come, in the evening or at midnight, or at cockcrow, or in the morning—³⁶lest the sovereign come suddenly and find you asleep. ³⁷And what I say to you I say to all: Watch.

°RSV *Son*. See Appendix.
*Addition to the text. See "Metaphor" and "God the Father and Mother" in the Appendix.
□RSV *master of the house*. See Appendix.

ADVENT 2

Lesson 1 ~ Isaiah 40:1-11

The prophet announces the coming of God.

¹Comfort, comfort my people,
    says your God.
²Speak tenderly to Jerusalem,
    and cry to it
that its warfare is ended,
    that its iniquity is pardoned,
that it has received from GOD's hand
    double for all its sins.
³A voice cries:
    "In the wilderness prepare the way of the SOVEREIGN ONE,
    make straight in the desert a highway for our God.
⁴Every valley shall be lifted up,
    and every mountain and hill be made low;
the uneven ground shall become level,
    and the rough places a plain.
⁵And the glory of GOD shall be revealed,
    and all flesh shall see it together,
    for the mouth of GOD has spoken."
⁶A voice says, "Cry!"
    And I said, "What shall I cry?"
All flesh is grass,
    and all its beauty is like the flower of the field.
⁷The grass withers, the flower fades,
    when the breath of GOD blows upon it;
    surely the people is grass.
⁸The grass withers, the flower fades;
    but the word of our God will stand for ever.
⁹Get you up to a high mountain,
    O Zion, herald of good tidings;
lift up your voice with strength,
    O Jerusalem, herald of good tidings,
    lift it up, fear not;
say to the cities of Judah,
    "Behold your God!"
¹⁰Behold, the Sovereign GOD comes with might,
    and rules with a mighty arm;
behold, God's reward is with God,
    and God's recompense before God.

[11]God will feed the flock like a shepherd,
   gather the lambs in God's arms,
 carry them in God's bosom,
   and gently lead those that are with young.

Psalm 85:8-13

[8]Let me hear what God the Sovereign One will speak,
   for God will speak peace to God's people,
     to God's saints, to those who turn to God in their hearts.
[9]Surely salvation is at hand for those who fear God,
   that glory may dwell in our land.
[10]Steadfast love and faithfulness will meet;
   righteousness and peace will kiss each other.
[11]Faithfulness will spring up from the ground,
   and righteousness will look down from the sky.
[12]The Sovereign One will give what is good,
   and our land will yield its increase.
[13]Righteousness will go before God,
   and make God's footsteps a way.

Lesson 2 ~ 2 Peter 3:8-15a

The author tells Christians they are to wait for the day of God and the coming of the Sovereign.

[8]But do not ignore this one fact, beloved, that with the Sovereign□ one day is as a thousand years, and a thousand years as one day. [9]The Sovereign□ is not slow in fulfilling the promise as some count slowness, but is forbearing toward you, not wishing that any should perish, but that all should reach repentance. [10]But the day of the Sovereign□ will come like a thief, and then the heavens will pass away with a loud noise, and the elements will be dissolved with fire, and the earth and the works that are upon it will be burned up.

[11]Since all these things are thus to be dissolved, what sort of persons ought you to be in lives of holiness and godliness, [12]waiting for and hastening the coming of the day of God, because of which the heavens will be kindled and dissolved, and the elements will melt with fire! [13]But according to the Sovereign's promise we wait for new heavens and a new earth in which righteousness dwells.

□RSV *Lord.* See Appendix.

¹⁴Therefore, beloved, since you wait for these, be zealous to be found by the Sovereign without spot or blemish, and at peace. ¹⁵And count the forbearance of our Sovereign□ as salvation.

Gospel ~ Mark 1:1-8

Mark begins the Gospel with the announcement of the coming of John the Baptist.

¹The beginning of the gospel of Jesus Christ, the Child◇ of God.
²As it is written in Isaiah the prophet,
"Behold, I send my messenger before your face,
who shall prepare your way;
³ the voice of one crying in the wilderness:
Prepare the way of the Sovereign,□
make the paths of the Sovereign straight—"
⁴John the baptizer appeared in the wilderness, preaching a baptism of repentance for the forgiveness of sins. ⁵And there went out to John all the country of Judea, and all the people of Jerusalem; and they were baptized by him in the river Jordan, confessing their sins. ⁶Now John was clothed with camel's hair, and had a leather girdle around his waist, and ate locusts and wild honey. ⁷And he preached, saying, "After me comes the one who is mightier than I, the thong of whose sandals I am not worthy to stoop down and untie. ⁸I have baptized you with water; but the one who comes will baptize you with the Holy Spirit."

□RSV *Lord*. See Appendix.
◇RSV *Son*. See Appendix.

ADVENT 3

The one whom God has anointed proclaims good news.

¹The Spirit of the Sovereign God is upon me,
  because God has anointed me
 to bring good tidings to the afflicted;
  God has sent me to bind up the brokenhearted,
 to proclaim liberty to the captives,
  and the opening of the prison to those who are bound;
²to proclaim the year of God's favor,
  and the day of vengeance of our God;
  to comfort all who mourn;
³to grant to those who mourn in Zion—
  to give them a garland instead of ashes,
 the oil of gladness instead of mourning,
  the mantle of praise instead of a faint spirit;
 that they may be called oaks of righteousness,
  the planting of God, that God may be glorified.
⁴They shall build up the ancient ruins,
  they shall raise up the former devastations;
 they shall repair the ruined cities,
  the devastations of many generations.
⁸For I the Sovereign One love justice,
  I hate robbery and wrong;
 I will faithfully give them their recompense,
  and I will make an everlasting covenant with them.
⁹Their descendants shall be known among the nations,
  and their offspring in the midst of the peoples;
 all who see them shall acknowledge them,
  that they are a people whom God has blessed.
¹⁰I will greatly rejoice in the Sovereign One,
  my soul shall exult in my God,
 who has clothed me with the garments of salvation,
  and covered me with the robe of righteousness,
 as a bridegroom decks himself with a garland,
  and as a bride adorns herself with her jewels.
¹¹For as the earth brings forth its shoots,
  and as a garden causes what is sown in it to spring up,
 so the Sovereign God will cause righteousness and praise
  to spring forth before all the nations.

Canticle ~ Luke 1:46b-55

Mary, the mother of Jesus, sings a song of praise.

⁴⁶My soul magnifies the Sovereign,□
⁴⁷and my spirit rejoices in God my Savior,
⁴⁸for God has regarded the low estate of God's handmaiden.
  For behold, henceforth all generations will call me blessed;
⁴⁹for God who is mighty has done great things for me,
  and holy is God's name.
⁵⁰And God's mercy is on those who fear God
  from generation to generation
⁵¹God has shown strength with God's arm,
  has scattered the proud in the imagination of their hearts,
⁵²has put down the mighty from their thrones,
  and exalted those of low degree;
⁵³God has filled the hungry with good things,
  and has sent the rich empty away.
⁵⁴God has helped God's servant Israel,
  in remembrance of God's mercy,
⁵⁵having spoken to our ancestors,
  to Abraham [*and Sarah**] and to their posterity for ever.

Lesson 2 ~ 1 Thessalonians 5:16-24

Paul admonishes the church at Thessalonica.

¹⁶Rejoice always, ¹⁷pray constantly, ¹⁸give thanks in all circumstances; for this is the will of God in Christ Jesus for you. ¹⁹Do not quench the Spirit, ²⁰do not despise prophesying, ²¹but test everything; hold fast what is good, ²²abstain from every form of evil.

²³May the God of peace sanctify you wholly; and may your spirit and soul and body be kept sound and blameless at the coming of our Sovereign□ Jesus Christ. ²⁴The one who calls you is faithful, and will do it.

□RSV *Lord*. See Appendix.
*Addition to the text. See Appendix.

Gospel ~ John 1:6-8, 19-28

John the Baptist, sent from God, proclaims that he is not the Christ, but is the voice of the one who announces the Christ.

[6]There was a man sent from God, whose name was John. [7]John came for testimony, to bear witness to the light, that all might believe through him. [8]John was not the light, but came to bear witness to the light.

[19]And this is the testimony of John, when the Jews sent priests and Levites from Jerusalem to ask him, "Who are you?" [20]John confessed, he did not deny, but confessed, "I am not the Christ." [21]And they asked, "What then? Are you Elijah?" John said, "I am not." "Are you the prophet?" And he answered, "No." [22]They said then, "Who are you? Let us have an answer for those who sent us. What do you say about yourself?" [23]John said, "I am the voice of one crying in the wilderness, 'Make straight the way of the Sovereign,▫' as the prophet Isaiah said."

[24]Now they had been sent from the Pharisees. [25]They asked John, "Then why are you baptizing, if you are neither the Christ, nor Elijah, nor the prophet?" [26]John answered them, "I baptize with water; but among you stands one whom you do not know, [27]even the one who comes after me, the thong of whose sandal I am not worthy to untie." [28]This took place in Bethany beyond the Jordan, where John was baptizing.

▫RSV *Lord.* See Appendix.

ADVENT 4

Lesson 1 ~ 2 Samuel 7:8-16

The word of God, sent to Nathan, announces a kingdom—not for the whole family of David but for Solomon.

⁸Now therefore thus you shall say to my servant David, "Thus says the GOD of hosts, I took you from the pasture, from following the sheep, that you should be prince over my people Israel; ⁹and I have been with you wherever you went, and have cut off all your enemies from before you; and I will make for you a great name, like the name of the great ones of the earth. ¹⁰And I will appoint a place for my people Israel, and will plant them, that they may dwell in their own place, and be disturbed no more; and the violent shall afflict them no more, as formerly, ¹¹from the time that I appointed judges over my people Israel; and I will give you rest from all your enemies. Moreover GOD declares to you that GOD will make you a house. ¹²When your days are fulfilled and you lie down with your ancestors, I will raise up your offspring after you, who shall come forth from your body, and I will establish a kingdom for that offspring, ¹³who shall build a house for my name, and I will establish the throne of that kingdom for ever. ¹⁴I will be parent to your child, and your child shall be my child. When your child commits iniquity, I will chasten that one with a rod of human discipline, with stripes of human hands; ¹⁵but I will not take away my steadfast love as I took it from Saul, whom I put away from before you. ¹⁶And your house and your kingdom shall be made sure for ever before me; your throne shall be established for ever."

Psalm 89:1-4, 19-24

¹I will sing of your steadfast love, O GOD, for ever;
     with my mouth I will proclaim your faithfulness to all generations.
²For your steadfast love was established for ever,
     your faithfulness is firm as the heavens.
³You have said, "I have made a covenant with my chosen one,
     I have sworn to David my servant:
⁴'I will establish your descendants for ever,
     and build your throne for all generations.' "
¹⁹Of old you spoke in a vision
     to your faithful one, and said:
"I have set the crown upon one who is mighty,
     I have exalted one chosen from the people.

^{20}I have found David, my servant;
   with my holy oil I have anointed him;
^{21}so that my hand shall ever abide with David,
   my arm also shall strengthen him.
^{22}The enemy shall not outwit him,
   the wicked shall not humble him.
^{23}I will crush David's foes before him
   and strike down those who hate him.
^{24}My faithfulness and my steadfast love shall be with him,
   and in my name shall David's horn be exalted."

Lesson 2 ~ Romans 16:25-27

Paul's letter to the Romans closes with this ascription.

^{25}Now to the one who is able to strengthen you according to my gospel and the preaching of Jesus Christ, according to the revelation of the mystery which was kept secret for long ages ^{26}but is now disclosed and through the prophetic writings is made known to all nations, according to the command of the eternal God, to bring about the obedience of faith—^{27}to the only wise God be glory for evermore through Jesus Christ! Amen.

Gospel ~ Luke 1:26-38

The angel Gabriel announces to Mary that she will bear the child of God.

^{26}In the sixth month the angel Gabriel was sent from God to a city of Galilee named Nazareth, ^{27}to a virgin betrothed to a man whose name was Joseph, of the house of David; and her name was Mary. ^{28}And the angel came to her and said, "Hail, O favored one, God$^\square$ is with you!" ^{29}But she was greatly troubled at the saying, and considered in her mind what sort of greeting this might be. ^{30}And the angel said to her, "Do not be afraid, Mary, for you have found favor with God. ^{31}And behold, you will conceive in your womb and bear a child, whose name you shall call Jesus.

$^\square$RSV *the Lord.* See Appendix.

³²This one will be great, and will be called the Child° of the Most High;
and the Sovereign□ God will give to that Child the throne of David, the
ancestor of the Child,
³³to reign over the house of Jacob for ever;
and of that reign* there will be no end."
³⁴And Mary said to the angel, "How shall this be, since I have no husband?"
³⁵And the angel said to her,
"The Holy Spirit will come upon you,
and the power of the Most High will overshadow you;
therefore the child to be born will be called holy,
the Child° of God.
³⁶And behold, your kinswoman Elizabeth in her old age has also conceived
a child; and this is the sixth month with her who was called barren. ³⁷For
with God nothing will be impossible." ³⁸And Mary said, "Behold, I am the
handmaid of God;□ let it be to me according to your word." And the angel
departed from her.

°RSV *Son*. See Appendix.
□RSV v. 32 *Lord;* v. 38 *the Lord*. See Appendix.
*RSV *his kingdom*. See Appendix.

CHRISTMAS EVE/DAY

Lesson 1 ~ Isaiah 9:2-7

This is the oracle of the messianic ruler, of the coming of one who brings a new age of peace and justice.

²The people who walked in gloom
  have seen a great light;
 those who dwelt in a land of deep shadows,
  on them has light shined.
³You have multiplied the nation,
  you have increased its joy;
 they rejoice before you
  as with joy at the harvest,
  as victors rejoice when they divide the spoil.
⁴For the yoke of Israel's burden,
  and the staff for its shoulder,
  the rod of its oppressor,
  you have broken as on the day of Midian.
⁵For every boot of the tramping warrior in battle tumult
  and every garment rolled in blood
  will be burned as fuel for the fire.
⁶For to us a child is born,
  to us an heir is given;
 and the government will be upon the shoulder
  of that one whose name will be called
 "Wonderful Counselor, Mighty God,
  Everlasting Father [*and Mother**], Prince of Peace."
⁷Of the increase of that government and of peace
  there will be no end,
 upon the throne of David, and over David's kingdom,
  to establish it, and to uphold it
 with justice and with righteousness
  from this time forth and for evermore.
 The zeal of the GOD of hosts will do this.

---

*Addition to the text. See "Metaphor" and "God the Father and Mother" in the Appendix.

Psalm 96

1O sing to GOD a new song;
　　sing to GOD, all the earth!
2Sing to GOD, bless God's name;
　　tell of God's salvation from day to day.
3Declare God's glory among the nations,
　　and marvelous works among all the peoples!
4For great is GOD, and greatly to be praised,
　　indeed, to be feared above all gods.
5For all the gods of the peoples are idols;
　　but the SOVEREIGN ONE made the heavens.
6Honor and majesty are before God;
　　strength and beauty are in God's sanctuary.
7Ascribe to GOD, O families of the peoples,
　　ascribe to GOD glory and strength!
8Ascribe to GOD the glory due God's name;
　　bring an offering, and come into God's courts!
9Worship GOD in holy array;
　　tremble before God, all the earth!
10Say among the nations, "GOD reigns!
　　The world is established, it shall never be moved;
　　God will judge the peoples with equity."
11Let the heavens be glad, and let the earth rejoice;
　　let the sea roar, and all that fills it;
12　let the field exult, and everything in it!
　Then shall all the trees of the wood sing for joy
13　before GOD, who comes,
　　who comes to judge the earth,
　and will judge the world with righteousness,
　　and the peoples with God's truth.

Lesson 2 ~ Titus 2:11-14

The letter to Titus points to the meaning of Christ's appearance.

11For the grace of God has appeared for the salvation of all, 12training us to renounce irreligion and worldly passions, and to live sober, upright, and godly lives in this world, 13awaiting our blessed hope, the appearing of the glory of our great God and Savior Jesus Christ, 14who gave up self for us to redeem us from all iniquity and to purify for Christ's self a chosen people who are zealous for good deeds.

Gospel ~ Luke 2:1-20

Luke describes the birth of Jesus.

¹In those days a decree went out from Caesar Augustus that all the world should be enrolled. ²This was the first enrollment, when Quirinius was governor of Syria. ³And all went to be enrolled, each to their own city. ⁴And Joseph also went up from Galilee, from the city of Nazareth, to Judea, to the city of David, which is called Bethlehem, because he was of the house and lineage of David, ⁵to be enrolled with Mary, his betrothed, who was with child. ⁶And while they were there, the time came for her to be delivered. ⁷And she gave birth to her first-born child, whom she wrapped in swaddling cloths and laid in a manger, because there was no place for them in the inn.

⁸And in that region there were shepherds out in the field, keeping watch over their flock by night. ⁹And an angel of God□ appeared to them, and the glory of God□ shone around them, and they were filled with fear. ¹⁰And the angel said to them, "Be not afraid; for behold, I bring you good news of a great joy which will come to all the people; ¹¹for to you is born this day in the city of David a Savior, who is Christ the Sovereign.□ ¹²And this will be a sign for you: you will find a babe wrapped in swaddling cloths and lying in a manger." ¹³And suddenly there was with the angel a multitude of the heavenly host praising God and saying,
¹⁴"Glory to God in the highest,
　and on earth peace among those with whom God is pleased!"

¹⁵When the angels went away from them into heaven, the shepherds said to one another, "Let us go over to Bethlehem and see this thing that has happened, which God□ has made known to us." ¹⁶And they went with haste, and found Mary and Joseph, and the babe lying in a manger. ¹⁷And when they saw it they made known the saying which had been told them concerning this child; ¹⁸and all who heard it wondered at what the shepherds told them. ¹⁹But Mary kept all these things, pondering them in her heart. ²⁰And the shepherds returned, glorifying and praising God for all they had heard and seen, as it had been told them.

□RSV vs. 9, 15 *the Lord;* v. 11 *Lord.* See Appendix.

CHRISTMAS DAY, Additional Lections, First Set

Lesson 1 ~ Isaiah 62:6-7, 10-12

God sets watchers on the walls of Zion to contemplate the return of the exiles to the holy city.

> ⁶Upon your walls, O Jerusalem,
>> I have set watchers;
> all the day and all the night
>> they shall never be silent.
> You who put GOD in remembrance,
>> take no rest,
> ⁷and give God no rest
>> until Jerusalem is established
>> and is made a praise in the earth.
> ¹⁰Go through, go through the gates,
>> prepare the way for the people;
> build up, build up the highway,
>> clear it of stones,
>> lift up an ensign over the peoples.
> ¹¹Behold, GOD has proclaimed
>> to the end of the earth:
> Say to the children of Zion,
>> "Behold, your salvation comes;
> behold, God's reward is with God,
>> and God's recompense goes before God."
> ¹²And they shall be called The holy people,
>> The redeemed of GOD;
> and you shall be called Sought out,
>> a city not forsaken.

Psalm 97

> ¹The SOVEREIGN ONE reigns; let the earth rejoice;
>> let the many coastlands be glad!
> ²Clouds and thick darkness are round about God;
>> righteousness and justice are the foundation of God's throne.
> ³Fire goes before God,
>> and burns up God's adversaries round about.
> ⁴God's lightnings lighten the world;
>> the earth sees and trembles.

⁵The mountains melt like wax before the Sovereign One,
  before the God of all the earth.
⁶The heavens proclaim God's righteousness;
  and all the peoples behold God's glory.
⁷All worshipers of images are put to shame,
  who make their boast in worthless idols;
  all gods bow down before God.
⁸Zion hears and is glad,
  and the daughters of Judah rejoice,
  because of your judgments, O God.
⁹For you, O Sovereign One, are most high over all the earth;
  you are exalted far above all gods.
¹⁰God loves those who hate evil,
  preserves the lives of the saints,
  and delivers them from the hand of the wicked.
¹¹Light dawns for the righteous,
  and joy for the upright in heart.
¹²Rejoice in God, O you righteous,
  and give thanks to God's holy name!

Lesson 2 ~ Titus 3:4-7

The author of the letter to Titus writes of how all things are changed because of the mercy of God.

⁴When the goodness and loving kindness of God our Savior appeared, ⁵we were saved, not because of deeds done by us in righteousness, but in virtue of God's mercy, by the washing of regeneration and renewal in the Holy Spirit, ⁶which God poured out upon us richly through Jesus Christ our Savior, ⁷so that we might be justified by God's grace and become heirs in hope of eternal life.

Gospel ~ Luke 2:8-20

Luke describes the birth of Jesus.

⁸And in that region there were shepherds out in the field, keeping watch over their flock by night. ⁹And an angel of God□ appeared to them, and the glory of God□ shone around them, and they were filled with fear. ¹⁰And the angel said to them, "Be not afraid; for behold, I bring you good news of a great joy which will come to all the people; ¹¹for to you is born this day in the city of David a Savior, who is Christ the Sovereign.□ ¹²And this will be a sign for you: you will find a babe wrapped in swaddling cloths and lying in a manger." ¹³And suddenly there was with the angel a multitude of the heavenly host praising God and saying,
¹⁴"Glory to God in the highest,
    and on earth peace among those with whom God is pleased!"
¹⁵When the angels went away from them into heaven, the shepherds said to one another, "Let us go over to Bethlehem and see this thing that has happened, which God□ has made known to us." ¹⁶And they went with haste, and found Mary and Joseph, and the babe lying in a manger. ¹⁷And when they saw it they made known the saying which had been told them concerning this child; ¹⁸and all who heard it wondered at what the shepherds told them. ¹⁹But Mary kept all these things, pondering them in her heart. ²⁰And the shepherds returned, glorifying and praising God for all they had heard and seen, as it had been told them.

□RSV vs. 9, 15 *the Lord;* v. 11 *Lord.* See Appendix.

CHRISTMAS DAY, Additional Lections, Second Set

Lesson 1 ~ Isaiah 52:7-10

Isaiah brings God's word of promise to Israel.

⁷How beautiful upon the mountains
    are the feet of the one who brings good tidings,
who publishes peace, who brings good tidings of good,
    who publishes salvation,
    who says to Zion, "Your God reigns."
⁸Hark, your watchers lift up their voice,
    together they sing for joy;
for eye to eye they see
    the return of GOD to Zion.
⁹Break forth together into singing,
    you waste places of Jerusalem;
for GOD has comforted God's people,
    and has redeemed Jerusalem.
¹⁰GOD has bared God's holy arm
    before the eyes of all the nations;
and all the ends of the earth shall see
    the salvation of our God.

Psalm 98

¹O sing a new song to GOD,
    who has done marvelous things,
whose right hand and holy arm
    have gained the victory.
²GOD has made known the victory,
    and has revealed God's vindication in the sight of the nations.
³God has remembered God's steadfast love and faithfulness
    to the house of Israel.
All the ends of the earth have seen
    the victory of our God.
⁴Make a joyful noise to GOD, all the earth;
    break forth into joyous song and sing praises!
⁵Sing praises to GOD with the lyre,
    with the lyre and the sound of melody!

⁶With trumpets and the sound of the horn
    make a joyful noise before the Ruler,□ the Sᴏᴠᴇʀᴇɪɢɴ Oɴᴇ!
⁷Let the sea roar, and all that fills it;
    the world and those who dwell in it!
⁸Let the floods clap their hands;
    let the hills sing for joy together
⁹before the Sᴏᴠᴇʀᴇɪɢɴ Oɴᴇ, for God comes
    to judge the earth,
  to judge the world with righteousness,
    and the peoples with equity.

Lesson 2 ~ Hebrews 1:1-12

The author of the letter to the Hebrews begins by emphasizing the superiority of Jesus Christ to the prophets and to the angels.

¹In many and various ways God spoke of old to our forebears by the prophets; ²but in these last days God has spoken to us by a Child,◇ whom God appointed the heir of all things, through whom also God created the world. ³This Child, by whose word of power the universe is upheld, reflects the glory of God and bears the very stamp of God's nature. Having made purification for sins, the Child sat down at the right hand of the Majesty on high, ⁴having become as much superior to angels as the name the Child has obtained is more excellent than theirs.

⁵For to what angel did God ever say,
    "You are my Child,◇
    today I have begotten you"?
Or again,
    "I will be to the Child a parent,
    and the Child shall be my very own"?
⁶And again, when bringing the first-born into the world, God says,
    "Let all God's angels worship the Child."
⁷Of the angels it is said,
    "Who makes God's angels winds,
    and God's servants flames of fire."
⁸But of the Child◇ it is said,
    "Your throne, O God, is for ever and ever,
    the righteous scepter is the scepter of your realm.✶

□RSV *King.* See Appendix.
◇RSV *Son.* See Appendix.
✶RSV *kingdom.* See Appendix.

⁹You have loved righteousness and hated lawlessness;
   therefore God, your God, has anointed you
   with the oil of gladness beyond your comrades."
¹⁰And,
   "You, O Sovereign,□ founded the earth in the beginning,
   and the heavens are the work of your hands;
¹¹they will perish, but you remain;
   they will all grow old like a garment,
¹²like a mantle you will roll them up,
   and they will be changed.
   But you are the same,
   and your years will never end."

Gospel ~ John 1:1-14

John unfolds the mystery of the incarnation.

¹In the beginning was the Word, and the Word was with God, and the Word was God. ²The Word was in the beginning with God; ³all things were made through the Word, and without the Word was not anything made that was made. ⁴In the Word was life, and the life was the light of all. ⁵The light shines in the deepest night, and the night has not overcome it.

⁶There was a man sent from God, whose name was John. ⁷John came for testimony, to bear witness to the light, that all might believe through him. ⁸John was not the light, but came to bear witness to the light.

⁹The true light that enlightens every one was coming into the world. ¹⁰The Word was in the world, and the world was made through the Word, yet the world did not know the Word. ¹¹The Word came to the Word's own home, but those to whom the Word came did not receive the Word. ¹²But to all who did receive the Word, who believed in the name of the Word, power was given to become children of God; ¹³who were born, not of blood nor of the will of the flesh nor of human will, but of God.

¹⁴And the Word became flesh and dwelt among us, full of grace and truth; we have beheld the Word's glory, glory as of the only Child◇ from [*God*] the Father [*and Mother**].

□RSV *Lord.* See Appendix.
◇RSV *Son.* See Appendix.
*Addition to the text. See "Metaphor" and "God the Father and Mother" in the Appendix.

CHRISTMAS 1
(Or the lections for Epiphany)

Lesson 1 ~ Isaiah 61:10–62:3

Isaiah extols the glory of God.

¹⁰I will greatly rejoice in the Sovereign One,
  my soul shall exult in my God,
 who has clothed me with the garments of salvation,
  and covered me with the robe of righteousness,
 as a bridegroom decks himself with a garland,
  and as a bride adorns herself with her jewels.
¹¹For as the earth brings forth its shoots,
  and as a garden causes what is sown in it to spring up,
 so the Sovereign God will cause righteousness and praise
  to spring forth before all the nations.
^{62:1}For Zion's sake I will not keep silent,
  and for Jerusalem's sake I will not rest,
 until its vindication goes forth as brightness,
  and its salvation as a burning torch.
²The nations shall see your vindication,
  and all the monarchs□ your glory;
 and you shall be called by a new name
  which the mouth of God will give.
³You shall be a crown of beauty in the hand of the Sovereign One,
  and a royal diadem in the hand of your God.

Psalm 111

¹Praise God.
 I will give thanks to God with my whole heart,
  in the company of the upright, in the congregation.
²Great are the works of God,
  studied by all who have pleasure in them.
³Full of honor and majesty is God's work,
  and God's righteousness endures for ever.
⁴God has caused God's wonderful works to be remembered,
  and is gracious and merciful,
⁵providing food for those who fear God
  and being ever mindful of the covenant.

□RSV *kings.* See Appendix.

⁶God has shown God's people the power of God's works,
    in giving them the heritage of the nations.
⁷The works of God's hands are faithful and just;
    all God's precepts are trustworthy,
⁸they are established for ever and ever,
    to be performed with faithfulness and uprightness.
⁹God sent redemption to God's people
    and has commanded the covenant for ever.
    Holy and terrible is God's name!
¹⁰The fear of GOD is the beginning of wisdom;
    a good understanding have all those who practice it.
    God's praise endures for ever!

Lesson 2 ~ Galatians 4:4-7

Paul writes to the Galatians about the time of Christ's coming.

⁴But when the time had fully come, God sent forth the Child,° born of woman, born under the law, ⁵to redeem those who were under the law, so that we might receive adoption as children. ⁶And because you are children, God has sent the Spirit of the Child° into our hearts, crying, "[*God! my Mother and*ᵃ] Father!" ⁷So through God you are no longer a slave but a child, and if a child then an heir.

Gospel ~ Luke 2:22-40

Mary and Joseph take the infant Jesus to the temple in Jerusalem and the child is met there by Simeon and Anna.

²²And when the time came for their purification according to the law of Moses, they brought the child Jesus up to Jerusalem to be presented to God,□ ²³(as it is written in the law of God,□ "Every male that opens the womb shall be called holy to God□") ²⁴and to offer a sacrifice according to what is said in the law of God,□ "a pair of turtledoves, or two young pigeons." ²⁵Now there was a man in Jerusalem, whose name was Simeon, who was righteous and devout, looking for the consolation of Israel, and the Holy Spirit was upon him. ²⁶And it had been revealed to Simeon by the Holy Spirit that he should not see death before he had seen the Christ of God.□ ²⁷And inspired by the Spirit Simeon came into the temple; and

---

°RSV *Son.* See Appendix.
ᵃAddition to the text. RSV *Abba!* See Notes, p. 249.
□RSV vs. 22, 23, 24 *the Lord;* v. 26 *Lord's Christ.* See Appendix.

when the parents brought in the child Jesus, to do for him according to the custom of the law, [28]Simeon took the child in his arms and blessed God and said,

[29]"O God,□ now let your servant depart in peace,
   according to your word;
[30]for my eyes have seen your salvation
[31]which you have prepared in the presence of all peoples,
[32]a light for revelation to the Gentiles,
   and for glory to your people Israel."

[33]And Jesus' father and mother marveled at what was said about their child; [34]and Simeon blessed them and said to Mary, Jesus' mother,

   "Behold, this child is set for the fall and rising of many in Israel,
   and for a sign that is spoken against
[35](and a sword will pierce through your own soul also),
   that thoughts out of many hearts may be revealed."

[36]And there was a prophet, Anna, the daughter of Phanuel, of the tribe of Asher; she was of a great age, having lived with her husband for seven years, [37]and as a widow till she was eighty-four. She did not depart from the temple, worshiping with fasting and prayer night and day. [38]And coming up at that very hour she gave thanks to God, and spoke about the child to all who were looking for the redemption of Jerusalem.

[39]And when Mary and Joseph had performed everything according to the law of God,□ they returned into Galilee, to their own city, Nazareth. [40]And the child grew and became strong, filled with wisdom; and the favor of God was upon the child.

□RSV v. 29 *Lord;* v. 39 *the Lord.*

JANUARY 1 (New Year)

Lesson 1 ~ Ecclesiastes 3:1-13

The Preacher speaks of times and seasons.

¹For everything there is a season, and a time for every matter under heaven:
²a time to be born, and a time to die;
 a time to plant, and a time to pluck up what is planted;
³a time to kill, and a time to heal;
 a time to break down, and a time to build up;
⁴a time to weep, and a time to laugh;
 a time to mourn, and a time to dance;
⁵a time to cast away stones, and a time to gather stones together;
 a time to embrace, and a time to refrain from embracing;
⁶a time to seek, and a time to lose;
 a time to keep, and a time to cast away;
⁷a time to rend, and a time to sew;
 a time to keep silence, and a time to speak;
⁸a time to love, and a time to hate;
 a time for war, and a time for peace.
⁹What gain have the workers from their toil?

¹⁰I have seen the business that God has given to the human race to be busy with. ¹¹God has made everything beautiful in its time, and has put eternity into human minds, yet they cannot find out what God has done from the beginning to the end. ¹²I know that there is nothing better for them than to be happy and enjoy themselves as long as they live; ¹³also that it is God's gift to humanity that all should eat and drink and take pleasure in all their toil.

Psalm 8

¹O SOVEREIGN ONE, our God,
   how majestic is your name in all the earth!
 You whose glory above the heavens is chanted
²   by the mouth of babes and infants,
   you have founded a bulwark because of your foes,
     to still the enemy and the avenger.
³When I look at your heavens, the work of your fingers,
     the moon and the stars which you have established;
⁴what are human beings that you are mindful of them,
     and mortals that you care for them?

⁵Yet you have made them little less than God,
  and crowned them with glory and honor.
⁶You have given them dominion over the works of your hands;
  you have put all things under their feet,
⁷all sheep and oxen,
  and also the beasts of the field,
⁸the birds of the air, and the fish of the sea,
  whatever passes along the paths of the sea.
⁹O SOVEREIGN ONE, our God,
  how majestic is your name in all the earth!

Lesson 2 ~ Colossians 2:1-7

Paul sends a message of encouragement to the church at Colossae.

¹For I want you to know how greatly I strive for you, and for those at Laodicea, and for all who have not seen my face, ²that their hearts may be encouraged as they are knit together in love, to have all the riches of assured understanding and the knowledge of God's mystery, of Christ, ³in whom are hid all the treasures of wisdom and knowledge. ⁴I say this in order that no one may delude you with beguiling speech. ⁵For though I am absent in body, yet I am with you in spirit, rejoicing to see your good order and the firmness of your faith in Christ.

⁶As therefore you received Christ Jesus the Sovereign,◻ so live in Christ, ⁷rooted and built up in Christ and established in the faith, just as you were taught, abounding in thanksgiving.

Gospel ~ Matthew 9:14-17

Jesus teaches John's disciples about the radically new age that has begun.

¹⁴Then the disciples of John came to Jesus, saying, "Why do we and the Pharisees fast, but your disciples do not fast?" ¹⁵And Jesus said to them, "Can the wedding guests mourn as long as the bridegroom is with them? The days will come, when the bridegroom is taken away from them, and then they will fast. ¹⁶And no one puts a piece of unshrunk cloth on an old garment, for the patch tears away from the garment, and a worse tear is made. ¹⁷Neither is new wine put into old wineskins; if it is, the skins burst, and the wine is spilled, and the skins are destroyed; but new wine is put into fresh wineskins, and so both are preserved."

◻RSV *Lord*. See Appendix.

JANUARY 1 Holy Name of Jesus; Solemnity of Mary, Mother of God

Lesson 1 ~ Numbers 6:22-27

Moses learns how Aaron is to bless the people of Israel.

²²GOD said to Moses, ²³"Say to Aaron and his offspring, Thus you shall bless the people of Israel: you shall say to them,
²⁴GOD bless you and keep you:
²⁵GOD make God's face to shine upon you, and be gracious to you:
²⁶GOD lift up God's countenance upon you, and give you peace.
   ²⁷"So shall they put my name upon the people of Israel, and I will bless them."

Psalm 67

¹May God be gracious to us and bless us
   and make God's face to shine upon us,
²that your way may be known upon earth,
   your saving power among all nations.
³Let the peoples praise you, O God;
   let all the peoples praise you!
⁴Let the nations be glad and sing for joy,
   for you judge the peoples with equity
   and guide the nations upon earth.
⁵Let the peoples praise you, O God;
   let all the peoples praise you!
⁶The earth has yielded its increase;
   God, our God, has blessed us.
⁷God has blessed us;
   let all the ends of the earth fear God!

Lesson 2 ~ Galatians 4:4-7

Paul writes to the Galatians about the time of Christ's coming.

⁴But when the time had fully come, God sent forth the Child,[◇] born of woman, born under the law, ⁵to redeem those who were under the law, so that we might receive adoption as children. ⁶And because you are children,

---

◇RSV *his Son*. See Appendix.

God has sent the Spirit of the Child° into our hearts, crying, "[*God! my Mother and*ª] Father!" ⁷So through God you are no longer a slave but a child, and if a child then an heir.

Lesson 2 (alternate) ~ Philippians 2:9-13

Paul reflects on Christ's example of humility and obedience.

⁹Therefore God has highly exalted Jesus and bestowed on Jesus the name which is above every name, ¹⁰that at the name of Jesus every knee should bow, in heaven and on earth and under the earth, ¹¹and every tongue confess that Jesus Christ is Sovereign,□ to the glory of God the Father [*and Mother**].
¹²Therefore, my beloved, as you have always obeyed, so now, not only as in my presence but much more in my absence, work out your own salvation with fear and trembling; ¹³for God is at work in you, both to will and to work for God's good pleasure.

Gospel ~ Luke 2:15-21

Luke describes the shepherds' visit to Bethlehem.

¹⁵When the angels went away from them into heaven, the shepherds said to one another, "Let us go over to Bethlehem and see this thing that has happened, which God□ has made known to us." ¹⁶And they went with haste, and found Mary and Joseph, and the babe lying in a manger. ¹⁷And when they saw it they made known the saying which had been told them concerning this child; ¹⁸and all who heard it wondered at what the shepherds told them. ¹⁹But Mary kept all these things, pondering them in her heart. ²⁰And the shepherds returned, glorifying and praising God for all they had heard and seen, as it had been told them.
²¹And at the end of eight days, the child was circumcised and was called Jesus, the name given by the angel before he was conceived in the womb.

CHRISTMAS 2
(Or the lections for Epiphany if not otherwise used)

Lesson 1 ~ Jeremiah 31:7-14

The prophet Jeremiah tells how Israel's suffering and despair will be turned to dancing and joy by God's deliverance and salvation.

⁷For thus says the SOVEREIGN ONE:
"Sing aloud with gladness for Jacob,
    and raise shouts for the chief of the nations;
proclaim, give praise, and say,
    'GOD has saved the people,
    the remnant of Israel.'
⁸Behold, I will bring them from the north country,
    and gather them from the farthest parts of the earth,
among them those who are blind and those who are lame,
    the woman with child and the woman in travail, together;
a great company, they shall return here.
⁹With weeping they shall come,
    and with consolations I will lead them back,
I will make them walk by brooks of water,
    in a straight path in which they shall not stumble;
for I am a father [*and a mother**] to Israel,
    and Ephraim is my first-born.
¹⁰Hear the word of GOD, O nations,
    and declare it in the coastlands afar off;
say, 'The one who scattered Israel will gather them,
    and will keep them as a shepherd keeps a flock.'
¹¹For GOD has ransomed Jacob,
    and has redeemed them from hands too strong for them.
¹²They shall come and sing aloud on the height of Zion,
    and they shall be radiant over the goodness of GOD,
over the grain, the wine, and the oil,
    and over the young of the flock and the herd;
their life shall be like a watered garden,
    and they shall languish no more.
¹³Then shall the maidens rejoice in the dance,
    and the young men and the old shall be merry.
I will turn their mourning into joy,
    I will comfort them, and give them gladness for sorrow.
¹⁴I will feast the soul of the priests with abundance,
    and my people shall be satisfied with my goodness,
                   says the SOVEREIGN ONE."

---

*Addition to the text.

Lesson 1 (alternate) ~ Ecclesiasticus (Sirach) 24:1-4, 12-16

Sirach writes of Wisdom at work in creation.

¹Wisdom will praise herself,
  and will glory in the midst of her people.
²In the assembly of the Most High she will open her mouth,
  and in the presence of the host of the Most High she will glory:
³"I came forth from the mouth of the Most High,
  and covered the earth like a mist.
⁴I dwelt in high places,
  and my throne was in a pillar of cloud.
¹²So I took root in an honored people,
  in the portion of the Most High, who is their inheritance.
¹³I grew tall like a cedar in Lebanon,
  and like a cypress on the heights of Hermon.
¹⁴I grew tall like a palm tree in Engedi,
  and like rose plants in Jericho;
like a beautiful olive tree in the field,
  and like a plane tree I grew tall.
¹⁵Like cassia and camel's thorn I gave forth the aroma of spices,
  and like choice myrrh I spread a pleasant odor,
like galbanum, onycha, and stacte,
  and like the fragrance of frankincense in the tabernacle.
¹⁶Like a terebinth I spread out my branches,
  and my branches are glorious and graceful."

Psalm 147:12-20

¹²Praise GOD, O Jerusalem!
  Praise your God, O Zion,
¹³for God strengthens the bars of your gates,
  and blesses your children within you,
¹⁴making peace in your borders,
  and filling you with the finest of the wheat.
¹⁵God sends forth a command to the earth;
  God's word runs swiftly.
¹⁶God gives snow like wool,
  scattering hoarfrost like ashes,
¹⁷and casting forth ice like morsels;
  who can stand before God's cold?
¹⁸God sends forth God's word, and melts them,
  making the wind blow, and the waters flow.

¹⁹God declares God's word to Jacob,
    God's statutes and ordinances to Israel.
²⁰God has not dealt thus with any other nation;
    they do not know the ordinances.
Praise GOD!

Lesson 2 ~ Ephesians 1:3-6, 15-18

The writer of the letter to the Ephesians begins by praising God's glorious grace in Jesus Christ.

³Blessed be God the Father [*and Mother**] of our Sovereign□ Jesus Christ, who has blessed us in Christ with every spiritual blessing in the heavenly places, ⁴even as God chose us in Christ before the foundation of the world, that we should be holy and blameless before God, ⁵who destined us in love to be God's children through Jesus Christ, according to the purpose of God's will, ⁶to the praise of God's glorious grace freely bestowed on us in the Beloved.

¹⁵For this reason, because I have heard of your faith in the Sovereign□ Jesus and your love toward all the saints, ¹⁶I do not cease to give thanks for you, remembering you in my prayers, ¹⁷that the God of our Sovereign□ Jesus Christ, the Father [*and Mother**] of glory, may give you a spirit of wisdom and of revelation in the knowledge of God, ¹⁸having the eyes of your hearts enlightened, that you may know what is the hope to which you have been called, what are the riches of God's glorious inheritance in the saints.

Gospel ~ John 1:1-18

John unfolds the mystery of the incarnation.

¹In the beginning was the Word, and the Word was with God, and the Word was God. ²The Word was in the beginning with God; ³all things were made through the Word, and without the Word was not anything made that was made. ⁴In the Word was life, and the life was the light of all. ⁵The light shines in the deepest night, and the night has not overcome it.

⁶There was a man sent from God, whose name was John. ⁷John came for testimony, to bear witness to the light, that all might believe through him. ⁸John was not the light, but came to bear witness to the light.

---

*Addition to the text. RSV v. 3 *the God and Father*; v. 17 *the Father*. See "Metaphor" and "God the Father and Mother" in the Appendix.
□RSV *Lord*. See Appendix.

⁹The true light that enlightens every one was coming into the world. ¹⁰The Word was in the world, and the world was made through the Word, yet the world did not know the Word. ¹¹The Word came to the Word's own home, but those to whom the Word came did not receive the Word. ¹²But to all who received the Word, who believed in the name of the Word, power was given to become children of God; ¹³who were born, not of blood nor of the will of the flesh nor of human will, but of God.

¹⁴And the Word became flesh and dwelt among us, full of grace and truth; we have beheld the Word's glory, glory as of the only Child° from [God] the Father [and Mother*]. ¹⁵(John bore witness to the Child, and cried, "This was the one of whom I said, 'The one who comes after me ranks before me, for that one was before me.'") ¹⁶And from the fulness of the Child have we all received, grace upon grace. ¹⁷For the law was given through Moses; grace and truth came through Jesus Christ. ¹⁸No one has ever seen God; the only Child,° who is in the bosom of [God] the [Mother and*] Father, that one has made God known.

———————

°RSV Son. See Appendix.
*Addition to the text. See "Metaphor" and "God the Father and Mother" in the Appendix.

EPIPHANY

Lesson 1 ~ Isaiah 60:1-6

Isaiah tells of the coming of God's glory to the people.

¹Arise, shine; for your light has come,
  and the glory of God has risen upon you.
²For behold, shadows shall cover the earth,
  and thick shadows the peoples;
 but God will arise upon you,
  and the glory of God will be seen upon you.
³And nations shall come to your light,
  and rulers□ to the brightness of your rising.
⁴Lift up your eyes round about, to see;
  they all gather together, they come to you;
 your sons shall come from far,
  and your daughters shall be carried in the arms.
⁵Then you shall see and be radiant,
  your heart shall thrill and rejoice;
 because the abundance of the sea shall be turned to you,
  the wealth of the nations shall come to you.
⁶A multitude of camels shall cover you,
  the young camels of Midian and Ephah;
 all those from Sheba shall come.
They shall bring gold and frankincense,
  and shall proclaim the praise of God.

Psalm 72:1-14

¹Give the ruler□ your justice, O God,
  and your righteousness to the royal heir!
²May the ruler judge your people with righteousness,
  and your poor with justice!
³Let the mountains bear prosperity for the people,
  and the hills, in righteousness!
⁴May the ruler defend the cause of the poor of the people,
  give deliverance to the needy,
  and crush the oppressor!
⁵May the ruler live while the sun endures,
  and as long as the moon, throughout all generations!
⁶May the ruler be like rain that falls on the mown grass,
  like showers that water the earth!

□RSV Isa. 60:3 *kings;* Ps. 72:1 *king.* See Appendix.

[7]In the ruler's days may righteousness flourish,
  and peace abound, till the moon be no more!
[8]May the ruler have dominion from sea to sea,
  and from the River to the ends of the earth!
[9]May the foes of the ruler bow down,
  and the enemies lick the dust!
[10]May the kings of Tarshish and of the isles
  render tribute,
 may the kings of Sheba and Seba
  bring gifts!
[11]May all kings bow down
  and all nations serve the ruler!
[12]For the ruler delivers the needy when they call,
  the poor and those who have no helper,
[13]has pity on the weak and the needy,
  and saves the lives of the needy.
[14]The ruler redeems their lives from oppression and violence,
  and their blood is precious in the ruler's sight.

Lesson 2 ~ Ephesians 3:1-12

The Ephesians learn about ministry that is rooted in Christ.

[1]For this reason I, Paul, a prisoner for Christ Jesus on behalf of you Gentiles—[2]assuming that you have heard of the stewardship of God's grace that was given to me for you, [3]how the mystery was made known to me by revelation, as I have written briefly. [4]When you read this you can perceive my insight into the mystery of Christ, [5]which was not made known to the human race in other generations as it has now been revealed to Christ's holy apostles and prophets by the Spirit; [6]that is, how the Gentiles are joint heirs, members of the same body, and partakers of the promise in Christ Jesus through the gospel.

[7]Of this gospel I was made a minister according to the gift of God's grace which was given me by the working of God's power. [8]To me, though I am the very least of all the saints, this grace was given, to preach to the Gentiles the unsearchable riches of Christ, [9]and to make every one see what is the plan of the mystery hidden for ages in God who created all things; [10]that through the church the manifold wisdom of God might now be made known to the principalities and powers in the heavenly places. [11]This was according to the eternal purpose which God has realized in Christ Jesus our Sovereign,□ [12]in whom we have boldness and confidence of access through our faith in Christ.

□RSV *Lord.* See Appendix.

Matthew describes the visit of the magi to the child.

¹Now when Jesus was born in Bethlehem of Judea in the days of Herod the king, behold, magi from the East came to Jerusalem, saying, ²"Where is the one who has been born ruler☐ of the Jews? For we have seen the star in the East, and have come to worship the newborn child." ³And hearing this, Herod the king was troubled, and all Jerusalem as well; ⁴and assembling all the chief priests and scribes of the people, he inquired of them where the Christ was to be born. ⁵They told Herod, "In Bethlehem of Judea; for so it is written by the prophet:
⁶'And you, O Bethlehem, in the land of Judah,
are by no means least among the rulers of Judah,
for from you shall come a ruler
who will govern my people Israel.' "
⁷Then Herod summoned the magi secretly, ascertained from them what time the star appeared, and ⁸sent them to Bethlehem, saying, "Go and search diligently, and when you have found the child bring me word, that I too may come and worship him." ⁹When they had heard the king they went their way; and lo, the star which they had seen in the East went before them, till it came to rest over the place where the child was. ¹⁰When they saw the star, they rejoiced exceedingly with great joy; ¹¹and going into the house they saw the child with Mary his mother, and they fell down and worshiped him. Then, opening their treasures, they offered the child gifts, gold and frankincense and myrrh. ¹²And being warned in a dream not to return to Herod, they departed to their own country by another way.

☐RSV *king.* See Appendix.

BAPTISM OF OUR SOVEREIGN

Lesson 1 ~ Genesis 1:1-5

This is the account of God's creation of the world.

¹In the beginning God created the heavens and the earth. ²The earth was without form and void, and darkness was upon the face of the deep; and the Spirit of God was moving over the face of the waters.

³And God said, "Let there be light"; and there was light. ⁴And God saw that the light was good; and God distinguished between the light and the darkness. ⁵God called the light Day, and the darkness Night. And there was evening and there was morning, one day.

Psalm 29

¹Ascribe to GOD, O heavenly beings,
   ascribe to GOD glory and strength.
²Ascribe to GOD the glory of God's name;
   worship GOD in holy array.
³The voice of GOD is upon the waters;
   the God of glory thunders,
   GOD, upon many waters.
⁴The voice of GOD is powerful,
   the voice of GOD is full of majesty.
⁵The voice of GOD breaks the cedars,
   GOD breaks the cedars of Lebanon,
⁶making Lebanon to skip like a calf,
   and Sirion like a young wild ox.
⁷The voice of GOD flashes forth flames of fire.
⁸The voice of GOD shakes the wilderness,
   GOD shakes the wilderness of Kadesh.
⁹The voice of GOD makes the oaks to whirl,
   and strips the forests bare;
   and in God's temple all cry, "Glory!"
¹⁰GOD sits enthroned over the flood;
   GOD sits enthroned as ruler▢ for ever.
¹¹May GOD give strength to God's people!
   May GOD bless the people with peace!

▢RSV *king.* See Appendix.

Lesson 2 ~ Acts 19:1-7

Paul baptizes in the name of the Sovereign Jesus.

[1]While Apollos was at Corinth, Paul passed through the upper country and came to Ephesus. There Paul found some disciples, [2]and said to them, "Did you receive the Holy Spirit when you believed?" And they said, "No, we have never even heard that there is a Holy Spirit." [3]And Paul said, "Into what then were you baptized?" They said, "Into John's baptism." [4]And Paul said, "John baptized with the baptism of repentance, telling the people to believe in the one who was to come after him, that is, Jesus." [5]On hearing this, they were baptized in the name of the Sovereign□ Jesus. [6]And when Paul had laid his hands upon them, the Holy Spirit came on them; and they spoke with tongues and prophesied. [7]There were about twelve of them in all.

Gospel ~ Mark 1:4-11

Mark tells of Jesus' baptism by John.

[4]John the baptizer appeared in the wilderness, preaching a baptism of repentance for the forgiveness of sins. [5]And there went out to John all the country of Judea, and all the people of Jerusalem; and they were baptized by him in the river Jordan, confessing their sins. [6]Now John was clothed with camel's hair, and had a leather girdle around his waist, and ate locusts and wild honey. [7]And he preached, saying, "After me comes the one who is mightier than I, the thong of whose sandals I am not worthy to stoop down and untie. [8]I have baptized you with water; but the one who comes will baptize you with the Holy Spirit."

[9]In those days Jesus came from Nazareth of Galilee and was baptized by John in the Jordan. [10]And having come up out of the water, immediately Jesus saw the heavens opened and the Spirit descending upon him like a dove; [11]and a voice came from heaven, "You are my beloved Child;◇ with you I am well pleased."

□RSV *Lord.* See Appendix.
◇RSV *Son.* See Appendix.

EPIPHANY 2

Lesson 1 ~ 1 Samuel 3:1-10, (11-20)

The boy Samuel is called by God and established as a prophet.

¹Now the boy Samuel was ministering to GOD under Eli. And the word of GOD was rare in those days; there was no frequent vision. ²At that time Eli, whose eyesight had begun to grow dim, so that he could not see, was lying down in his own place; ³the lamp of God had not yet gone out, and Samuel was lying down within the temple of GOD, where the ark of God was. ⁴Then GOD called, "Samuel! Samuel!" and Samuel said, "Here I am!" ⁵and ran to Eli, and said, "Here I am, for you called me." But Eli said, "I did not call; lie down again." So Samuel went and lay down. ⁶And GOD called again, "Samuel!" And Samuel arose and went to Eli, and said, "Here I am, for you called me." But Eli said, "I did not call, my son; lie down again." ⁷Now Samuel did not yet know GOD, and the word of GOD had not yet been revealed to Samuel. ⁸And GOD called Samuel again the third time. And Samuel arose and went to Eli, and said, "Here I am, for you called me." Then Eli perceived that GOD was calling the boy. ⁹Therefore Eli said to Samuel, "Go, lie down; and if GOD calls you, you shall say, 'Speak, O SOVEREIGN ONE, for your servant hears.'" So Samuel went and lay down in his place.

¹⁰And GOD came and stood forth, calling as at other times, "Samuel! Samuel!" And Samuel said, "Speak, for your servant hears." ¹¹Then GOD said to Samuel, "Behold, I am about to do a thing in Israel, at which the two ears of every one that hears it will tingle. ¹²On that day I will fulfil against Eli all that I have spoken concerning his house, from beginning to end. ¹³And I tell Eli that I am about to punish his house for ever, for the iniquity which he knew, because his sons were blaspheming God, and Eli did not restrain them. ¹⁴Therefore I swear to the house of Eli that the iniquity of Eli's house shall not be expiated by sacrifice or offering for ever."

¹⁵Samuel lay until morning; then he opened the doors of the house of GOD. And Samuel was afraid to tell the vision to Eli. ¹⁶But Eli called Samuel and said, "Samuel, my son." And Samuel said, "Here I am." ¹⁷And Eli said, "What was it that God told you? Do not hide it from me. May God do so to you and more also, if you hide anything from me of all that God told you." ¹⁸So Samuel told Eli everything and hid nothing from him. And Eli said, "It is the SOVEREIGN ONE; let God do what seems good."

¹⁹And Samuel grew, and GOD was with him and let none of Samuel's words fall to the ground. ²⁰And all Israel from Dan to Beersheba knew that Samuel was established as a prophet of GOD.

Psalm 63:1-8

[1]O God, you are my God, I seek you,
  my soul thirsts for you;
 my flesh faints for you,
  as in a dry and weary land where no water is.
[2]So I have looked upon you in the sanctuary,
  beholding your power and glory.
[3]Because your steadfast love is better than life,
  my lips will praise you.
[4]So I will bless you as long as I live;
  I will lift up my hands and call on your name.
[5]My soul is feasted as with marrow and fat,
  and my mouth praises you with joyful lips,
[6]when I think of you upon my bed,
  and meditate on you in the watches of the night;
[7]for you have been my help,
  and in the shadow of your wings I sing for joy.
[8]My soul clings to you;
  your right hand upholds me.

Lesson 2 (alternate) ~ Romans 16:1-7[+]

Paul commends Phoebe and greets other co-workers in the church at Rome.

[1]I commend to you our sister Phoebe, a deacon of the church at Cenchreae, [2]that you may receive her in the Sovereign[□] as befits the saints, and help her in whatever she may require from you, for she has been a helper of many and of myself as well.

[3]Greet Prisca and Aquila, my co-workers in Christ Jesus, [4]who risked their necks for my life, to whom not only I but also all the churches of the Gentiles give thanks; [5]greet also the church in their house. Greet my beloved Epaenetus, who was the first convert in Asia for Christ. [6]Greet Mary, who has worked hard among you. [7]Greet Andronicus and Junia,[‡] my kinsfolk and prisoners with me; they are noteworthy among the apostles, and they were in Christ before me.

[+]Lection added. See Appendix, p. 248.
[□]RSV *Lord*. See Appendix.
[‡]RSV *Junias*.

Lesson 2 ~ 1 Corinthians 6:12-15a, 19-20[+]

Paul writes to the Corinthians that they are members of Christ.

[12]"All things are lawful for me," but not all things are helpful. "All things are lawful for me," but I will not be enslaved by anything. [13]"Food is meant for the stomach and the stomach for food"—and God will destroy both one and the other. The body is not meant for immorality, but for Christ,□ and Christ□ for the body. [14]And God raised Christ□ and will also raise us up by God's power. [15]Do you not know that your bodies are members of Christ? [19]Do you not know that your body is a temple of the Holy Spirit within you, which you have from God? You are not your own; [20]you were bought with a price. So glorify God in your body.

Gospel ~ John 1:35-42

Two of John's disciples follow Jesus, testifying that Jesus is the Messiah.

[35]The next day again John was standing with two of his disciples, [36]and looking at Jesus walking by, said, "Behold, the Lamb of God!" [37]The two disciples heard John say this, and they followed Jesus. [38]Jesus turned, and saw them following, and said to them, "What do you seek?" And they said, "Rabbi" (which means Teacher), "where are you staying?" [39]Jesus said to them, "Come and see." They came and saw where Jesus was staying; and they stayed with him that day, for it was about the tenth hour. [40]One of the two who heard John speak, and followed Jesus, was Andrew, Simon Peter's brother. [41]Andrew first found his brother Simon, and said to him, "We have found the Messiah" (which means Christ). [42]Andrew brought Simon to Jesus. Jesus looked at him, and said, "So you are Simon the son of John? You shall be called Cephas" (which means Peter).

[+]The NACCL reads 1 Cor. 6:12-20. See Appendix, p. 248.
□RSV *the Lord.* See Appendix.

EPIPHANY 3

Lesson 1 ~ Jonah 3:1-5, 10

Jonah's second call to preach to Nineveh results in the conversion of its inhabitants.

¹Then the word of GOD came to Jonah the second time, saying, ²"Arise, go to Nineveh, that great city, and proclaim to it the message that I tell you." ³So Jonah arose and went to Nineveh, according to the word of GOD. Now Nineveh was an exceedingly great city, three days' journey in breadth. ⁴Jonah began to go into the city, going a day's journey. And he cried, "Yet forty days, and Nineveh shall be overthrown!" ⁵And the people of Nineveh believed God; they proclaimed a fast, and put on sackcloth, from the greatest of them to the least of them.

¹⁰When God saw what they did, how they turned from their evil way, God repented of the evil which God had vowed to do to them, and did not do it.

Psalm 62:5-12

⁵For God alone my soul waits in silence,
  for my hope is from God,
⁶who alone is my rock and my salvation,
  my fortress; I shall not be shaken.
⁷On God rests my deliverance and my honor;
  my mighty rock, my refuge is God.
⁸Trust in God at all times, O people;
  pour out your heart before God,
  who is a refuge for us.
⁹Those of low estate are but a breath,
  those of high estate are a delusion;
 in the balances they go up;
  they are together lighter than a breath.
¹⁰Put no confidence in extortion,
  set no vain hopes on robbery;
  if riches increase, set not your heart on them.
¹¹Once God has spoken;
  twice have I heard this:
 that power belongs to God;
¹² and that to you, O God, belongs steadfast love.
 For you repay all people
  according to their work.

Lesson 2 ~ 1 Corinthians 7:29-31, (32-35)

Paul writes to the Corinthians about living in the time when the form of this world is passing away.

29I mean, sisters and brothers, the appointed time has grown very short; from now on, let those who are married live as though they were not, 30and those who mourn as though they were not mourning, and those who rejoice as though they were not rejoicing, and those who buy as though they had no goods, 31and those who deal with the world as though they had no dealings with it. For the form of this world is passing away.

32I want you to be free from anxieties. The unmarried man is anxious about the affairs of the Sovereign,□ how to please the Sovereign;□ 33 but the married man is anxious about worldly affairs, how to please his wife, 34and his interests are divided. And the unmarried woman or young girl is anxious about the affairs of the Sovereign,□ how to be holy in body and spirit; but the married woman is anxious about worldly affairs, how to please her husband. 35I say this for your own benefit, not to lay any restraint upon you, but to promote good order and to secure your undivided devotion to the Sovereign.□

Gospel ~ Mark 1:14-20

Jesus calls Simon and Andrew.

14Now after John was arrested, Jesus came into Galilee, preaching the gospel of God, 15and saying, "The time is fulfilled, and the realm* of God is at hand; repent, and believe in the gospel."

16And passing along by the Sea of Galilee, Jesus saw Simon and Andrew the brother of Simon casting a net in the sea; for they were fishers. 17And Jesus said to them, "Follow me and I will make you become fishers of people." 18And immediately they left their nets and followed him. 19And going on a little farther, Jesus saw James the son of Zebedee and John his brother, who were in their boat mending the nets. 20And immediately Jesus called them; and they left their father Zebedee in the boat with the hired servants, and followed Jesus.

□RSV *Lord*. See Appendix.
*RSV *kingdom*. See Appendix.

EPIPHANY 4

Lesson 1 ~ Deuteronomy 18:15-20

God promises to send a prophet like Moses.

¹⁵The SOVEREIGN ONE your God will raise up for you a prophet like me from among you, from your own people—that prophet you shall heed—¹⁶just as you desired of the SOVEREIGN ONE your God at Horeb on the day of the assembly, when you said, "Let me not hear again the voice of the SOVEREIGN ONE my God, or see this great fire any more, lest I die." ¹⁷And GOD said to me, "They have rightly said all that they have spoken. ¹⁸I will raise up for them a prophet like you from among their people; and I will put my words in the mouth of that prophet, who shall speak to them all that I command. ¹⁹And whoever will not give heed to my words which the prophet shall speak in my name, I myself will require it of them. ²⁰But the prophet who presumes to speak a word in my name which I have not commanded to be spoken, or who speaks in the name of other gods, that same prophet shall die."

Psalm 111

¹Praise GOD.
I will give thanks to GOD with my whole heart,
    in the company of the upright, in the congregation.
²Great are the works of GOD,
    studied by all who have pleasure in them.
³Full of honor and majesty is God's work,
    and God's righteousness endures for ever.
⁴God has caused God's wonderful works to be remembered,
    and is gracious and merciful,
⁵providing food for those who fear God
    and being ever mindful of the covenant.
⁶God has shown God's people the power of God's works,
    in giving them the heritage of the nations.
⁷The works of God's hands are faithful and just;
    all God's precepts are trustworthy,
⁸they are established for ever and ever,
    to be performed with faithfulness and uprightness.

⁹God sent redemption to God's people,
  and has commanded the covenant for ever.
  Holy and terrible is God's name!
¹⁰The fear of GOD is the beginning of wisdom;
  a good understanding have all those who practice it.
  God's praise endures for ever!

Lesson 2 ~ 1 Corinthians 8:1-13

Paul writes to the Corinthians about their ethical responsibilities to one another.

¹Now concerning food offered to idols: we know that "all of us possess knowledge." "Knowledge" puffs up, but love builds up. ²If any imagine that they know something, they do not yet know as they ought to know. ³But if one loves God, one is known by God.

⁴Hence, as to the eating of food offered to idols, we know that "an idol has no real existence," and that "there is no God but one." ⁵For although there may be so-called gods in heaven or on earth—as indeed there are many "gods" and many "sovereigns□" ⁶yet for us there is one God, the Father [*and Mother**], from whom are all things and for whom we exist, and one Sovereign,□ Jesus Christ, through whom are all things and through whom we exist.

⁷However, not all possess this knowledge. But some, through being hitherto accustomed to idols, eat food as really offered to an idol; and their conscience, being weak, is defiled. ⁸Food will not commend us to God. We are no worse off if we do not eat, and no better off if we do. ⁹Only take care lest this liberty of yours somehow become a stumbling block to the weak. ¹⁰For if any one, having a weak conscience, sees you, a person of knowledge, at table in an idol's temple, might that one not be encouraged to eat food offered to idols? ¹¹And so by your knowledge this weak person is destroyed, the sister or brother for whom Christ died. ¹²Thus, sinning against your brothers or sisters and wounding their conscience when it is weak, you sin against Christ. ¹³Therefore, if food is a cause of my sister's or brother's falling, I will never eat meat, lest I cause that person to fall.

□RSV v. 5 *"lords"*; v. 6 *Lord*. See Appendix.
*Addition to the text. See "Metaphor" and "God the Father and Mother" in the Appendix.

Jesus speaks with authority to an unclean spirit.

[21]And they went into Capernaum; and immediately on the sabbath Jesus entered the synagogue and taught. [22]And they were astonished at Jesus' teaching, for he taught them as one who had authority, and not as the scribes. [23]And immediately there was in their synagogue some one with an unclean spirit [24]who cried out, "What have you to do with us, Jesus of Nazareth? Have you come to destroy us? I know who you are, the Holy One of God." [25]But Jesus rebuked the spirit, saying, "Be silent, and come out!" [26]And the unclean spirit, convulsing the person and crying with a loud voice, came out. [27]And they were all amazed, so that they questioned among themselves, saying, "What is this? A new teaching! With authority Jesus commands even the unclean spirits, and they obey." [28]And at once Jesus' fame spread everywhere throughout all the surrounding region of Galilee.

EPIPHANY 5

Lesson 1 ~ Job 7:1-7

Job speaks about the pain of human life.

¹Have not human beings a hard service upon earth,
   and are not their days like the days of a hireling?
²Like a slave who longs for the shadow of evening,
   and like a hireling who looks for wages,
³so I am allotted months of emptiness,
   and nights of misery are apportioned to me.
⁴When I lie down I say, "When shall I arise?"
   But the night is long,
   and I am full of tossing till the dawn.
⁵My flesh is clothed with worms and dirt;
   my skin hardens, then breaks out afresh.
⁶My days are swifter than a weaver's shuttle,
   and come to their end without hope.
⁷Remember that my life is a breath;
   my eye will never again see good.

Psalm 147:1-11

¹Praise GOD!
 For it is good to sing praises to our God;
   for God is gracious, and a song of praise is seemly.
²GOD builds up Jerusalem,
   and gathers the outcasts of Israel,
³heals the brokenhearted,
   and binds up their wounds,
⁴determines the number of the stars,
   and gives to all of them their names.
⁵Great is our GOD, and abundant in power,
   with understanding beyond measure.
⁶GOD lifts up the downtrodden,
   and casts the wicked to the ground.
⁷Sing to GOD with thanksgiving;
   make melody upon the lyre to our God,
⁸who covers the heavens with clouds,
   prepares rain for the earth,
   and makes grass grow upon the hills,

9who gives to the beasts their food,
    and to the young ravens which cry!
10God does not delight in the strength of the horse,
    nor take pleasure in the might of a human being;
11but GOD takes pleasure in those who fear God,
    in those who hope in God's steadfast love.

Lesson 2 ~ 1 Corinthians 9:16-23

Paul writes about his mandate to preach the gospel under all circumstances.

16For if I preach the gospel, that gives me no ground for boasting. For necessity is laid upon me. Woe to me if I do not preach the gospel! 17For if I do this of my own will, I have a reward; but if not of my own will, I am entrusted with a commission. 18What then is my reward? Just this: that in my preaching I may make the gospel free of charge, not making full use of my right in the gospel.

19For though I am free from all people, I have made myself a slave to all, that I might win the more. 20To the Jews I became as a Jew, in order to win Jews; to those under the law I became as one under the law—though not being myself under the law—that I might win those under the law. 21To those outside the law I became as one outside the law—not being without law toward God but under the law of Christ—that I might win those outside the law. 22To the weak I became weak, that I might win the weak. I have become all things to all people, that I might by all means save some. 23I do it all for the sake of the gospel, that I may share in its blessings.

Gospel ~ Mark 1:29-39

Jesus is engaged in a ministry of healing.

29And immediately Jesus left the synagogue, and entered the house of Simon and Andrew, with James and John. 30Now Simon's mother-in-law lay sick with a fever, and immediately they told Jesus of her. 31And Jesus came and took her by the hand and lifted her up, and the fever left her; and she served them.

32That evening, at sundown, they brought to Jesus all who were sick or possessed with demons. 33And the whole city was gathered together about the door. 34And Jesus healed many who were sick with various diseases, and cast out many demons, and would not permit the demons to speak, because they knew him.

[35]And in the morning, a great while before day, Jesus rose and went out to a lonely place, and there Jesus prayed. [36]And Simon and those who were with him pursued Jesus, [37]and they found him and said, "Every one is searching for you." [38]And Jesus replied, "Let us go on to the next towns, that I may preach there also; for that is why I came out." [39]And Jesus went throughout all Galilee, preaching in their synagogues and casting out demons.

EPIPHANY 6

Lesson 1 ~ 2 Kings 5:1-14

Naaman is cured of leprosy.

[1]Naaman, commander of the army of the king of Syria, was a great man with his ruler and in high favor, because by Naaman GOD had given victory to Syria. Naaman was a mighty man of valor, but he had leprosy. [2]Now the Syrians on one of their raids had carried off a little maid from the land of Israel, and she waited on Naaman's wife. [3] She said to her mistress, "Would that my lord were with the prophet who is in Samaria! The prophet would cure Naaman of leprosy." [4]So Naaman went in and told his lord, "Thus and so spoke the maiden from the land of Israel." [5]And the king of Syria said, "Go now, and I will send a letter to the king of Israel."

So Naaman went, taking ten talents of silver, six thousand shekels of gold, and ten festal garments. [6]And Naaman brought the letter to the king of Israel, which read, "When this letter reaches you, know that I have sent to you Naaman my servant, that you may cure him of leprosy." [7]And when the king of Israel read the letter, he rent his clothes and said, "Am I God, to kill and to make alive, that the king of Syria sends word to me to cure some one of leprosy? Only consider, and see how that king is seeking a quarrel with me."

[8]But when Elisha the prophet of God heard that the king of Israel had rent his clothes, Elisha sent to the king, saying, "Why have you rent your clothes? Let Naaman come now to me, that he may know that there is a prophet in Israel." [9]So Naaman came with horses and chariots, and halted at the door of Elisha's house. [10]And Elisha sent a messenger to Naaman, saying, "Go and wash in the Jordan seven times, and your flesh shall be restored, and you shall be clean." [11]But Naaman was angry, and went away, saying, "Behold, I thought that Elisha would surely come out to me, and stand, and call on the name of the SOVEREIGN ONE his God, and wave his hand over the place, and cure the one with leprosy. [12]Are not Abana and Pharpar, the rivers of Damascus, better than all the waters of Israel? Could I not wash in them, and be clean?" So Naaman turned and went away in a rage. [13]But his servants came near and said to Naaman, "My father, if the prophet had commanded you to do some great thing, would you not have done it? How much rather, then, when Elisha says to you, 'Wash, and be clean'?" [14]So Naaman went down and dipped himself seven times in the Jordan, according to the word of the prophet of God; and Naaman's flesh was restored like the flesh of a little child, and he was clean.

Psalm 32

¹Blessed is the one whose transgression is forgiven,
    whose sin is covered.
²Blessed is the person to whom GOD imputes no iniquity,
    and in whose spirit there is no deceit.
³When I declared not my sin, my body wasted away
    through my groaning all day long.
⁴For day and night your hand was heavy upon me;
    my strength was dried up as by the heat of summer.
⁵I acknowledged my sin to you,
    and I did not hide my iniquity;
 I said, "I will confess my transgressions to GOD";
    then you forgave the guilt of my sin.
⁶Therefore let all who are godly
    offer prayer to you;
 at a time of distress, the rush of great waters
    shall not reach them.
⁷You are a hiding place for me,
    you preserve me from trouble;
    you encompass me with deliverance.
⁸I will instruct you and teach you
    the way you should go;
    I will counsel you with my eye upon you.
⁹Be not like a horse or a mule, without understanding,
    which must be curbed with bit and bridle,
    else it will not keep with you.
¹⁰Many are the pangs of the wicked;
    but steadfast love surrounds the one who trusts in GOD.
¹¹Be glad in GOD, and rejoice, O righteous,
    and shout for joy, all you upright in heart!

Lesson 2 ~ 1 Corinthians 9:24-27

Paul speaks about the importance of self-discipline.

²⁴Do you not know that in a race all the runners compete, but only one receives the prize? So run that you may obtain it. ²⁵Every athlete exercises self-control in all things. They do it to receive a perishable wreath, but we an imperishable. ²⁶Well, I do not run aimlessly, I do not box as one beating the air; ²⁷but I pommel my body and subdue it, lest after preaching to others I myself should be disqualified.

Gospel ~ Mark 1:40-45

A person with leprosy comes to Jesus for healing.

[40]A person with leprosy came beseeching Jesus, and kneeling said to him, "If you will, you can make me clean." [41]Moved with pity, Jesus reached out and touched the person, and said, "I will; be clean." [42]And immediately the leprosy went away and the person was made clean. [43]And Jesus sternly charged and sent away the one whom he had healed, [44]saying, "See that you tell nothing about this to any one; but go, show yourself to the priest, and offer for your cleansing what Moses commanded, for a proof to the people." [45]But the one who had been healed went out and began to talk freely about it, and to spread the news, so that Jesus could no longer openly enter a town, but was out in the country; and people came to Jesus from every quarter.

EPIPHANY 7

Lesson 1 ~ Isaiah 43:18-25

Isaiah announces God's forgiveness and redemption.

18Remember not the former things,
  nor consider the things of old.
19Behold, I am doing a new thing;
  now it springs forth, do you not perceive it?
 I will make a way in the wilderness
  and rivers in the desert.
20The wild beasts will honor me,
  the jackals and the ostriches;
 for I give water in the wilderness,
  rivers in the desert,
 to give drink to my chosen people,
21   the people whom I formed for myself
  that they might declare my praise.
22Yet you did not call upon me, O Jacob;
  but you have been weary of me, O Israel!
23You have not brought me your sheep for burnt offerings,
  or honored me with your sacrifices.
 I have not burdened you with offerings,
  or wearied you with frankincense.
24You have not bought me sweet cane with money,
  or satisfied me with the fat of your sacrifices.
 But you have burdened me with your sins,
  you have wearied me with your iniquities.
25I, I am the One
  who blots out your transgressions for my own sake,
  and I will not remember your sins.

Psalm 41

1Blessed are those who consider the poor!
  GOD delivers them in the day of trouble;
2GOD protects them and keeps them alive;
  they are called blessed in the land;
  you do not give them up to the will of their enemies.
3GOD sustains them on their sickbed;
  in their illness you heal all their infirmities.

⁴As for me, I said, "O GOD, be gracious to me;
  heal me, for I have sinned against you!"
⁵My enemies say of me in malice:
  "When will that one die, and that name perish?"
⁶And when people come to see me, uttering empty words,
  their heart gathers mischief;
  and when they go out, they tell it abroad.
⁷All who hate me whisper together about me;
  they imagine the worst for me.
⁸They say, "A deadly thing has fastened upon that one,
  who has lain down never to rise again."
⁹Even my bosom friend in whom I trusted,
  who ate of my bread, has betrayed me.
¹⁰But you, O GOD, be gracious to me,
  and raise me up, that I may repay them!
¹¹By this I know that you are pleased with me,
  in that my enemy has not triumphed over me.
¹²But you have upheld me because of my integrity,
  and set me in your presence for ever.
¹³Blessed be the SOVEREIGN ONE, the God of Israel,
  from everlasting to everlasting!
  Amen and Amen.

Lesson 2 ~ 2 Corinthians 1:18-22

All God's promises are affirmed in Christ.

¹⁸As surely as God is faithful, our word to you has not been Yes and
No. ¹⁹For the Child◇ of God, Jesus Christ, whom we preached among
you, Silvanus and Timothy and I, was not Yes and No; but in Christ it is
always Yes. ²⁰For all the promises of God find their Yes in Christ. That
is why we utter the Amen through Jesus Christ, to the glory of God.
²¹But it is God who establishes us with you in Christ, and has
commissioned us; ²²God has put God's seal upon us and given us the
Spirit of God in our hearts as a guarantee.

◇RSV *Son.* See Appendix.

Mark tells the story of Jesus' healing someone who was paralyzed.

[1]And when Jesus returned to Capernaum after some days, it was reported that he was at home. [2]And many were gathered together, so that there was no longer room for them, not even about the door; and Jesus was preaching the word to them. [3]And some people came, bringing to Jesus a person who was paralyzed, carried by four men. [4]And when they could not get near Jesus because of the crowd, they removed the roof above him; and when they had made an opening, they let down the pallet on which the person lay. [5]And having seen their faith, Jesus said to the one who was paralyzed, "My child, your sins are forgiven." [6]Now some of the scribes were sitting there, questioning in their hearts, [7]"Why does this man speak thus? It is blasphemy! Who can forgive sins but God alone?" [8]And immediately Jesus, perceiving in his spirit that they thus questioned within themselves, said to them, "Why do you question thus in your hearts? [9]Which is easier, to say to the one paralyzed, 'Your sins are forgiven,' or to say, 'Rise, take up your pallet and walk'? [10]But that you may know that the Human One° has authority on earth to forgive sins"—Jesus said to the one who was paralyzed— [11]"I say to you, rise, take up your pallet and go home." [12]And the one who had been paralyzed arose, and immediately took up the pallet and went out before them all; so that they were all amazed and glorified God, saying, "We never saw anything like this!"

°RSV *Son of man.* See Appendix.

EPIPHANY 8

Lesson 1 ~ Hosea 2:14-20

Through the prophet Hosea, God speaks of God's love for Israel.

¹⁴Therefore, behold, I will allure Israel,
    and bring them into the wilderness,
    and speak tenderly to them.
¹⁵And there I will give Israel vineyards,
    and make the Valley of Achor a door of hope.
  And there Israel shall answer as in the days of their youth,
    as at the time when they came out of the land of Egypt.
¹⁶And in that day, says the SOVEREIGN ONE, you will call me, "My beloved,"
and no longer will you call me, "My Baal." ¹⁷For I will remove the names of
the Baals from Israel's mouth, and they shall be mentioned by name no
more. ¹⁸And I will make for you a covenant on that day with the beasts of
the field, the birds of the air, and the creeping things of the ground; and I
will abolish the bow, the sword, and war from the land; and I will make you
lie down in safety. ¹⁹And I will join you to me for ever; I will join you to me
in righteousness and in justice, in steadfast love, and in mercy. ²⁰I will join
you to me in faithfulness; and you shall know the SOVEREIGN ONE.

Psalm 103:1-13

¹Bless GOD, O my soul;
    and all that is within me, bless God's holy name!
²Bless GOD, O my soul,
    and forget not all God's benefits,
³who forgives all your iniquity,
    who heals all your diseases,
⁴who redeems your life from the Pit,
    who crowns you with steadfast love and mercy,
⁵who satisfies you with good as long as you live
    so that your youth is renewed like the eagle's.
⁶GOD works vindication
    and justice for all who are oppressed.
⁷God made known God's ways to Moses,
    God's acts to the people of Israel.
⁸GOD is merciful and gracious,
    slow to anger and abounding in steadfast love,

⁹not always chiding,
>nor remaining angry for ever.
¹⁰GOD does not deal with us according to our sins,
>nor repay us according to our iniquities.
¹¹For as the heavens are high above the earth,
>so great is God's steadfast love toward those who fear God;
¹²as far as the east is from the west,
>so far does God remove our transgressions from us.
¹³As parents pity their children,
>so GOD pities those who fear God.

Lesson 2 ~ 2 Corinthians 3:1-6

Paul defends his apostolic authority.

¹Are we beginning to commend ourselves again? Or do we need, as some do, letters of recommendation to you, or from you? ²You yourselves are our letter of recommendation, written on your hearts, to be known and read by all; ³and you show that you are a letter from Christ delivered by us, written not with ink but with the Spirit of the living God, not on tablets of stone but on tablets of human hearts.

⁴Such is the confidence that we have through Christ toward God. ⁵Not that we are competent of ourselves to claim anything as coming from us; our competence is from God, ⁶who has made us competent to be ministers of a new covenant, not in a written code but in the Spirit; for the written code kills, but the Spirit gives life.

Gospel ~ Mark 2:18-22

Jesus responds to a question about why his disciples do not fast.

¹⁸Now John's disciples and the Pharisees were fasting; and people came and said to Jesus, "Why do John's disciples and the disciples of the Pharisees fast, but your disciples do not fast?" ¹⁹And Jesus said to them, "Can the wedding guests fast while the bridegroom is with them? As long as they have the bridegroom with them, they cannot fast. ²⁰The days will come, when the bridegroom is taken away from them, and then they will fast in that day. ²¹No one sews a piece of unshrunk cloth on an old garment; if one does, the patch tears away from it, the new from the old, and a worse tear is made. ²²And no one puts new wine into old wineskins; if one does, the wine will burst the skins, and the wine is lost, and so are the skins; but new wine is for fresh skins."

LAST SUNDAY AFTER EPIPHANY

Lesson 1 ~ 2 Kings 2:1-12a

Elijah passes the responsibilities of leadership to Elisha.

¹Now when GOD was about to take Elijah up to heaven by a whirlwind, Elijah and Elisha were on their way from Gilgal. ²And Elijah said to Elisha, "Tarry here, I pray you; for GOD has sent me as far as Bethel." But Elisha said, "As GOD lives, and as you yourself live, I will not leave you." So they went down to Bethel. ³And the prophets who were in Bethel came out to Elisha, and said, "Do you know that today GOD will take away your teacher from over you?" And Elisha said, "Yes, I know it; hold your peace."

⁴Elijah said to him, "Elisha, tarry here, I pray you; for GOD has sent me to Jericho." But Elisha said, "As GOD lives, and as you yourself live, I will not leave you." So they came to Jericho. ⁵The prophets who were at Jericho drew near to Elisha, and said to him, "Do you know that today GOD will take away your teacher from over you?" And Elisha answered, "Yes, I know it; hold your peace."

⁶Then Elijah said to Elisha, "Tarry here, I pray you; for GOD has sent me to the Jordan." But Elisha said, "As GOD lives, and as you yourself live, I will not leave you." So the two of them went on. ⁷Fifty of the prophets also went, and stood at some distance from them, as they both were standing by the Jordan. ⁸Then Elijah took his mantle, and rolled it up, and struck the water, and the water was parted to the one side and to the other, till the two of them could go over on dry ground.

⁹When they had crossed, Elijah said to Elisha, "Ask what I shall do for you, before I am taken from you." And Elisha said, "I pray you, let me inherit a double share of your spirit." ¹⁰And Elijah said, "You have asked a hard thing; yet, if you see me as I am being taken from you, it shall be so for you; but if you do not see me, it shall not be so." ¹¹And as they still went on and talked, behold, a chariot of fire and horses of fire separated the two of them. And Elijah went up by a whirlwind into heaven. ¹²And Elisha saw it and cried out, "My teacher, my teacher! the chariots of Israel and its riders!"

Psalm 50:1-6

¹The Mighty One, God the SOVEREIGN ONE,
　　speaks and summons the earth
　　from the rising of the sun to its setting.
²Out of Zion, the perfection of beauty,
　　God shines forth.

³Our God comes and does not keep silence,
   before God is a devouring fire,
   round about God a mighty tempest.
⁴God calls to the heavens above
   and to the earth, in order to judge God's people:
⁵"Gather to me my faithful ones,
   who made a covenant with me by sacrifice!"
⁶The heavens declare God's righteousness,
   for it is God who judges!

Lesson 2 ~ 2 Corinthians 4:3-6

Paul clarifies for the Corinthians the meaning of the gospel.

³And even if our gospel is veiled, it is veiled only to those who are perishing. ⁴In their case the god of this world has blinded the minds of the unbelievers, to keep them from seeing the light of the gospel of the glory of Christ, who is the likeness of God. ⁵For what we preach is not ourselves, but Jesus Christ as Sovereign,□ with ourselves as your servants for Jesus' sake. ⁶For it is the God who said, "Let light shine out of darkness," who has shone in our hearts to give the light of the knowledge of the glory of God in the face of Christ.

Gospel ~ Mark 9:2-9

Mark records the transfiguration of Jesus.

²And after six days Jesus took with him Peter and James and John, and led them up a high mountain apart by themselves; and Jesus was transfigured before them, ³and Jesus' garments became glistening, intensely white, as no one on earth could bleach them. ⁴And there appeared to them Elijah with Moses; and they were talking to Jesus. ⁵And Peter said to Jesus, "Rabbi, it is well that we are here; let us make three booths, one for you and one for Moses and one for Elijah." ⁶For Peter did not know what to say, for they were exceedingly afraid. ⁷And a cloud overshadowed them, and a voice came out of the cloud, "This is my beloved Child;◇ to this one you shall listen." ⁸And suddenly looking around they no longer saw any one with them but Jesus only.

⁹And as they were coming down the mountain, Jesus charged them to tell no one what they had seen, until the Human One○ should have risen from the dead.

□RSV *Lord.* See Appendix.
◇RSV *Son.* See Appendix.
○RSV *Son of man.* See Appendix.

ASH WEDNESDAY

God calls the people to fasting and repentance.

¹Blow the trumpet in Zion;
    sound the alarm on my holy mountain!
Let all the inhabitants of the land tremble,
    for the day of GOD is coming, it is near,
²a day of shadow and gloom,
    a day of clouds and dense shadow!
Like a blanket there is spread upon the mountains
    a great and powerful people;
their like has never been from of old,
    nor will be again after them
    through the years of all generations.
¹²"Yet even now," says the SOVEREIGN ONE,
    "return to me with all your heart,
with fasting, with weeping, and with mourning;
¹³   and rend your hearts and not your garments."
Return to the SOVEREIGN ONE, your God,
    for God is gracious and merciful,
slow to anger, and abounding in steadfast love,
    and repents of evil.
¹⁴Who knows whether God will not turn and repent,
    and leave a blessing behind,
a cereal offering and a drink offering
    for the SOVEREIGN ONE, your God?
¹⁵Blow the trumpet in Zion;
    sanctify a fast;
call a solemn assembly;
¹⁶   gather the people.
Sanctify the congregation;
    assemble the elders;
gather the children,
    even nursing infants.
Let the bridegroom leave his room,
    and the bride her chamber.
¹⁷Between the vestibule and the altar
    let the priests, the ministers of GOD, weep
and say, "Spare your people, O SOVEREIGN ONE,
    and make not your heritage a reproach,
    a byword among the nations."

Psalm 51:1-12

[1]Have mercy on me, O God, according to your steadfast love;
  according to your abundant mercy blot out my transgressions.
[2]Wash me thoroughly from my iniquity,
  and cleanse me from my sin!
[3]For I know my transgressions,
  and my sin is ever before me.
[4]Against you, you only, have I sinned,
  and done that which is evil in your sight,
so that you are justified in your sentence
  and blameless in your judgment.
[5]Behold, I was brought forth in iniquity,
  and in sin did my mother conceive me.
[6]Behold, you desire truth in the inward being;
  therefore teach me wisdom in my secret heart.
[7]Purge me with hyssop, and I shall be clean;
  wash me, and I shall be cleaner than snow.
[8]Fill me with joy and gladness;
  let the bones which you have broken rejoice.
[9]Hide your face from my sins,
  and blot out all my iniquities.
[10]Create in me a clean heart, O God,
  and put a new and right spirit within me.
[11]Cast me not away from your presence,
  and take not your holy Spirit from me.
[12]Restore to me the joy of your salvation,
  and uphold me with a willing spirit.

Lesson 2 ~ 2 Corinthians 5:20b–6:2, (3-10)

Paul writes to the Corinthians of his ministry of reconciliation.

[20]We beseech you on behalf of Christ, be reconciled to God. [21]For our sake God made Christ to be sin who knew no sin, so that in Christ we might become the righteousness of God.
  [6:1]Working together with God, then, we entreat you not to accept the grace of God in vain. [2]For God says,
  "At the acceptable time I have listened to you,
  and helped you on the day of salvation."
Behold,·now is the acceptable time; behold, now is the day of salvation.

3We put no obstacle in any one's way, so that no fault may be found with our ministry, 4but as servants of God we commend ourselves in every way: through great endurance, in afflictions, hardships, calamities, 5beatings, imprisonments, tumults, labors, watching, hunger; 6by purity, knowledge, forbearance, kindness, the Holy Spirit, genuine love, 7truthful speech, and the power of God; with the weapons of righteousness for the right hand and for the left; 8in honor and dishonor, in ill repute and good repute. We are treated as impostors, and yet are true; 9as unknown, and yet well known; as dying, and behold we live; as punished, and yet not killed; 10as sorrowful, yet always rejoicing; as poor, yet making many rich; as having nothing, and yet possessing everything.

Gospel ~ Matthew 6:1-6, 16-21

Jesus tells the disciples to lay up treasure in heaven.

1Beware of practicing your piety before others in order to be seen by them; for then you will have no reward from [God] your Father [and Mother*] who is in heaven.

2Thus, when you give alms, sound no trumpet before you, as the hypocrites do in the synagogues and in the streets, that they may be praised by others. Truly, I say to you, they have received their reward. 3But when you give alms, do not let your left hand know what your right hand is doing, 4so that your alms may be in secret; and God who sees in secret will reward you.

5And when you pray, you must not be like the hypocrites; for they love to stand and pray in the synagogues and at the street corners, that they may be seen by others. Truly, I say to you, they have received their reward. 6But when you pray, go into your room and shut the door and pray to God who is in secret; and God who sees in secret will reward you.

16And when you fast, do not look dismal, like the hypocrites, for they disfigure their faces that their fasting may be seen by others. Truly, I say to you, they have received their reward. 17But when you fast, anoint your head and wash your face, 18that your fasting may not be seen by others but by God who is in secret; and God who sees in secret will reward you.

19Do not lay up for yourselves treasures on earth, where moth and rust consume and where thieves break in and steal, 20but lay up for yourselves treasures in heaven, where neither moth nor rust consumes and where thieves do not break in and steal. 21For where your treasure is, there will your heart be also.

---

*Addition to the text. See "Metaphor" and "God the Father and Mother" in the Appendix.

LENT 1

Lesson 1 ~ Genesis 9:8-17

After the flood, God establishes a new covenant with Noah.

[8]Then God said to Noah and to his children, [9]"Behold, I establish my covenant with you and your descendants after you, [10]and with every living creature that is with you, the birds, the cattle, and every beast of the earth with you, as many as came out of the ark. [11]I establish my covenant with you, that never again shall all flesh be cut off by the waters of a flood, and never again shall there be a flood to destroy the earth." [12]And God said, "This is the sign of the covenant which I make between me and you and every living creature that is with you, for all future generations: [13]I set my bow in the cloud, and it shall be a sign of the covenant between me and the earth. [14]When I bring clouds over the earth and the bow is seen in the clouds, [15]I will remember my covenant which is between me and you and every living creature of all flesh; and the waters shall never again become a flood to destroy all flesh. [16]When the bow is in the clouds, I will look upon it and remember the everlasting covenant between God and every living creature of all flesh that is upon the earth." [17]God said to Noah, "This is the sign of the covenant which I have established between me and all flesh that is upon the earth."

Psalm 25:1-10

[1]To you, O GOD, I lift up my soul.
[2]O my God, in you I trust,
    let me not be put to shame;
    let not my enemies exult over me.
[3]Let none that wait for you be put to shame;
    let them be ashamed who are wantonly treacherous.
[4]Make me to know your ways, O GOD;
    teach me your paths.
[5]Lead me in your truth, and teach me,
    for you are the God of my salvation;
    for you I wait all the day long.
[6]Be mindful of your mercy, O GOD, and of your steadfast love,
    for they have been from of old.
[7]Remember not the sins of my youth, or my transgressions;
    according to your steadfast love remember me,
    for your goodness' sake, O GOD!

⁸Good and upright is G<small>OD</small>,
　　who therefore instructs sinners in the way,
⁹who leads the humble in what is right,
　　and teaches the humble God's way.
¹⁰All the paths of G<small>OD</small> are steadfast love and faithfulness,
　　for those who keep God's covenant and testimonies.

Lesson 2 ~ 1 Peter 3:18-22

The author writes of the saving work of baptism through Jesus' resurrection.

¹⁸For Christ also died for sins once for all, the righteous for the unrighteous, in order to bring us to God, being put to death in the flesh but made alive in the spirit; ¹⁹in which Christ went and preached to the spirits in prison, ²⁰who formerly did not obey, when God's patience waited in the days of Noah, during the building of the ark, in which a few, that is, eight persons, were saved through water. ²¹Baptism, which corresponds to this, now saves you, not as a removal of dirt from the body but as an appeal to God for a clear conscience, through the resurrection of Jesus Christ, ²²who has gone into heaven and is at the right hand of God, and rules over angels, authorities, and powers.

Gospel ~ Mark 1:9-15

Mark writes about Jesus' baptism and temptation, and about the beginning of Jesus' ministry.

⁹In those days Jesus came from Nazareth of Galilee and was baptized by John in the Jordan. ¹⁰And having come up out of the water, immediately Jesus saw the heavens opened and the Spirit descending upon him like a dove; ¹¹and a voice came from heaven, "You are my beloved Child;[◇] with you I am well pleased."

¹²The Spirit immediately drove Jesus out into the wilderness. ¹³And Jesus was in the wilderness forty days, tempted by Satan; and was with the wild beasts; and the angels ministered to him.

¹⁴Now after John was arrested, Jesus came into Galilee, preaching the gospel of God, ¹⁵and saying, "The time is fulfilled, and the realm* of God is at hand; repent, and believe in the gospel."

◇RSV *Son.* See Appendix.
*RSV *kingdom.* See Appendix.

72

LENT 2

Lesson 1 ~ Genesis 17:1-10, 15-19

God makes a covenant with Abraham, and bestows blessings upon both Abraham and Sarah.

¹When Abram was ninety-nine years old the SOVEREIGN ONE appeared to Abram, and said, "I am God Almighty; walk before me, and be blameless. ²And I will make my covenant between me and you, and will multiply you exceedingly." ³Then Abram fell on his face; and God said, ⁴"Behold, my covenant is with you, and you shall be the ancestor of a multitude of nations. ⁵No longer shall your name be Abram, but your name shall be Abraham; for I have made you the ancestor of a multitude of nations. ⁶I will make you exceedingly fruitful; and I will make nations of you, and rulers☐ shall come forth from you. ⁷And I will establish my covenant between me and you and your descendants after you throughout their generations for an everlasting covenant, to be God to you and to your descendants after you. ⁸And I will give to you, and to your descendants after you, the land of your sojournings, all the land of Canaan, for an everlasting possession; and I will be their God."

⁹And God said to Abraham, "As for you, you shall keep my covenant, you and your descendants after you throughout their generations. ¹⁰This is my covenant, which you shall keep, between me and you and your descendants after you: Every male among you shall be circumcised."

¹⁵And God said to Abraham, "As for Sarai your wife, you shall not call her name Sarai, but Sarah shall be her name. ¹⁶I will bless her, and moreover I will give you a child by her; I will bless her, and she shall be a mother of nations; rulers☐ of peoples shall come from her." ¹⁷Then Abraham fell on his face and laughed, and said to himself, "Shall a child be born to a man who is a hundred years old? Shall Sarah, who is ninety years old, bear a child?" ¹⁸And Abraham said to God, "O that Ishmael might live in your sight!" ¹⁹God said, "No, but Sarah your wife shall bear you a son, and you shall call his name Isaac. I will establish my covenant with Isaac as an everlasting covenant for his descendants."

☐RSV *kings.* See Appendix.

¹O give thanks to GOD, call on God's name,
    make known God's deeds among the peoples!
²Sing to God, sing praises to God,
    tell of all God's wonderful works!
³Glory in God's holy name;
    let the hearts of those who seek GOD rejoice!
⁴Seek GOD and God's strength,
    seek God's presence continually!
⁵Remember the wonderful works that God has done,
    God's miracles, and the judgments GOD uttered,
⁶O offspring of Abraham [*and Sarah,**] God's servants,
    children of Jacob, [*Rachel, and Leah,**] God's chosen ones!
⁷This is the SOVEREIGN ONE our God,
    whose judgments are in all the earth.
⁸God is mindful of the covenant for ever,
    of the word that God commanded, for a thousand generations,
⁹the covenant which God made with Abraham,
    God's sworn promise to Isaac,
¹⁰confirmed to Jacob as a statute,
    to Israel as an everlasting covenant,
¹¹saying, "To you I will give the land of Canaan
    as your portion for an inheritance."

Lesson 2 ~ Romans 4:16-25

Paul writes that our justification, like Abraham's, is by faith, not by obedience to the law.

¹⁶That is why it depends on faith, in order that the promise may rest on grace and be guaranteed to all the descendants of Abraham [*and Sarah**]—not only to the adherents of the law but also to those who share the faith of Abraham, who is the ancestor of us all, ¹⁷as it is written, "I have made you the ancestor of many nations"—in the presence of the God in whom Abraham believed, who gives life to the dead and calls into existence the things that do not exist. ¹⁸In hope Abraham believed against hope, in order to become the ancestor of many nations; as he had been told, "So shall your descendants be." ¹⁹Abraham, being about a hundred years old, did not weaken in faith when considering his own body to be as good as dead, or

*Addition to the text. RSV Ps. 105:6a *Abraham his servant;* v. 6b *sons of Jacob, his chosen ones!*; Rom. 4:16 *descendants of Abraham.* See Appendix.

when considering the barrenness of Sarah's womb. [20]No distrust made Abraham waver concerning the promise of God, but he grew strong in faith, giving glory to God, [21]fully convinced that God was able to do what God had promised. [22]That is why Abraham's faith was "reckoned to him as righteousness." [23]But the words, "it was reckoned to him," were written not for Abraham's sake alone, [24]but for ours also. It will be reckoned to us who believe in the one who raised from the dead Jesus our Sovereign,[□] [25]who was put to death for our trespasses and raised for our justification.

Gospel ~ Mark 8:31-38

Jesus speaks about the passion and teaches about discipleship.

[31]And Jesus began to teach them that the Human One[○] must suffer many things, and be rejected by the elders and the chief priests and the scribes, and be killed, and after three days rise again. [32]And he said this plainly. And Peter took Jesus, and began to rebuke him. [33]But turning and seeing his disciples, Jesus rebuked Peter, and said, "Get behind me, Satan! For you are not on God's side, but on the human side."

[34]And Jesus summoned the multitude with the disciples, and said to them, "If any would come after me, let them deny themselves and take up their cross and follow me. [35]For those who would save their life will lose it; and those who lose their life for my sake and the gospel's will save it. [36]For what is one profited, if one gains the whole world and forfeits one's life? [37]For what shall one give in return for one's life? [38]For whoever is ashamed of me and of my words in this adulterous and sinful generation, of that one will the Human One[○] also be ashamed, when the Human One[○] comes in the glory of God[⊗] with the holy angels."

[□]RSV *Lord.* See Appendix.
[○]RSV *Son of man.* See Appendix.
[⊗]RSV *his Father.*

Mark records the transfiguration of Jesus.

¹And Jesus said to them, "Truly, I say to you, there are some standing here who will not taste death before they see that the realm* of God has come with power."

²And after six days Jesus took Peter and James and John, and led them up a high mountain apart by themselves; and Jesus was transfigured before them, ³and Jesus' garments became glistening, intensely white, as no one on earth could bleach them. ⁴And there appeared to them Elijah with Moses; and they were talking to Jesus. ⁵And Peter said to Jesus, "Rabbi, it is well that we are here; let us make three booths, one for you and one for Moses and one for Elijah." ⁶For Peter did not know what to say, for they were exceedingly afraid. ⁷And a cloud overshadowed them, and a voice came out of the cloud, "This is my beloved Child;° to this one you shall listen." ⁸And suddenly looking around they no longer saw any one with them but Jesus only.

⁹And as they were coming down the mountain, Jesus charged them to tell no one what they had seen, until the Human One° should have risen from the dead.

---

*RSV *kingdom.* See Appendix.
°RSV *Son.* See Appendix.
°RSV *Son of man.* See Appendix.

LENT 3

Lesson 1 ~ Exodus 20:1-17

God gives the Ten Commandments to Moses.

¹And God spoke all these words, saying,

²"I am the SOVEREIGN ONE your God, who brought you out of the land of Egypt, out of the house of bondage.

³"You shall have no other gods before me.

⁴"You shall not make for yourself a graven image, or any likeness of anything that is in heaven above, or that is in the earth beneath, or that is in the water under the earth; ⁵you shall not bow down to them or serve them; for I the SOVEREIGN ONE your God am a jealous God, visiting the iniquity of the parents upon the children to the third and the fourth generation of those who hate me, ⁶but showing steadfast love to thousands of those who love me and keep my commandments.

⁷"You shall not take the name of the SOVEREIGN ONE your God in vain; for GOD will not hold any one guiltless who takes God's name in vain.

⁸"Remember the sabbath day, to keep it holy. ⁹Six days you shall labor, and do all your work; ¹⁰but the seventh day is a sabbath to the SOVEREIGN ONE your God; in it you shall not do any work, you, or your son, or your daughter, your manservant, or your maidservant, or your cattle, or the sojourner who is within your gates; ¹¹for in six days GOD made heaven and earth, the sea, and all that is in them, and rested the seventh day; therefore GOD blessed the sabbath day and hallowed it.

¹²"Honor your father and your mother, that your days may be long in the land which the SOVEREIGN ONE your God gives you.

¹³"You shall not kill.

¹⁴"You shall not commit adultery.

¹⁵"You shall not steal.

¹⁶"You shall not bear false witness against your neighbor.

¹⁷"You shall not covet your neighbor's house; you shall not covet your neighbor's wife, [*or husband,**] or manservant, or maidservant, or ox, or ass, or anything that is your neighbor's."

---

*Addition to the text.

Psalm 19:7-14

⁷The law of GOD is perfect,
  reviving the soul;
the testimony of GOD is sure,
  making wise the simple;
⁸the precepts of GOD are right,
  rejoicing the heart;
the commandment of GOD is pure,
  enlightening the eyes;
⁹the fear of GOD is clean,
  enduring for ever;
the ordinances of GOD are true,
  and righteous altogether.
¹⁰More to be desired are they than gold,
  even much fine gold;
sweeter also than honey
  and drippings of the honeycomb.
¹¹Moreover by them is your servant warned;
  in keeping them there is great reward.
¹²But who can discern their errors?
  Clear me from hidden faults.
¹³Keep back your servant also from presumptuous sins;
  let them not have dominion over me!
Then I shall be blameless,
  and innocent of great transgression.
¹⁴Let the words of my mouth and the meditation of my heart
  be acceptable in your sight,
  O GOD, my rock and my redeemer.

Lesson 2 ~ 1 Corinthians 1:22-25

Paul writes that the wisdom of God is wiser than human wisdom.

²²For Jews demand signs and Greeks seek wisdom, ²³but we preach Christ crucified, a stumbling block to Jews and folly to Gentiles, ²⁴but to those who are called, both Jews and Greeks, Christ the power of God and the wisdom of God. ²⁵For the foolishness of God is wiser than human wisdom, and the weakness of God is stronger than human strength.

Jesus cleanses the temple.

¹³The Passover was at hand, and Jesus went up to Jerusalem. ¹⁴In the temple Jesus found those who were selling oxen and sheep and pigeons, and the money-changers at their business. ¹⁵And making a whip of cords, Jesus drove them all, with the sheep and oxen, out of the temple, pouring out the coins of the money-changers and overturning their tables. ¹⁶And Jesus told those who sold the pigeons, "Take these things away; you shall not make God's⊗ house a house of trade." ¹⁷The disciples remembered that it was written, "Zeal for your house will consume me." ¹⁸The religious authorities▽ then said to Jesus, "What sign have you to show us for doing this?" ¹⁹Jesus answered them, "Destroy this temple, and in three days I will raise it up." ²⁰Then the religious authorities▽ said, "It has taken forty-six years to build this temple, and will you raise it up in three days?" ²¹But Jesus spoke of the temple of his body. ²²When therefore Jesus was raised from the dead, the disciples remembered that Jesus had said this; and they believed the scripture and the word which Jesus had spoken.

⊗RSV *my Father's.*
▽RSV v. 18 *The Jews;* v. 20 *the Jews.* See Appendix.

LENT 4

Lesson 1 (alternate) ~ Judges 4:4-9[+]

Deborah, a prophet and judge of Israel, fearlessly leads her people into battle.

⁴Now Deborah, a prophet, the wife of Lappidoth, was judging Israel at that time. ⁵She used to sit under the palm of Deborah between Ramah and Bethel in the hill country of Ephraim; and the people of Israel came up to her for judgment. ⁶She sent and summoned Barak the son of Abinoam from Kedesh in Naphtali, and said to him, "The SOVEREIGN ONE, the God of Israel, commands you, 'Go, gather your soldiers at Mount Tabor, taking ten thousand from the tribe of Naphtali and the tribe of Zebulun. ⁷And I will draw out Sisera, the general of Jabin's army, to meet you by the river Kishon with chariots and troops; and I will give Sisera into your hand.' " ⁸Barak said to Deborah, "If you will go with me, I will go; but if you will not go with me, I will not go." ⁹And she said, "I will surely go with you; nevertheless, the road on which you are going will not lead to your glory, for GOD will sell Sisera into the hand of a woman." Then Deborah arose, and went with Barak to Kedesh.

Lesson 1 ~ 2 Chronicles 36:14-23

God judges the transgressions of the nation Judah.

¹⁴All the leading priests and the people likewise were exceedingly unfaithful, following all the abominations of the nations; and they polluted the house of GOD which God had hallowed in Jerusalem.

¹⁵The SOVEREIGN ONE, the God of their ancestors, sent persistently to them by messengers, because God had compassion on the people and on God's dwelling place; ¹⁶but they kept mocking the messengers of God, despising God's words, and scoffing at God's prophets, till the wrath of the SOVEREIGN ONE rose against God's people, till there was no remedy.

¹⁷Therefore God brought up against them the king of the Chaldeans, who slew their young men with the sword in the house of their sanctuary, and had no compassion on young man or young woman, old people or aged; God gave them all into the king's hand. ¹⁸And all the vessels of the house of God, great and small, and the treasures of the house of GOD, and the treasures of the king and of his princes, all these the king of the Chaldeans

---

[+]Lection added. See Appendix, p. 248.

brought to Babylon. ¹⁹And they burned the house of God, and broke down the wall of Jerusalem, and burned all its palaces with fire, and destroyed all its precious vessels. ²⁰He took into exile in Babylon those who had escaped from the sword, and they became servants to the king and to his offspring until the establishment of the kingdom of Persia, ²¹to fulfil the word of God by the mouth of Jeremiah, until the land had enjoyed its sabbaths. All the days that it lay desolate it kept sabbath, to fulfil seventy years.

²²Now in the first year of Cyrus, king of Persia, that the word of God by the mouth of Jeremiah might be accomplished, God stirred up the spirit of Cyrus king of Persia so that Cyrus made a proclamation throughout all the kingdom and also put it in writing: ²³"Thus says Cyrus king of Persia, 'The SOVEREIGN ONE, the God of heaven, has given me all the kingdoms of the earth and has charged me to build for God a house at Jerusalem, which is in Judah. All who are among you of all God's people, may the SOVEREIGN ONE their God be with them. Let them go up.' "

Psalm 137:1-6

¹By the waters of Babylon,
    there we sat down and wept,
    when we remembered Zion.
²On the willows there
    we hung up our lyres.
³For there our captors
    required of us songs,
  and our tormentors, mirth, saying,
    "Sing us one of the songs of Zion!"
⁴How shall we sing God's song
    in a foreign land?
⁵If I forget you, O Jerusalem,
    let my right hand wither!
⁶Let my tongue cleave to the roof of my mouth,
    if I do not remember you,
  if I do not set Jerusalem
    above my highest joy!

Lesson 2 ~ Ephesians 2:4-10

Salvation in Christ is declared to be the gift of God.

⁴But God, who is rich in mercy, out of the great love with which God loved us, ⁵even when we were dead through our trespasses, made us alive together with Christ (by grace you have been saved), ⁶and raised us up with Christ, and made us sit with Christ in the heavenly places in Christ Jesus, ⁷that in the coming ages God might show the immeasurable riches of God's grace in kindness toward us in Christ Jesus. ⁸For by grace you have been saved through faith; and this is not your own doing, it is the gift of God—⁹not because of works, lest any one should boast. ¹⁰For we are God's handiwork, created in Christ Jesus for good works, which God prepared beforehand, that we should walk in them.

Gospel ~ John 3:14-21

Acceptance or rejection of God's love in Jesus Christ brings its own consequence.

¹⁴And as Moses lifted up the serpent in the wilderness, so must the Human One° be lifted up, ¹⁵that whoever believes in the Human One may have eternal life.

¹⁶For God so loved the world that God gave God's only Child,◇ that whoever believes in that Child should not perish but have eternal life. ¹⁷For God sent that Child◇ into the world, not to condemn the world, but that through that Child the world might be saved. ¹⁸Whoever believes in the Child [*of God**] is not condemned; whoever does not believe is condemned already, for not having believed in the name of the only Child◇ of God. ¹⁹And this is the judgment, that the light has come into the world, and people loved the shadows rather than the light, because their deeds were evil. ²⁰For all who do evil hate the light, and do not come to the light, lest their deeds should be exposed. ²¹But all who do what is true come to the light, that it may be clearly seen that their deeds have been wrought in God.

°RSV *Son of man.* See Appendix.
◇RSV, vs. 16, 18 *Son;* v. 17 *the Son.* See Appendix.
*Addition to the text.

LENT 5

Lesson 1 ~ Jeremiah 31:31-34

God promises a new covenant with the house of Israel.

³¹Behold, the days are coming, says the SOVEREIGN ONE, when I will make a new covenant with the house of Israel and the house of Judah, ³²not like the covenant which I made with their ancestors when I took them by the hand to bring them out of the land of Egypt, my covenant which they broke, though I was married to them, says the SOVEREIGN ONE. ³³But this is the covenant which I will make with the house of Israel after those days, says the SOVEREIGN ONE: I will put my law within them, and I will write it upon their hearts; and I will be their God, and they shall be my people. ³⁴And no longer shall each one teach a neighbor and each a brother or sister, saying, "Know GOD," for they shall all know me, from the least of them to the greatest, says the SOVEREIGN ONE; for I will forgive their iniquity, and I will remember their sin no more.

Psalm 51:10-17

¹⁰Create in me a clean heart, O God,
   and put a new and right spirit within me.
¹¹Cast me not away from your presence,
   and take not your holy Spirit from me.
¹²Restore to me the joy of your salvation,
   and uphold me with a willing spirit.
¹³Then I will teach transgressors your ways,
   and sinners will return to you.
¹⁴Deliver me from bloodguiltiness, O God,
   the God of my salvation,
   and my tongue will sing aloud of your deliverance.
¹⁵O GOD, open my lips,
   and my mouth shall show forth your praise.
¹⁶For you have no delight in sacrifice;
   were I to give a burnt offering, you would not be pleased.
¹⁷The sacrifice acceptable to God is a broken spirit;
   a broken and contrite heart, O God, you will not despise.

Lesson 2 ~ Hebrews 5:7-10

Salvation is given through Jesus Christ, the suffering high priest.

[7]While in the flesh, Jesus offered up prayers and supplications, with loud cries and tears, to the one who was able to save him from death, and Jesus was heard for his godly fear. [8]Although the Child° [*of God**], Jesus learned obedience through suffering, [9]and being made perfect, became the source of eternal salvation to all who obey Jesus Christ, [10]having been designated by God a high priest after the order of Melchizedek.

Gospel ~ John 12:20-33

John speaks of the glorification of the Human One.

[20]Now among those who went up to worship at the feast were some Greeks. [21]So these came to Philip, who was from Bethsaida in Galilee, and said, "Sir, we wish to see Jesus." [22]Philip went and told Andrew; Andrew went with Philip and they told Jesus. [23]And Jesus answered them, "The hour has come for the Human One° to be glorified. [24]Truly, truly, I say to you, unless a grain of wheat falls into the earth and dies, it remains alone; but if it dies, it bears much fruit. [25]Whoever loves their life loses it, and whoever hates their life in this world will keep it for eternal life. [26]Any one who serves me must follow me; and where I am, there shall my servant be also; any one who serves me will be honored by God.⊗

[27]"Now is my soul troubled. And what shall I say? 'O God,⊗ save me from this hour'? No, for this purpose I have come to this hour. [28] O God,⊗ glorify your name." Then a voice came from heaven, "I have glorified it, and I will glorify it again." [29]The crowd standing by heard it and said that it had thundered. Others said, "An angel has spoken to Jesus." [30]Jesus answered, "This voice has come for your sake, not for mine. [31]Now is the judgment of this world, now shall the ruler of this world be cast out; [32]and I, when I am lifted up from the earth, will draw all people to myself." [33]Jesus said this to show by what death he was to die.

°RSV *a Son.* See Appendix.
*Addition to the text.
°RSV *Son of man.* See Appendix.
⊗RSV v. 26 *the Father;* vs. 27, 28 *Father.* See Appendix.

LENT 6, PASSION SUNDAY

Lesson 1 ~ Isaiah 50:4-9a

The prophet Isaiah tells of the suffering of the one who obeys God.

⁴The Sovereign GOD has given me
    the tongue of those who are taught,
that I may know how to sustain with a word
    one who is weary.
Morning by morning God wakens,
    God wakens my ear
to hear as those who are taught.
⁵The Sovereign GOD has opened my ear,
    and I was not rebellious,
    I turned not backward.
⁶I gave my back to the smiters,
    and my cheeks to those who pulled out my beard;
I hid not my face
    from shame and spitting.
⁷For the Sovereign GOD helps me;
    therefore I have not been confounded;
therefore I have set my face like a flint,
    and I know that I shall not be put to shame;
⁸ the one who vindicates me is near.
Who will contend with me?
    Let us stand together.
Who are my adversaries?
    Let them come near to me.
⁹Behold, the Sovereign GOD helps me;
    who will declare me guilty?

Psalm 31:9-16

⁹Be gracious to me, O GOD, for I am in distress;
    my eye is wasted from grief,
    my soul and my body also.
¹⁰For my life is spent with sorrow,
    and my years with sighing;
my strength fails because of my misery,
    and my bones waste away.

¹¹I am the scorn of all my adversaries,
    a horror to my neighbors,
  an object of dread to my acquaintances;
    those who see me in the street flee from me.
¹²I have passed out of mind like one who is dead;
    I have become like a broken vessel.
¹³For I hear the whispering of many—
    terror on every side!—
  as they scheme together against me,
    as they plot to take my life.
¹⁴But I trust in you, O GOD,
    I say, "You are my God."
¹⁵My times are in your hand;
    deliver me from the hand of my enemies and persecutors!
¹⁶Let your face shine on your servant;
    save me in your steadfast love!

Lesson 2 ~ Philippians 2:5-11

Paul speaks about the Sovereign Jesus Christ.

⁵Have this mind among yourselves, which is yours in Christ Jesus, ⁶who, though being in the form of God, did not count equality with God a thing to be grasped, ⁷but emptied self, taking the form of a servant, being born in the likeness of human beings. ⁸And being found in human form Christ humbled self and became obedient unto death, even death on a cross. ⁹Therefore God has highly exalted Jesus and bestowed on Jesus the name which is above every name, ¹⁰that at the name of Jesus every knee should bow, in heaven and on earth and under the earth, ¹¹and every tongue confess that Jesus Christ is Sovereign,[□] to the glory of God the Father [*and Mother**].

Gospel ~ Mark 14–15 (or 15:1-39)

Mark gives an account of the final events of Jesus' earthly life.

¹It was now two days before the Passover and the feast of Unleavened Bread. And the chief priests and the scribes were seeking how to arrest Jesus by stealth, and kill him; ²for they said, "Not during the feast, lest there be a tumult of the people."

□RSV *Lord*. See Appendix.
*Addition to the text. See "Metaphor" and "God the Father and Mother" in the Appendix.

³And while Jesus was at Bethany sitting at table in the house of Simon—a man who had leprosy, a woman came with an alabaster flask of ointment of pure nard, very costly, and she broke the flask and poured it over Jesus' head. ⁴But there were some who said to themselves indignantly, "Why was the ointment thus wasted? ⁵For this ointment might have been sold for more than three hundred denarii, and given to the poor." And they reproached her. ⁶But Jesus said, "Let her alone; why do you trouble her? She has done a beautiful thing to me. ⁷For you always have the poor with you, and whenever you will, you can do good to them; but you will not aways have me. ⁸She has done what she could; she has anointed my body beforehand for burying. ⁹And truly, I say to you, wherever the gospel is preached in the whole world, what she has done will be told in memory of her."

¹⁰Then Judas Iscariot, who was one of the twelve, went to the chief priests in order to betray Jesus to them. ¹¹And when they heard it they were glad, and promised to give Judas money. And Judas sought an opportunity to betray Jesus.

¹²And on the first day of Unleavened Bread, when they sacrificed the passover lamb, the disciples said to Jesus, "Where will you have us go and prepare for you to eat the passover?" ¹³And Jesus sent two of the disciples, and said to them, "Go into the city, and a man carrying a jar of water will meet you; follow him, ¹⁴and wherever he enters, say to the householder, 'The Teacher says, Where is my guest room, where I am to eat the passover with my disciples?' ¹⁵And the householder will show you a large upper room furnished and ready; there prepare for us." ¹⁶And the disciples set out and went to the city, and found it as Jesus had told them; and they prepared the passover.

¹⁷And when it was evening Jesus came with the twelve. ¹⁸And as they were at table eating, Jesus said, "Truly, I say to you, one of you will betray me, one who is eating with me." ¹⁹They began to be sorrowful, and to say to Jesus one after another, "Is it I?" ²⁰Jesus said to them, "It is one of the twelve, one who is dipping bread into the dish with me. ²¹For the Human One° goes as it is written, but woe to that person by whom the Human One° is betrayed! It would have been better for that person not to have been born."

²²And as they were eating, Jesus took bread, and blessed, and broke it, and gave it to them, and said, "Take; this is my body." ²³And Jesus took a cup, and after giving thanks, gave it to them, and they all drank of it. ²⁴And Jesus said to them, "This is my blood of the covenant, which is poured out for many. ²⁵Truly, I say to you, I shall not drink again of the fruit of the vine until that day when I drink it new in the realm* of God."

° RSV *Son of man*. See Appendix.
* RSV *kingdom*. See Appendix.

²⁶And when they had sung a hymn, they went out to the Mount of Olives. ²⁷And Jesus said to them, "You will all fall away; for it is written, 'I will strike the shepherd, and the sheep will be scattered.' ²⁸But after I am raised up, I will go before you to Galilee." ²⁹Peter said to Jesus, "Even though they all fall away, I will not." ³⁰And Jesus said to Peter, "Truly, I say to you, this very night, before the cock crows twice, you will deny me three times." ³¹But Peter said vehemently, "If I must die with you, I will not deny you." And they all said the same.

³²And they went to a place which was called Gethsemane; and Jesus said to the disciples, "Sit here, while I pray." ³³And taking Peter and James and John, Jesus began to be greatly distressed and troubled. ³⁴And Jesus said to them, "My soul is very sorrowful, even to death; remain here, and watch." ³⁵And going a little farther, Jesus fell on the ground and prayed that, if it were possible, the hour might pass from him. ³⁶And Jesus said, "[*God, my Mother and*ᵃ] Father, all things are possible to you; remove this cup from me; yet not what I will, but what you will." ³⁷And Jesus came and found them sleeping, and said to Peter, "Simon, are you asleep? Could you not watch one hour? ³⁸Watch and pray that you may not enter into temptation; the spirit indeed is willing, but the flesh is weak." ³⁹And again Jesus went away and prayed, saying the same words. ⁴⁰And again he came and found them sleeping, for their eyes were very heavy; and they did not know what to answer. ⁴¹And Jesus came the third time, and said to them, "Are you still sleeping and taking your rest? It is enough; the hour has come; the Human One° is betrayed into the hands of sinners. ⁴²Rise, let us be going; see, my betrayer is at hand."

⁴³And immediately, while Jesus was still speaking, Judas came, one of the twelve, and with him a crowd with swords and clubs, from the chief priests and the scribes and the elders. ⁴⁴Now the betrayer had given them a sign, saying, "The one I shall kiss is the man; seize him and lead him away under guard." ⁴⁵And when Judas came, he went up to Jesus at once, and said, "Rabbi!" And Judas kissed Jesus. ⁴⁶And they laid hands on Jesus and seized him. ⁴⁷But one of those who stood by drew a sword, and struck the slave of the high priest and cut off his ear. ⁴⁸And Jesus said to them, "Have you come out as against a robber, with swords and clubs to capture me? ⁴⁹Day after day I was with you in the temple teaching, and you did not seize me. But let the scriptures be fulfilled." ⁵⁰And they all forsook Jesus, and fled.

⁵¹And a young man followed Jesus, with nothing but a linen cloth about his body; and they seized him, ⁵²but he left the linen cloth and ran away naked.

ᵃAddition to the text. RSV *Abba*. See Notes, p. 249.
°RSV *Son of man*. See Appendix.

[53]And they led Jesus to the high priest; and all the chief priests and the elders and the scribes were assembled. [54]And Peter had followed Jesus at a distance, right into the courtyard of the high priest, and was sitting with the guards, warming himself at the fire. [55]Now the chief priests and the whole council sought testimony against Jesus to put him to death; but they found none. [56]For many bore false witness against Jesus, and their witness did not agree. [57]And some stood up and bore false witness, saying, [58]"We heard Jesus say, 'I will destroy this temple that is made with hands, and in three days I will build another, not made with hands.'" [59]Yet not even so did their testimony agree. [60]And the high priest stood up in the midst, and asked Jesus, "Have you no answer to make? What is it that these witnesses testify against you?" [61]But Jesus was silent and made no answer. Again the high priest asked Jesus, "Are you the Christ, the Child◇ of the Blessed?" [62]And Jesus said, "I am; and you will see the Human One° seated at the right hand of Power, and coming with the clouds of heaven." [63]And the high priest tore the priestly garments, and said, "Why do we still need witnesses? [64]You have heard his blasphemy. What is your decision?" And they all condemned Jesus as deserving death. [65]And some began to spit on Jesus, and to cover his face, and to strike him, saying, "Prophesy!" And the guards received Jesus with blows.

[66]And as Peter was below in the courtyard, one of the maids of the high priest came; [67]and seeing Peter warming himself, she looked at him, and said, "You also were with the Nazarene, Jesus." [68]But Peter denied it, saying, "I neither know nor understand what you mean." And he went out into the gateway. [69]And the maid saw him, and began again to say to the bystanders, "This is one of them." [70]But again Peter denied it. And after a little while again the bystanders said to Peter, "Certainly you are one of them; for you are a Galilean." [71]But Peter began to invoke a curse on himself and to swear, "I do not know this one of whom you speak." [72]And immediately the cock crowed a second time. And Peter remembered how Jesus had said, "Before the cock crows twice, you will deny me three times." And Peter broke down and wept.

[15:1]And as soon as it was morning the chief priests, with the elders and scribes, and the whole council held a consultation; and they bound Jesus and led him away and delivered him to Pilate. [2]And Pilate asked Jesus, "Are you the King of the Jews?" And Jesus answered, "You have said so." [3]And the chief priests accused Jesus of many things. [4]And Pilate again asked Jesus, "Have you no answer to make? See how many charges they bring against you." [5]But Jesus made no further answer, so that Pilate wondered.

◇RSV *Son.* See Appendix.
°RSV *Son of man.* See Appendix.

⁶Now at the feast Pilate used to release for them one prisoner for whom they asked. ⁷And among the rebels in prison, who had committed murder in the insurrection, there was a man called Barabbas. ⁸And the crowd came up and began to ask Pilate to do as he was wont to do for them. ⁹And Pilate answered them, "Do you want me to release for you the King of the Jews?" ¹⁰For Pilate perceived that it was out of envy that the chief priests had delivered Jesus up. ¹¹But the chief priests stirred up the crowd to have Pilate release for them Barabbas instead. ¹²And Pilate again said to them, "Then what shall I do with the one whom you call the King of the Jews?" ¹³And they cried out again, "Crucify him." ¹⁴And Pilate said to them, "Why, what evil has he done?" But they shouted all the more, "Crucify him." ¹⁵So Pilate, wishing to satisfy the crowd, released for them Barabbas; and having scourged Jesus, Pilate delivered him to be crucified.

¹⁶And the soldiers led Jesus away inside the palace (that is, the praetorium); and they called together the whole battalion. ¹⁷And they clothed Jesus in a purple cloak, and plaiting a crowd of thorns they put it on him. ¹⁸And they began to salute Jesus, "Hail, King of the Jews!" ¹⁹And they struck Jesus' head with a reed, and spat upon him, and they knelt down in homage to him. ²⁰And when they had mocked Jesus, they stripped him of the purple cloak, and put his own clothes on him. And they led Jesus out to be crucified.

²¹And they compelled a passer-by, Simon of Cyrene, who was coming in from the country, the father of Alexander and Rufus, to carry Jesus' cross. ²²And they brought Jesus to the place called Golgotha (which means the place of a skull). ²³And they offered Jesus wine mingled with myrrh; but he did not take it. ²⁴And they crucified Jesus, and divided his garments among them, casting lots for them, to decide what each should take. ²⁵And it was the third hour, when they crucified Jesus. ²⁶And the inscription of the charge against him read, "The King of the Jews." ²⁷And with Jesus they crucified two robbers, one on the right and one on the left. ²⁹And those who passed by derided Jesus, wagging their heads, and saying, "Aha! You who would destroy the temple and build it in three days, ³⁰save yourself, and come down from the cross!" ³¹So also the chief priests, together with the scribes, mocked Jesus, saying to one another, "He saved others, but cannot save himself. ³²Let the Christ, the King of Israel, come down now from the cross, that we may see and believe." Those who were crucified with Jesus also reviled him.

³³And when the sixth hour had come, there was darkness over the whole land until the ninth hour. ³⁴And at the ninth hour Jesus cried with a loud voice, "Eloi, Eloi, lama sabachthani?" which means, "My God, my God, why have you forsaken me?" ³⁵And some of the bystanders hearing it said, "Behold, Jesus is calling Elijah." ³⁶And one ran and, filling a sponge full of vinegar, put it on a reed and gave it to Jesus to drink, saying, "Wait, let us see whether Elijah will come to take Jesus down." ³⁷And Jesus uttered a

loud cry, and died. [38]And the curtain of the temple was torn in two, from top to bottom. [39]And when the centurion, who stood facing Jesus, saw that Jesus died in this way, he said, "Truly this was the Child° of God!"

[40]There were also women looking on from afar, among whom were Mary Magdalene, and Mary the mother of James the younger and of Joses, and Salome, [41]who, when Jesus was in Galilee, followed him, and ministered to him; and also many other women who came up with Jesus to Jerusalem.

[42]And when the evening had come, since it was the day of Preparation, that is, the day before the sabbath, [43]Joseph of Arimathea, a respected member of the council, who was also looking for the realm* of God, took courage and went to Pilate, and asked for the body of Jesus. [44]And Pilate wondered if Jesus were already dead; and summoning the centurion, Pilate asked the centurion whether Jesus were already dead. [45]And on learning from the centurion that Jesus was dead, Pilate granted the body to Joseph. [46]And Joseph bought a linen shroud, and taking him down, wrapped him in the linen shroud, and laid him in a tomb which had been hewn out of the rock; and Joseph rolled a stone against the door of the tomb. [47]Mary Magdalene and Mary the mother of Joses saw where Jesus was laid.

°RSV *Son.* See Appendix.
*RSV *kingdom.* See Appendix.

LENT 6, PALM SUNDAY

Lesson 1 ~ Isaiah 50:4-9a

The prophet Isaiah tells of the suffering of the one who obeys God.

⁴The Sovereign GOD has given me
    the tongue of those who are taught,
that I may know how to sustain with a word
    one who is weary.
  Morning by morning God wakens,
    God wakens my ear
    to hear as those who are taught.
⁵The Sovereign GOD has opened my ear,
    and I was not rebellious,
    I turned not backward.
⁶I gave my back to the smiters,
    and my cheeks to those who pulled out my beard;
  I hid not my face
    from shame and spitting.
⁷For the Sovereign GOD helps me;
    therefore I have not been confounded;
therefore I have set my face like a flint,
    and I know that I shall not be put to shame;
⁸ the one who vindicates me is near.
Who will contend with me?
    Let us stand together.
Who are my adversaries?
    Let them come near to me.
⁹Behold, the Sovereign GOD helps me;
    who will declare me guilty?

Psalm 118:19-29

¹⁹Open to me the gates of righteousness,
    that I may enter through them
    and give thanks to GOD.
²⁰This is the gate of GOD;
    the righteous shall enter through it.
²¹I thank you that you have answered me
    and have become my salvation.
²²The stone which the builders rejected
    has become the head of the corner.

²³This is GOD's doing;
    it is marvelous in our eyes.
²⁴This is the day which GOD has made;
    let us rejoice and be glad in it.
²⁵Save us, we beseech you, O GOD!
    O GOD, we beseech you, give us success!
²⁶Blessed be the one who enters in the name of GOD!
    We bless you from the house of GOD.
²⁷The SOVEREIGN ONE is God,
    who has caused light to shine upon us.
Bind the festal procession with branches,
    up to the horns of the altar!
²⁸You are my God, and I will give thanks to you;
    you are my God, I will extol you.
²⁹O give thanks to GOD, for God is good;
    for God's steadfast love endures for ever!

Lesson 2 ~ Philippians 2:5-11

Paul speaks about the Sovereign Jesus Christ.

⁵Have this mind among yourselves, which is yours in Christ Jesus, ⁶who, though being in the form of God, did not count equality with God a thing to be grasped, ⁷but emptied self, taking the form of a servant, being born in the likeness of human beings. ⁸And being found in human form Christ humbled self and became obedient unto death, even death on a cross. ⁹Therefore God has highly exalted Jesus and bestowed on Jesus the name which is above every name, ¹⁰that at the name of Jesus every knee should bow, in heaven and on earth and under the earth, ¹¹and every tongue confess that Jesus Christ is Sovereign,□ to the glory of God the Father [*and Mother**].

□RSV *Lord.* See Appendix.
*Addition to the text. See "Metaphor" and "God the Father and Mother" in the Appendix.

Gospel ～ Mark 11:1-11

Jesus enters Jerusalem amid the shouts of the people.

¹And when they drew near to Jerusalem, to Bethphage and Bethany, at the Mount of Olives, Jesus sent two of the disciples, ²and said to them, "Go into the village opposite you, and immediately as you enter it you will find a colt tied, on which no one has ever sat; untie it and bring it. ³If any one says to you, 'Why are you doing this?' say, 'The Sovereign□ has need of it and will send it back here immediately.' " ⁴And they went away, and found a colt tied at the door out in the open street; and they untied it. ⁵And those who stood there said to them, "What are you doing, untying the colt?" ⁶And the disciples told them what Jesus had said; and they let the disciples go. ⁷And the disciples brought the colt to Jesus, and threw their garments on it; and Jesus sat upon it. ⁸And many spread their garments on the road, and others spread leafy branches which they had cut from the fields. ⁹And those who went before and those who followed cried out, "Hosanna! Blessed is the one who comes in the name of the Sovereign!□ ¹⁰Blessed is the realm* of our ancestor David! Hosanna in the highest!"

¹¹And Jesus entered Jerusalem, and went into the temple; and having looked round at everything, since it was already late, went out to Bethany with the twelve.

□RSV *Lord.* See Appendix.
*RSV *kingdom.* See Appendix.

MONDAY OF HOLY WEEK

Lesson 1 ~ Isaiah 42:1-9

God speaks through the prophet Isaiah about God's servant.

¹Behold my servant, whom I uphold,
　　my chosen, in whom my soul delights;
　I have put my Spirit upon my servant,
　　who will bring forth justice to the nations.
²My servant will not cry or speak out,
　　nor be heard in the street;
³a bruised reed my servant will not break,
　　nor quench a dimly burning wick,
　　but will faithfully bring forth justice.
⁴My servant will not fail or be discouraged
　　till justice has been established in the earth;
　　and the coastlands wait for the servant's law.
⁵Thus says God, the SOVEREIGN ONE,
　　who created the heavens and stretched them out,
　　who spread forth the earth and what comes from it,
　who gives breath to the people upon it
　　and spirit to those who walk in it:
⁶"I am the SOVEREIGN ONE, I have called you in righteousness,
　　I have taken you by the hand and kept you;
　I have given you as a covenant to the people,
　　a light to the nations,
⁷　to open the eyes that are blind,
　to bring out the prisoners from the dungeon,
　　from the prison those who sit in gloom.
⁸I am the SOVEREIGN ONE, that is my name;
　　my glory I give to no other,
　　nor my praise to graven images.
⁹Behold, the former things have come to pass,
　　and new things I now declare;
　before they spring forth
　　I tell you of them."

Psalm 36:5-10

[5]Your steadfast love, O GOD, extends to the heavens,
   your faithfulness to the clouds.
[6]Your righteousness is like the mountains of God,
   your judgments are like the great deep;
   all living things you save, O GOD.
[7]How precious is your steadfast love, O God!
   All people may take refuge in the shadow of your wings.
[8]They feast on the abundance of your house,
   and you give them drink from the river of your delights.
[9]For with you is the fountain of life;
   in your light do we see light.
[10]O continue your steadfast love to those who know you,
   and your salvation to the upright of heart!

Lesson 2 ~ Hebrews 9:11-15

Christ is the mediator of a new covenant.

[11]But when Christ appeared as a high priest of the good things that have come, then through the greater and more perfect tent (not made with hands, that is, not of this creation) [12]Christ entered once for all into the Holy Place, taking not the blood of goats and calves but Christ's own blood, thus securing an eternal redemption. [13]For if the sprinkling of defiled persons with the blood of goats and bulls and with the ashes of a heifer sanctifies for the purification of the flesh, [14]how much more shall the blood of Christ, who through the eternal Spirit offered a sacrifice of self without blemish to God, purify your conscience from dead works to serve the living God.

[15]Therefore Christ is the mediator of a new covenant, so that those who are called may receive the promised eternal inheritance, since a death has occurred which redeems them from the transgressions under the first covenant.

Gospel ~ John 12:1-11

Mary of Bethany anoints the feet of Jesus.

[1]Six days before the Passover, Jesus came to Bethany, where Lazarus was, whom Jesus had raised from the dead. [2]There they made Jesus a supper; Martha served, and Lazarus was one of those at the table. [3]Mary took a pound of costly ointment of pure nard and anointed the feet of Jesus and wiped them with her hair; and the house was filled with the fragrance of the ointment. [4]But Judas Iscariot, one of the disciples (the one who was to betray Jesus), said, [5]"Why was this ointment not sold for three hundred denarii and given to the poor?" [6]This Judas said, not that he cared for the poor but because he was a thief, and having the money box, he used to take what was put into it. [7]Jesus said, "Let her alone, let her keep it for the day of my burial. [8]The poor you always have with you, but you do not always have me."

[9]When the great crowd of the Jews learned that Jesus was there, they came, not only on account of Jesus but also to see Lazarus, whom Jesus had raised from the dead. [10]So the chief priests planned to put Lazarus also to death, [11]because on account of him many of the Jews were going away and believing in Jesus.

TUESDAY OF HOLY WEEK

Lesson 1 ~ Isaiah 49:1-7

The servant of God speaks through the prophet Isaiah.

¹Listen to me, O coastlands,
  and hearken, you peoples from afar.
God called me from the womb,
  from the body of my mother, God named my name.
²God made my mouth like a sharp sword,
  in the shadow of God's hand I was hidden;
God made me a polished arrow,
  in the quiver I was hidden away.
³And God said to me, "You are my servant,
  Israel, in whom I will be glorified."
⁴But I said, "I have labored in vain,
  I have spent my strength for nothing and vanity;
yet surely my right is with the Sovereign One,
  and my recompense with my God."
⁵And now God says,
  who formed me from the womb to be God's servant,
to bring Jacob back to God,
  and that Israel might be gathered to God,
for I am honored in the eyes of the Sovereign One,
  and my God has become my strength—
⁶God says:
"It is too light a thing that you should be my servant
  to raise up the tribes of Jacob
  and to restore the preserved of Israel;
I will give you as a light to the nations,
  that my salvation may reach to the end of the earth."
⁷Thus says the Sovereign One,
  the Redeemer of Israel and Israel's Holy One,
to one deeply despised, abhorred by the nations,
  the servant of rulers:
"Monarchs⊡ shall see and arise;
  rulers,◻ and they shall prostrate themselves;
because of the Sovereign One, who is faithful,
  the Holy One of Israel, who has chosen you."

⊡RSV *Kings.* See Appendix.
◻RSV *princes.*

¹In you, O GOD, do I take refuge;
    let me never be put to shame!
²In your righteousness deliver me and rescue me;
    incline your ear to me, and save me!
³Be to me a rock of refuge,
    a strong fortress, to save me,
    for you are my rock and my fortress.
⁴Rescue me, O my God, from the hand of the wicked,
    from the grasp of the unjust and the cruel.
⁵For you, O God, are my hope,
    my trust, O GOD, from my youth.
⁶Upon you I have leaned from my birth;
    you are the one who took me from my mother's womb.
My praise is continually of you.
⁷I have been as a portent to many;
    but you are my strong refuge.
⁸My mouth is filled with your praise,
    and with your glory all the day.
⁹Do not cast me off in the time of old age;
    forsake me not when my strength is spent.
¹⁰For my enemies speak concerning me,
    those who watch for my life consult together,
¹¹and say, "God has forsaken the one who trusted;
    pursue and seize the forsaken one,
    for there is no one to give deliverance."
¹²O God, be not far from me;
    O my God, make haste to help me!

Lesson 2 ~ 1 Corinthians 1:18-31

Paul writes to the Corinthian church about the wisdom of God.

¹⁸For the word of the cross is folly to those who are perishing, but to us who are being saved it is the power of God. ¹⁹For it is written,

"I will destroy the wisdom of the wise,
    and the cleverness of the clever I will thwart."

²⁰Where is the wise one? Where is the scribe? Where is the debater of this age? Has not God made foolish the wisdom of the world? ²¹For since, in the wisdom of God, the world did not know God through wisdom, it pleased God through the folly of what we preach to save those who believe. ²²For Jews demand signs and Greeks seek wisdom, ²³but we preach Christ

crucified, a stumbling block to Jews and folly to Gentiles, ²⁴but to those who are called, both Jews and Greeks, Christ the power of God and the wisdom of God. ²⁵For the foolishness of God is wiser than human wisdom, and the weakness of God is stronger than human strength.

²⁶For consider your call, my friends; not many of you were wise according to worldly standards, not many were powerful, not many were of noble birth; ²⁷but God chose what is foolish in the world to shame the wise, God chose what is weak in the world to shame the strong, ²⁸God chose what is low and despised in the world, even things that are not, to bring to nothing things that are, ²⁹so that no human being might boast in the presence of God. ³⁰God is the source of your life in Christ Jesus, whom God made our wisdom, our righteousness and sanctification and redemption; ³¹therefore, as it is written, "Let the one who boasts, boast of the Sovereign."□

Gospel ~ John 12:20-36

Jesus speaks of the glorification of the Human One.

²⁰Now among those who went up to worship at the feast were some Greeks. ²¹So these came to Philip, who was from Bethsaida in Galilee, and said, "Sir, we wish to see Jesus." ²²Philip went and told Andrew; Andrew went with Philip and they told Jesus. ²³And Jesus answered them, "The hour has come for the Human One° to be glorified. ²⁴Truly, truly, I say to you, unless a grain of wheat falls into the earth and dies, it remains alone; but if it dies, it bears much fruit. ²⁵Whoever loves their life loses it, and whoever hates their life in this world will keep it for eternal life. ²⁶Any one who serves me must follow me; and where I am, there shall my servant be also; any one who serves me will be honored by God.⊗

²⁷"Now is my soul troubled. And what shall I say? 'O God,⊗ save me from this hour'? No, for this purpose I have come to this hour. ²⁸O God,⊗ glorify your name." Then a voice came from heaven, "I have glorified it, and I will glorify it again." ²⁹The crowd standing by heard it and said that it had thundered. Others said, "An angel has spoken to Jesus." ³⁰Jesus answered, "This voice has come for your sake, not for mine. ³¹Now is the judgment of this world, now shall the ruler of this world be cast out; ³²and I, when I am lifted up from the earth, will draw all people to myself." ³³Jesus said this to show by what death he was to die. ³⁴The crowd answered, "We have heard

---

□RSV *Lord*. See Appendix.
°RSV *Son of man*. See Appendix.
⊗RSV v. 26 *the Father*; vs. 27, 28 *Father*. See Appendix.

from the law that the Christ remains for ever. How can you say that the Human One° must be lifted up? Who is this Human One°?" [35]Jesus said to them, "The light is with you for a little longer. Walk while you have the light, lest the night overtake you; those who walk in the night do not know where they are going. [36]While you have the light, believe in the light, that you may become children of light."

Having said this, Jesus departed and hid from them.

°RSV *Son of man*. See Appendix.

WEDNESDAY OF HOLY WEEK

Lesson 1 ~ Isaiah 50:4-9a

The prophet Isaiah tells of the suffering of the one who obeys God.

⁴The Sovereign GOD has given me
    the tongue of those who are taught,
that I may know how to sustain with a word
    one who is weary.
Morning by morning God wakens,
    God wakens my ear
    to hear as those who are taught.
⁵The Sovereign GOD has opened my ear,
    and I was not rebellious,
    I turned not backward.
⁶I gave my back to the smiters,
    and my cheeks to those who pulled out my beard;
I hid not my face
    from shame and spitting.
⁷For the Sovereign GOD helps me;
    therefore I have not been confounded;
therefore I have set my face like a flint,
    and I know that I shall not be put to shame;
⁸ the one who vindicates me is near.
Who will contend with me?
    Let us stand together.
Who are my adversaries?
    Let them come near to me.
⁹Behold, the Sovereign GOD helps me;
    who will declare me guilty?

Psalm 70

¹Be pleased, O God, to deliver me!
    O GOD, make haste to help me!
²Let them be put to shame and confusion
    who seek my life!
Let them be turned back and brought to dishonor
    who desire my hurt!
³Let them be appalled because of their shame
    who say, "Aha, Aha!"

⁴May all who seek you
  rejoice and be glad in you!
May those who love your salvation
  say evermore, "God is great!"
⁵But I am poor and needy;
  hasten to me, O God!
You are my help and my deliverer;
  O GOD, do not tarry!

Lesson 2 ~ Hebrews 12:1-3

The author encourages us to look to Jesus as the pioneer and the perfecter of our faith.

¹Therefore, since we are surrounded by so great a cloud of witnesses, let us also lay aside every weight, and sin which clings so closely, and let us run with perseverance the race that is set before us, ²looking to Jesus the pioneer and perfecter of our faith, who for the joy that was set before him endured the cross, despising the shame, and is seated at the right hand of the throne of God. ³Consider the one who endured from sinners such hostility against himself, so that you may not grow weary or fainthearted.

Gospel ~ John 13:21-30

Judas is identified as the one who will betray Jesus.

²¹Having spoken thus, Jesus was troubled in spirit, and testified, "Truly, truly, I say to you, one of you will betray me." ²²The disciples looked at one another, uncertain of whom Jesus spoke. ²³One of the disciples, whom Jesus loved, was lying close to the breast of Jesus; ²⁴so Simon Peter beckoned to that disciple and said, "Tell us who it is of whom Jesus speaks." ²⁵So lying thus, close to the breast of Jesus, the one whom Jesus loved said to Jesus, "Who is it?" ²⁶Jesus answered, "It is the one to whom I shall give this morsel when I have dipped it." Having dipped the morsel, he gave it to Judas, the son of Simon Iscariot. ²⁷Then after the morsel, Satan entered into Judas. Jesus said to him, "What you are going to do, do quickly." ²⁸Now no one at the table knew why Jesus said this to Judas. ²⁹Some thought that, because Judas had the money box, Jesus was telling him, "Buy what we need for the feast"; or, that Judas should give something to the poor. ³⁰So, after receiving the morsel, Judas immediately went out; and it was night.

MAUNDY THURSDAY

(For those who want the foot washing emphasis every year, the Series A readings are used each year.)

Lesson 1 ~ Exodus 24:3-8

The covenant is ratified by Moses and the people.

³Moses came and told the people all the words of GOD and all the ordinances; and all the people answered with one voice, and said, "All the words which GOD has spoken we will do." ⁴And Moses wrote all the words of GOD. And Moses rose early in the morning, and built an altar at the foot of the mountain, and twelve pillars, according to the twelve tribes of Israel. ⁵And Moses sent some young people of Israel to offer burnt offerings and to sacrifice peace offerings of oxen to GOD. ⁶And Moses took half of the blood and put it in basins, and half of the blood he threw against the altar. ⁷Then Moses took the book of the covenant, and read it in the hearing of the people; and they said, "All that GOD has spoken we will do, and we will be obedient." ⁸And Moses took the blood and threw it upon the people, and said, "Behold the blood of the covenant which GOD has made with you in accordance with all these words."

Psalm 116:12-19

(Psalm 116 is used at the Lord's Supper on Maundy (Holy) Thursday. Psalm 89:20-21, 24, 26, on page 162, is used at the "chrism" service.)

¹²What shall I render to GOD
    for all God's bounty to me?
¹³I will lift up the cup of salvation
    and call on the name of GOD,
¹⁴I will pay my vows to GOD
    in the presence of all God's people.
¹⁵Precious in the sight of GOD
    is the death of the saints.
¹⁶O GOD, I am your servant;
    I am your servant, the child of your handmaid.
    You have loosed my bonds.
¹⁷I will offer to you the sacrifice of thanksgiving
    and call on the name of GOD.
¹⁸I will pay my vows to GOD
    in the presence of all God's people,
¹⁹in the courts of the house of GOD,
    in your midst, O Jerusalem.
    Praise GOD!

Lesson 2 ~ 1 Corinthians 10:16-17

Partaking of the bread and the cup is an act of unity in Jesus Christ.

[16]The cup of blessing which we bless, is it not a participation in the blood of Christ? The bread which we break, is it not a participation in the body of Christ? [17]Because there is one bread, we who are many are one body, for we all partake of the one bread.

Gospel ~ Mark 14:12-26

Mark tells about Jesus' last supper with the disciples.

[12]And on the first day of Unleavened Bread, when they sacrificed the passover lamb, the disciples said to Jesus, "Where will you have us go and prepare for you to eat the passover?" [13]And Jesus sent two of the disciples, and said to them, "Go into the city, and a man carrying a jar of water will meet you; follow him, [14]and wherever he enters, say to the householder, 'The Teacher says, Where is my guest room, where I am to eat the passover with my disciples?' [15]And the householder will show you a large upper room furnished and ready; there prepare for us." [16]And the disciples set out and went to the city, and found it as Jesus had told them; and they prepared the passover.

[17]And when it was evening Jesus came with the twelve. [18]And as they were at table eating, Jesus said, "Truly, I say to you, one of you will betray me, one who is eating with me." [19]They began to be sorrowful, and to say to Jesus one after another, "Is it I?" [20]Jesus said to them, "It is one of the twelve, one who is dipping bread into the dish with me. [21]For the Human One° goes as it is written, but woe to that person by whom the Human One° is betrayed! It would have been better for that person not to have been born."

[22]And as they were eating, Jesus took bread, and blessed, and broke it, and gave it to them, and said, "Take; this is my body." [23]And Jesus took a cup, and after giving thanks, gave it to them, and they all drank of it. [24]And Jesus said to them, "This is my blood of the covenant, which is poured out for many. [25]Truly, I say to you, I shall not drink again of the fruit of the vine until that day when I drink it new in the realm* of God."

[26]And when they had sung a hymn, they went out to the Mount of Olives.

°RSV *Son of man.* See Appendix.
*RSV *kingdom.* See Appendix.

GOOD FRIDAY

Lesson 1 ~ Isaiah 52:13–53:12

Isaiah writes of the Suffering Servant.

¹³Behold, my servant shall prosper,
    shall be exalted and lifted up,
    and shall be very high.
¹⁴As many were astonished at the one
    whose appearance was so marred, beyond human semblance,
    and whose form beyond that of human beings,
¹⁵so many nations will be startled;
    rulers□ shall shut their mouths because of my servant;
  for that which has not been told them they shall see,
    and that which they have not heard they shall understand.
^{53:1}Who has believed what we have heard?
    And to whom has the arm of GOD been revealed?
  ²For the servant grew up before God like a young plant,
    and like a root out of dry ground,
  with no form or comeliness that we should admire,
    and no beauty that we should desire.
  ³The servant was despised and rejected by every one,
    was full of sorrows, and acquainted with grief,
  and as one from whom people hide their faces,
    was despised and not esteemed by us.
  ⁴Surely this one has borne our griefs
    and carried our sorrows;
  yet we esteemed the servant stricken,
    smitten by God, and afflicted.
  ⁵But this servant was wounded for our transgressions,
    was bruised for our iniquities,
  bore the chastisement that made us whole
    and the stripes by which we are healed.
  ⁶All we like sheep have gone astray;
    we have turned every one to our own way;
  and GOD has laid on this one
    the iniquity of us all.

□RSV *kings.* See Appendix.

⁷The servant was oppressed, and was afflicted,
  yet did not say a word;
 like a lamb that is led to the slaughter,
  and like a ewe that before her shearers is dumb,
  the servant did not say a word.
⁸By oppression and judgment the servant was taken away;
  and as for that one's generation, who considered
 that the servant was cut off out of the land of the living,
  stricken for the transgression of my people?
⁹Although the servant had done no violence
  and had spoken no deceit,
 the servant was buried with the wicked,
  and with the rich in death.
¹⁰Yet it was the will of GOD to bruise
  and put to grief this one,
 who, after choosing to become an offering for sin,
  shall see offspring, and enjoy long life;
 the will of GOD shall prosper in the servant's hand;
¹¹ my servant shall see the fruit of the soul's travail and be satisfied;
  by knowledge shall the righteous one, my servant,
   make many to be accounted righteous,
   and shall bear their iniquities.
¹²Therefore I will divide for this one a portion with the great,
  and my servant shall divide the spoil with the strong;
 because my servant poured out self unto death,
  and was numbered with the transgressors;
 yet bore the sin of many,
  and made intercession for the transgressors.

Psalm 22:1-18

¹My God, my God, why have you forsaken me?
  Why are you so far from helping me, from the words of my groaning?
²O my God, I cry by day, but you do not answer;
  and by night, but find no rest.
³Yet you are holy,
  enthroned on the praises of Israel.
⁴In you our ancestors trusted;
  they trusted, and you delivered them.
⁵To you they cried, and were saved;
  in you they trusted, and were not disappointed.
⁶But I am a worm, not human at all;
  scorned by every one, and despised by the people.

⁷All who seek me mock at me,
>   they make mouths at me, they wag their heads and say,
⁸"You trusted in GOD; let God deliver you,
>   let God rescue you, for God delights in you!"
⁹Yet you, O God, are the one who took me from the womb;
>   you kept me safe upon my mother's breasts.
¹⁰Upon you I was cast from my birth,
>   and since my mother bore me you have been my God.
¹¹Be not far from me,
>   for trouble is near
>   and there is none to help.
¹²Many bulls encompass me,
>   strong bulls of Bashan surround me;
¹³they open wide their mouths at me,
>   like a ravening and roaring lion.
¹⁴I am poured out like water,
>   and all my bones are out of joint;
> my heart is like wax,
>   it is melted within my breast;
¹⁵my strength is dried up like a potsherd,
>   and my tongue cleaves to my jaws;
>   you lay me in the dust of death.
¹⁶Even dogs are round about me;
>   a company of evildoers encircle me;
>   they have pierced my hands and feet—
¹⁷I can count all my bones—
>   they stare and gloat over me;
¹⁸they divide my garments among them,
>   and for my raiment they cast lots.

Lesson 2 ~ Hebrews 4:14-16; 5:7-9

Jesus the high priest learns obedience through suffering.

¹⁴Since then we have a great high priest who has passed through the heavens, Jesus, the Child° of God, let us hold fast our confession. ¹⁵For we have not a high priest who is unable to sympathize with our weaknesses, but one who in every respect has been tempted as we are, yet without sin. ¹⁶Let us then with confidence draw near to the throne of grace, that we may receive mercy and find grace to help in time of need.

°RSV *Son.* See Appendix.

5:7While in the flesh, Jesus offered up prayers and supplications, with loud cries and tears, to the one who was able to save him from death, and was heard for his godly fear. 8Although the Child° [of God*], Jesus learned obedience through suffering, 9and being made perfect, became the source of eternal salvation to all who obey Jesus Christ.

Gospel ~ John 18–19 (or 19:17-30)

John tells of the arrest and crucifixion of Jesus.

1After praying for the disciples, Jesus went forth with them across the Kidron valley, where there was a garden, which they entered. 2Now Judas, who betrayed Jesus, also knew the place; for Jesus often met there with the disciples. 3So Judas, procuring a band of soldiers and some officers from the chief priests and the Pharisees, went there with lanterns and torches and weapons. 4Then Jesus, knowing all that was to befall him, came forward and said to them, "Whom do you seek?" 5They answered, "Jesus of Nazareth." Jesus said to them, "I am the one." Judas, the betrayer, was standing with them. 6When Jesus said to them, "I am the one," they drew back and fell to the ground. 7Again Jesus asked them, "Whom do you seek?" And they said, "Jesus of Nazareth." 8Jesus answered, "I told you that I am the one; so, if you seek me, let these others go." 9This was to fulfil the word which Jesus had spoken, "Of those whom you gave me I lost not one." 10Then Simon Peter, having a sword, drew it and struck the high priest's slave and cut off his right ear. The slave's name was Malchus. 11Jesus said to Peter, "Put your sword into its sheath; shall I not drink the cup which [God] the Father [and Mother**] has given me?"

12So the band of soldiers and their captain and the officers of the Jews seized and bound Jesus. 13First they led him to Annas, who was the father-in-law of Caiaphas, the high priest that year. 14It was Caiaphas who had given counsel to the Jews that it was expedient that one person should die for the people.

15Simon Peter followed Jesus, and so did another disciple, who was known to the high priest, and who entered the court of the high priest along with Jesus, 16while Peter stood outside at the door. So the other disciple, who was known to the high priest, went out and spoke to the maid who kept the door, and brought Peter in. 17The maid who kept the door said to Peter, "Are not you also one of this person's disciples?" Peter said, "I am not." 18Now the servants and officers had made a charcoal fire, because it was

---

°RSV *he was a Son.* See Appendix.
*Addition to the text.
**Addition to the text. See "Metaphor" and "God the Father and Mother" in the Appendix.

cold, and they were standing and warming themselves; Peter also was with them, standing and warming himself.

¹⁹The high priest then questioned Jesus about his disciples and teaching. ²⁰Jesus answered the high priest, "I have spoken openly to the world; I have always taught in synagogues and in the temple, where all Jews come together; I have said nothing secretly. ²¹Why do you ask me? Ask those who have heard me, what I said to them; they know what I said." ²³When Jesus had said this, one of the officers standing by struck Jesus with his hand, saying, "Is that how you answer the high priest?" ²³Jesus answered the officer, "If I have spoken wrongly, bear witness to the wrong; but if I have spoken rightly, why do you strike me?" ²⁴Annas then sent Jesus bound to Caiaphas the high priest.

²⁵Now Simon Peter was standing and warming himself. They said to Peter, "Are not you also one of the disciples?" He denied it and said, "I am not." ²⁶One of the servants of the high priest, a relative of the slave whose ear Peter had cut off, asked, "Did I not see you in the garden with this person?" ²⁷Peter again denied it; and at once the cock crowed.

²⁸Then they led Jesus from the house of Caiaphas to the praetorium. It was early. They themselves did not enter the praetorium, so that they might not be defiled, but might eat the passover. ²⁹So Pilate went out to them and said, "What accusation do you bring against this person?" ³⁰They answered Pilate, "If this one were not an evildoer, we would not have handed him over." ³¹Pilate said to them, "Take him yourselves and make judgment by your own law." The Jews said to Pilate, "It is not lawful for us to put any one to death." ³²This was to fulfil the word which Jesus had spoken to show by what death he was to die.

³³Pilate entered the praetorium again and called Jesus, and said, "Are you the King of the Jews?" ³⁴Jesus answered, "Do you say this of your own accord, or did others say it to you about me?" ³⁵Pilate answered, "Am I one of you?⊕ Your own nation and the chief priests have handed you over to me; what have you done?" ³⁶Jesus answered, "My realm* is not of this world; if my realm* were of this world, my servants would fight, that I might not be handed over to the religious authorities;ᵛ but my realm* is not from the world." ³⁷Pilate said to Jesus, "So you are a king?" Jesus answered, "You say that I am a king. For this I was born, and for this I have come into the world, to bear witness to the truth. Every one who is of the truth hears my voice." ³⁸Pilate said to Jesus, "What is truth?"

And having said this, Pilate went out to the Jews again, and told them, "I find no crime in this person. ³⁹But you have a custom that I should release some one for you at the Passover; will you have me release for you

⊕RSV *"Am I a Jew?"*
*RSV *kingship.* See Appendix.
ᵛRSV *the Jews.* See Appendix.

the King of the Jews?" [40]They cried out again, "Not Jesus, but Barabbas!" Now Barabbas was a robber.

[19:1]Then Pilate had Jesus scourged. [2]And the soldiers plaited a crown of thorns, and put it on Jesus' head, and arrayed Jesus in a purple robe; [3]they came up, saying, "Hail, King of the Jews!" and struck Jesus with their hands. [4]Pilate went out again, and said to them, "See, I am bringing this person out to you, that you may know that I find no crime in him." [5]So Jesus came out, wearing the crown of thorns and the purple robe. Pilate said to them, "Here is the one!" [6]When the chief priests and the officers saw Jesus, they cried out, "Crucify, crucify!" Pilate said to them, "Take this one yourselves and crucify him, for I find no crime in him." [7]The Jews answered Pilate, "We have a law, and by that law Jesus ought to die, having made himself the Child° of God." [8]Hearing these words, Pilate was the more afraid. [9]Pilate entered the praetorium again and said to Jesus, "Where are you from?" But Jesus gave no answer. [10]Pilate therefore said to Jesus, "You will not speak to me? Do you not know that I have power to release you, and power to crucify you?" [11]Jesus answered Pilate, "You would have no power over me unless it had been given you from above; therefore the one who delivered me to you has the greater sin."

[12]Upon this Pilate sought to release Jesus, but the Jews cried out, "If you release this person, you are not Caesar's friend; every one who claims to be a king opposes Caesar." [13]Hearing these words, Pilate brought Jesus out and sat down on the judgment seat at a place called The Pavement, and in Hebrew, Gabbatha. [14]Now it was the day of Preparation of the Passover; it was about the sixth hour. Pilate said to the Jews, "Behold your King!" [15]They cried out, "Get on with it, get on with it, crucify Jesus!" Pilate said to them, "Shall I crucify your King?" The chief priests answered, "We have no king but Caesar." [16]Then Pilate handed Jesus over to them to be crucified.

[17]So they took Jesus, who went out bearing his own cross, to the place called the place of a skull, which is called in Hebrew Golgotha. [18]There they crucified Jesus, along with two others, one on either side, and Jesus between them. [19]Pilate also wrote a title and put it on the cross; it read, "Jesus of Nazareth, the King of the Jews." [20]Many of the Jews read this title, for the place where Jesus was crucified was near the city; and it was written in Hebrew, in Latin, and in Greek. [21]The chief priests of the Jews then said to Pilate, "Do not write, 'The King of the Jews,' but, 'This one said, I am King of the Jews.' " [22]Pilate answered, "What I have written I have written."

[23]When the soldiers had crucified Jesus they took his garments and made four parts, one for each soldier; also Jesus' tunic. But the tunic was

---

°RSV *Son*. See Appendix.

without seam, woven from top to bottom; ²⁴so they said to one another, "Let us not tear it, but cast lots for it to see whose it shall be." This was to fulfil the scripture,

"They parted my garments among them,
and for my clothing they cast lots."

²⁵So the soldiers did this. But standing by the cross of Jesus were his mother, and his mother's sister, Mary the wife of Clopas, and Mary Magdalene. ²⁶When Jesus saw his mother, and the disciple whom he loved standing near, Jesus said to his mother, "Woman, behold, your child!" ²⁷Then Jesus said to the disciple, "Behold, your mother!" And from that hour the disciple took her to his own home.

²⁸After this Jesus, knowing that all was now finished, said (to fulfil the scripture), "I thirst." ²⁹A bowl full of vinegar stood there; so they put a sponge full of the vinegar on hyssop and held it to Jesus' mouth. ³⁰After receiving the vinegar, Jesus said, "It is finished"; and Jesus bowed his head and gave up the spirit.

³¹Since it was the day of Preparation, in order to prevent the bodies from remaining on the cross on the sabbath (for that sabbath was a high day), the Jews asked Pilate that their legs might be broken, and that they might be taken away. ³²So the soldiers came and broke the legs of the first, and of the other who had been crucified with Jesus; ³³but when they came to Jesus and saw that he was already dead, they did not break his legs. ³⁴But one of the soldiers pierced Jesus' side with a spear, and at once there came out blood and water. ³⁵The one who saw it has borne witness—that testimony is true, and the witness knows that it is the truth—that you also may believe. ³⁶For these things took place that the scripture might be fulfilled, "Not a bone of that one shall be broken." ³⁷And again another scripture says, "They shall look on the one whom they have pierced."

³⁸After this Joseph of Arimathea, who was a disciple of Jesus, but secretly, for fear of the Jews, asked Pilate for permission to take away the body of Jesus, and Pilate granted it. So Joseph came and took away Jesus' body. ³⁹Nicodemus also, who had at first come to Jesus by night, came bringing a mixture of myrrh and aloes, about a hundred pounds' weight. ⁴⁰They took the body of Jesus, and bound it in linen cloths with the spices, as is the burial custom of the Jews. ⁴¹Now in the place where Jesus was crucified there was a garden, and in the garden a new tomb where no one had ever been laid. ⁴²So because of the Jewish day of Preparation, as the tomb was close at hand, they laid Jesus there.

EASTER

(If the first lection is read from the Old Testament, the lection from Acts should be the second lection.)

Lesson 1 ~ Acts 10:34-43

Peter preaches about Jesus' life, death, and resurrection.

[34]Peter proclaimed: "Truly I perceive that God shows no partiality, [35]but in every nation any one who fears God and does what is right is acceptable to God. [36]You know the word which God sent to Israel, preaching good news of peace by Jesus Christ (Christ is Sovereign[□] of all), [37]the word which was proclaimed throughout all Judea, beginning from Galilee after the baptism which John preached: [38]how God anointed Jesus of Nazareth with the Holy Spirit and with power; how Jesus went about doing good and healing all that were oppressed by the devil, for God was with Jesus. [39]And we are witnesses to all that Jesus did both in Judea and in Jerusalem. They put Jesus to death by hanging him on a tree; [40]but God raised Jesus on the third day and made Jesus manifest; [41]not to all the people but to us who were chosen by God as witnesses, who ate and drank with Jesus after Jesus' resurrection from the dead. [42]And Jesus commanded us to preach to the people, and to testify that this one is the one ordained by God to be judge of the living and the dead. [43]To this one all the prophets bear witness that every one who believes in Jesus Christ receives forgiveness of sins through this name."

Lesson 1 (alternate) ~ Isaiah 25:6-9

Isaiah speaks of God's victory over death.

[6]On this mountain the GOD of hosts will make for all peoples a feast of fat things, a feast of wine on the lees, of fat things full of marrow, of wine on the lees well refined. [7]And God will destroy on this mountain the covering that is cast over all peoples, the veil that is spread over all nations. [8]God will swallow up death for ever, and the Sovereign GOD will wipe away tears from all faces, and God will take away from all the earth the reproach of God's people; for GOD has spoken. [9]It will be said on that day, "This is our God, the one for whom we have waited, that we might be saved. This is the SOVEREIGN ONE for whom we have waited; let us be glad and rejoice in God's salvation."

□RSV *Lord.* See Appendix.

Psalm 118:14-24

[14]God is my strength and my song,
and has become my salvation.
[15]Hark, glad songs of victory
in the tents of the righteous:
"The right hand of God does valiantly,
[16] the right hand of God is exalted,
the right hand of God does valiantly!"
[17]I shall not die, but I shall live,
and recount the deeds of God.
[18]God has chastened me sorely,
but has not given me over to death.
[19]Open to me the gates of righteousness,
that I may enter through them
and give thanks to God.
[20]This is the gate of God;
the righteous shall enter through it.
[21]I thank you that you have answered me
and have become my salvation.
[22]The stone which the builders rejected
has become the head of the corner.
[23]This is God's doing;
it is marvelous in our eyes.
[24]This is the day which God has made;
let us rejoice and be glad in it.

Lesson 2 ~ 1 Corinthians 15:1-11

(If Isaiah 25:6-9 is read as the first lection, Acts 10:34-43 should be read as the second lection.)

Paul passes on the tradition of the appearances of the risen Christ.

[1]Now I would remind you, sisters and brothers, in what terms I
preached to you the gospel, which you received, in which you stand, [2]by
which you are saved, if you hold it fast—unless you believed in vain.
[3]For I delivered to you as of first importance what I also received, that
Christ died for our sins in accordance with the scriptures, [4]that Christ was
buried, that Christ was raised on the third day in accordance with the
scriptures, [5]and that Christ appeared to Cephas, then to the twelve. [6]Then
Christ appeared to more than five hundred followers at one time, most of
whom are still alive, though some have fallen asleep. [7]Then Christ
appeared to James, then to all the apostles. [8]Last of all, as to one untimely

born, Christ appeared also to me. [9]For I am the least of the apostles, unfit to be called an apostle, because I persecuted the church of God. [10]But by the grace of God I am what I am, and God's grace toward me was not in vain. On the contrary, I worked harder than any of them, though it was not I, but the grace of God which is with me. [11]Whether then it was I or they, so we preach and so you believed.

Gospel ~ John 20:1-18

The risen Christ appears to Mary Magdalene.

[1]Now on the first day of the week Mary Magdalene came to the tomb early, while it was still dark, and saw that the stone had been taken away from the tomb. [2]So she ran, and went to Simon Peter and the other disciple, the one whom Jesus loved, and said to them, "They have taken the Sovereign□ out of the tomb, and we do not know where they have laid him." [3]Peter then came out with the other disciple, and they went toward the tomb. [4]They both ran, but the other disciple outran Peter, reached the tomb first, [5]and stooping to look in, saw the linen cloths lying there, but did not go in. [6]Then Simon Peter came, following after, and went into the tomb; Peter saw the linen cloths lying, [7]and the napkin, which had been on Jesus' head, not lying with the linen cloths but rolled up in a place by itself. [8]Then the other disciple, who reached the tomb first, also went in, and saw and believed; [9]for as yet they did not know the scripture, that Jesus must rise from the dead. [10]Then the disciples went back to their homes.

[11]But Mary stood weeping outside the tomb, and as she wept she stooped to look into the tomb; [12]and she saw two angels in white, sitting where the body of Jesus had lain, one at the head and one at the feet. [13]They said to her, "Woman, why are you weeping?" She said to them, "Because they have taken away my Sovereign,□ and I do not know where they have laid him." [14]Saying this, she turned round and saw Jesus standing, but she did not know that it was Jesus. [15]Jesus said to her, "Woman, why are you weeping? Whom do you seek?" Supposing Jesus to be the gardener, she answered, "Sir, if you have carried Jesus away, tell me where you have laid him, and I will take him away." [16]Jesus said to her, "Mary." She turned and responded in Hebrew, "Rabboni!" (which means Teacher). [17]Jesus said to her, "Do not hold me, for I have not yet ascended to God; but go to my friends and say to them, I am ascending to [*God*] my Father [*and Mother**] and your Father [*and Mother**], my God and your God." [18]Mary Magdalene went and said to the disciples, "I have seen the Sovereign□"; and she told them that Jesus had said these things to her.

□RSV *Lord*. See Appendix.
*Addition to the text. See "Metaphor" and "God the Father and Mother" in the Appendix.

Gospel (alternate) ~ Mark 16:1-8

Several women are appointed to tell the disciples they will see the risen Jesus.

[1]And when the sabbath was past, Mary Magdalene, and Mary the mother of James, and Salome, bought spices, so that they might go and anoint Jesus. [2]And very early on the first day of the week they went to the tomb when the sun had risen. [3]And they were saying to one another, "Who will roll away the stone for us from the door of the tomb?" [4]And looking up, they saw that the stone was rolled back—it was very large. [5]And entering the tomb, they saw a youth sitting on the right side, dressed in a white robe; and they were amazed. [6]And the youth said to them, "Do not be amazed; you seek Jesus of Nazareth, who was crucified. Jesus has risen and is not here; see the place where they laid the body. [7]But go, tell the disciples and Peter that Jesus is going before you to Galilee; there you will see Jesus, as he told you." [8]And they went out and fled from the tomb; for trembling and astonishment had come upon them; and they said nothing to any one, for they were afraid.

EASTER EVENING

(If the first lection is read from the Old Testament, the lection from Acts should be the second lection.)

Lesson 1 ~ Acts 5:29-32

Peter and the apostles bear witness to the risen Christ.

²⁹But Peter and the apostles answered, "We must obey God rather than human beings. ³⁰The God of our ancestors raised Jesus whom you killed by hanging on a tree. ³¹God exalted the risen one at God's right hand as Leader and Savior, to give repentance to Israel and forgiveness of sins. ³²And we are witnesses to these things, and so is the Holy Spirit whom God has given to those who obey God."

Lesson 1 (alternate) ~ Daniel 12:1-3

Daniel prophesies the events of the end time.

¹At that time shall arise Michael, the great prince who has charge of your people. And there shall be a time of trouble, such as never has been since there was a nation till that time; but at that time your people shall be delivered, every one whose name shall be found written in the book. ²And many of those who sleep in the dust of the earth shall awake, some to everlasting life, and some to shame and everlasting contempt. ³And those who are wise shall shine like the brightness of the firmament; and those who turn many to righteousness, like the stars for ever and ever.

Psalm 150

¹Praise GOD!
 Praise God in the sanctuary;
  praise God in the mighty firmament!
²Praise God for mighty deeds;
  praise God according to God's exceeding greatness!
³Praise God with trumpet sound;
  praise God with lute and harp!
⁴Praise God with timbrel and dance;
  praise God with strings and pipe!
⁵Praise God with sounding cymbals;
  praise God with loud clashing cymbals!
⁶Let everything that breathes praise GOD!
 Praise GOD!

Lesson 2 ~ 1 Corinthians 5:6-8

(If Daniel 12:1-3 is read as the first lection, Acts 5:29-32 should be read as the second lection.)

Paul writes about the bread of the new passover.

⁶Your boasting is not good. Do you not know that a little leaven leavens the whole lump? ⁷Cleanse out the old leaven that you may be a new lump, as you really are unleavened. For Christ, our paschal lamb, has been sacrificed. ⁸Let us, therefore, celebrate the festival, not with the old leaven, the leaven of malice and evil, but with the unleavened bread of sincerity and truth.

Gospel ~ Luke 24:13-49

Jesus meets two disciples on the road to Emmaus.

¹³That very day two of the disciples were going to a village named Emmaus, about seven miles from Jerusalem, ¹⁴and talking with each other about all these things that had happened. ¹⁵While they were talking and discussing together, Jesus drew near and went with them. ¹⁶But their eyes were kept from recognizing Jesus, ¹⁷who said to them, "What is this conversation which you are holding with each other as you walk?" And they stood still, looking sad. ¹⁸Then one of them, named Cleopas, answered, "Are you the only visitor to Jerusalem who does not know the things that have happened there in these days?" ¹⁹And Jesus said to them, "What things?" And they said, "Concerning Jesus of Nazareth, who was a prophet mighty in deed and word before God and all the people, ²⁰and how our chief priests and rulers delivered up this Jesus to be condemned to death, and crucified him. ²¹But we had hoped that Jesus was the one to redeem Israel. Yes, and besides all this, it is now the third day since this happened. ²²Moreover, some women of our company amazed us. They were at the tomb early in the morning ²³and did not find Jesus' body; and they came back saying that they had even seen a vision of angels, who said that Jesus was alive. ²⁴Some of those who were with us went to the tomb, and found it just as the women had said; but Jesus they did not see."²⁵And Jesus said to them, "O foolish ones, and slow of heart to believe all that the prophets have spoken! ²⁶Was it not necessary that the Christ should suffer these things and be glorified?" ²⁷And beginning with Moses and all the prophets, he interpreted to them in all the scriptures the things concerning Jesus the Christ.

²⁸So they drew near to the village to which they were going. Jesus appeared to be going further, ²⁹but they urged against it, saying, "Stay with us, for it is toward evening and the day is now far spent." So Jesus went in to

stay with them. ³⁰While at table with them, Jesus took the bread and blessed, and broke it, and gave it to them. ³¹And their eyes were opened and they recognized Jesus, who then vanished out of their sight. ³²They said to each other, "Did not our hearts burn within us while Jesus talked to us on the road, and opened to us the scriptures?" ³³And they rose that same hour and returned to Jerusalem; and they found the eleven gathered together and those who were with them, ³⁴who said, "The Sovereign□ has risen indeed, and has appeared to Simon!" ³⁵Then they told what had happened on the road, and how Jesus was known to them in the breaking of the bread.

³⁶As they were saying this, that very Jesus stood among them. ³⁷But they were startled and frightened, and supposed that they saw a spirit. ³⁸And Jesus said to them, "Why are you troubled, and why do questionings rise in your hearts? ³⁹See my hands and my feet, that it is I myself; handle me, and see; for a spirit has not flesh and bones as you see that I have." ⁴¹And while they still disbelieved for joy, and wondered, Jesus said to them, "Have you anything here to eat?" ⁴²They gave Jesus a piece of broiled fish, ⁴³and Jesus took it and ate before them.

⁴⁴Then Jesus said to them, "These are my words which I spoke to you, while I was still with you, that everything written about me in the law of Moses and the prophets and the psalms must be fulfilled." ⁴⁵Then Jesus opened their minds to understand the scriptures, ⁴⁶and said to them, "Thus it is written, that the Christ should suffer and on the third day rise from the dead, ⁴⁷and that repentance and forgiveness of sins should be preached in Christ's name to all nations, beginning from Jerusalem. ⁴⁸You are witnesses of these things. ⁴⁹And behold, I send upon you the promise of [God] my Father [and Mother*]; but stay in the city, until you are clothed with power from on high."

□RSV *Lord.* See Appendix.
*Addition to the text. See "Metaphor" and "God the Father and Mother" in the Appendix.

EASTER 2

Lesson 1 ~ Acts 4:32-35

The author describes life in the early church.

³²Now the company of those who believed were of one heart and soul, and no one claimed personal ownership of any possessions, but they had everything in common. ³³And with great power the apostles gave their testimony to the resurrection of the Sovereign□ Jesus, and great grace was upon them all. ³⁴There was not a needy person among them, for as many as were possessors of lands or houses sold them, and brought the proceeds of what was sold ³⁵and laid it at the apostles' feet; and distribution was made to each as any had need.

Psalm 133

¹Behold, how good and pleasant it is
    when brothers and sisters dwell in unity!
²It is like fragrant oil upon the head,
    running down upon the face,
upon the face of Aaron,
    running down on the collar of the robes!
³It is like the dew of Hermon,
    which falls on the mountains of Zion!
For there GOD has commanded the blessing,
    life for evermore.

Lesson 2 ~ 1 John 1:1-2:2

Eternal life is partnership with God and with one another.

¹That which was from the beginning, which we have heard, which we have seen with our eyes, which we have looked upon and touched with our hands, concerning the word of life— ²the life was made manifest, and we saw it, and testify to it, and proclaim to you the eternal life which was with God and was made manifest to us— ³that which we have seen and heard we proclaim also to you, so that you may be partners with us; and our partnership is with [God] the Father [and Mother*] and with God's Child◇ Jesus Christ. ⁴And we are writing this that our joy may be complete.

□RSV *Lord.* See Appendix.
*Addition to the text. See "Metaphor" and "God the Father and Mother" in the Appendix.
◇RSV *his Son.* See Appendix.

⁵This is the message we have heard from Jesus Christ and proclaim to you, that God is light and in God is no shadow at all. ⁶If we say we are partners with God while we walk in shadows, we lie and do not live according to the truth; ⁷but if we walk in the light as God is in the light, we have partnership with one another, and the blood of Jesus, God's Child,◇ cleanses us from all sin. ⁸If we say we have no sin, we deceive ourselves, and the truth is not in us. ⁹If we confess our sins, God is faithful and just, and will forgive our sins and cleanse us from all unrighteousness. ¹⁰If we say we have not sinned, we make God a liar, and God's word is not in us.

²:¹My little children, I am writing this to you so that you may not sin; but if any one does sin, we have an advocate with God,⊗ Jesus Christ the righteous, ²who is the expiation for our sins, and not for ours only but also for the sins of the whole world.

Gospel ~ John 20:19-31

The risen Christ appears to Thomas.

¹⁹On the evening of that day, the first day of the week, the doors being shut where the disciples were, for fear of the Jewish authorities, Jesus came and stood among them and said to them, "Peace be with you." ²⁰Having said this, Jesus showed them his hands and side. Then the disciples were glad when they saw the Sovereign.□ ²¹Jesus said to them again, "Peace be with you. As [God] the [Mother and*] Father has sent me, even so I send you." ²²Having said this, Jesus breathed on them, and said to them, "Receive the Holy Spirit. ²³If you forgive the sins of any, they are forgiven; if you retain the sins of any, they are retained."

²⁴Now Thomas, one of the twelve, called the Twin, was not with them when Jesus came. ²⁵So the other disciples told him, "We have seen the Sovereign.□" But Thomas said to them, "Unless I see in Jesus' hands the print of the nails, and place my finger in the mark of the nails, and place my hand in Jesus' side, I will not believe."

²⁶Eight days later, the disciples were again in the house, and Thomas was with them. The doors were shut, but Jesus came and stood among them, and said, "Peace be with you." ²⁷Then Jesus said to Thomas, "Put your finger here, and see my hands; and put out your hand, and place it in my side; do not be faithless, but believing." ²⁸Thomas answered, "My

---

◇RSV *his Son.* See Appendix.
⊗RSV *the Father.*
□RSV *Lord.* See Appendix.
*Addition to the text. See "Metaphor" and "God the Father and Mother" in the Appendix.

Sovereign☐ and my God!" ²⁹Jesus said to Thomas, "Have you believed because you have seen me? Blessed are those who have not seen and yet believe."

³⁰Now Jesus did many other signs in the presence of the disciples, which are not written in this book; ³¹but these are written that you may believe that Jesus is the Christ, the Child◇ of God, and that believing you may have life in Christ's name.

☐RSV *Lord.* See Appendix.
◇RSV *Son.* See Appendix.

EASTER 3

Lesson 1 ~ Acts 3:12-19

After healing a person who had been lame since birth, Peter addresses the people at the gate of the temple.

¹²Peter said, "People of Israel, why do you wonder at this, or why do you stare at us, as though by our own power or piety we had made this person walk? ¹³The God of Abraham [*and Sarah**], of Isaac [*and Rebekah**], of Jacob, [*Leah, and Rachel**], the God of our ancestors, glorified God's servant Jesus, whom you delivered up and denied in the presence of Pilate, when he had decided to release Jesus. ¹⁴But you denied the Holy and Righteous One, and asked for a murderer to be granted to you, ¹⁵and killed the Author of life, whom God raised from the dead. To this we are witnesses. ¹⁶And Jesus' name, by faith in that name, has made this person strong whom you see and know; and the faith which is through Jesus has given the person this perfect health in the presence of you all.

¹⁷"And now, sisters and brothers, I know that you acted in ignorance, as did also your rulers. ¹⁸But what God foretold by the mouth of all the prophets, that the Christ of God should suffer, God thus fulfilled. ¹⁹Repent therefore, and turn again, that your sins may be blotted out, that times of refreshing may come from the presence of the Sovereign.□"

Psalm 4

¹Answer me when I call, O God of my right!
    You gave me room when I was in distress.
    Be gracious to me, and hear my prayer.
²O people, how long shall my honor suffer shame?
    How long will you love vain words, and seek after lies?
³But know that GOD has set apart the godly;
    GOD hears when I call.
⁴Be angry, but sin not;
    commune with your own hearts on your beds, and be silent.
⁵Offer right sacrifices,
    and put your trust in GOD.
⁶There are many who say, "O that we might see some good!
    Lift up the light of your countenance upon us, O GOD!"

---

*Addition to the text. See Appendix.
□RSV *Lord.* See Appendix.

⁷You have put more joy in my heart
  than they have when their grain and wine abound.
⁸In peace I will both lie down and sleep;
  for you alone, O GOD, make me dwell in safety.

Lesson 2 ~ 1 John 3:1-7

The love of God beckons us to a new life.

¹See what [*God*] the Father [*and Mother**] has given us, that we should be called children of God; and so we are. The reason why the world does not know us is that it did not know Christ. ²Beloved, we are God's children now; it does not yet appear what we shall be, but we know that when Christ appears we shall be like Christ, for we shall see Christ just as Christ is. ³And all who thus hope in Christ purify themselves as Christ is pure.

⁴Every one who commits sin is guilty of lawlessness; sin is lawlessness. ⁵You know that Christ, in whom there is no sin, appeared to take away sins. ⁶No one who abides in Christ sins; no one who sins has either seen or known Christ. ⁷Little children, let no one deceive you. The person who does right is righteous, as Christ is righteous.

Gospel ~ Luke 24:35-48

The risen Jesus appears to the disciples and sends them out to preach the gospel.

³⁵Then they told what had happened on the road, and how Jesus was known to them in the breaking of the bread.

³⁶As they were saying this, that very Jesus stood among them. ³⁷But they were startled and frightened, and supposed that they saw a spirit. ³⁸And Jesus said to them, "Why are you troubled, and why do questionings rise in your hearts? ³⁹See my hands and my feet, that it is I myself; handle me, and see; for a spirit has not flesh and bones as you see that I have." ⁴¹And while they still disbelieved for joy, and wondered, Jesus said to them, "Have you anything here to eat?" ⁴²They gave Jesus a piece of broiled fish, ⁴³and Jesus took it and ate before them.

⁴⁴Then Jesus said to them, "These are my words which I spoke to you, while I was still with you, that everything written about me in the law of

---

*Addition to the text. See "Metaphor" and "God the Father and Mother" in the Appendix.

124

Moses and the prophets and the psalms must be fulfilled." [45]Then Jesus opened their minds to understand the scriptures, [46]and said to them, "Thus it is written, that the Christ should suffer and on the third day rise from the dead, [47]and that repentance and forgiveness of sins should be preached in Christ's name to all nations, beginning from Jerusalem. [48]You are witnesses of these things."

EASTER 4

Lesson 1 ~ Acts 4:8-12

Peter speaks about the true source of the healing of the person who was born lame.

⁸Then Peter, filled with the Holy Spirit, said to them, "Rulers of the people and elders, ⁹if we are being examined today concerning a good deed done to one who was sick, by what means this person has been healed, ¹⁰be it known to you all, and to all the people of Israel, that by the name of Jesus Christ of Nazareth, whom you crucified, whom God raised from the dead, by that name this person is standing before you well. ¹¹This is the stone which was rejected by you builders, but which has become the head of the corner. ¹²And there is salvation in no one else, for there is no other name under heaven given among humankind by which we must be saved."

Psalm 23

¹GOD is my shepherd, I shall not want;
² God makes me lie down in green pastures,
and leads me beside still waters;
³ God restores my soul.
God leads me in paths of righteousness
for God's name sake.
⁴Even though I walk through the valley of the shadow of death,
I fear no evil;
for you are with me;
your rod and your staff,
they comfort me.
⁵You prepare a table before me
in the presence of my enemies;
you anoint my head with oil,
my cup overflows.
⁶Surely goodness and mercy shall follow me
all the days of my life;
and I shall dwell in the house of GOD
for ever.

Lesson 2 ~ 1 John 3:18-24

God's commandment is that we believe in Jesus Christ and that we love one another.

[18]Little children, let us not love in word or speech but in deed and in truth.

[19]By this we shall know that we are of the truth, and reassure our hearts before God [20]whenever our hearts condemn us; for God is greater than our hearts, and knows everything. [21]Beloved, if our hearts do not condemn us, we have confidence before God; [22]and we receive from God whatever we ask, because we keep the commandments and do what pleases God. [23]And this is God's commandment, that we should believe in the name of God's own Child◇ Jesus Christ and love one another, just as God has commanded us. [24]All who keep the commandments abide in God, and God in them. And by this we know that God abides in us, by the Spirit which God has given us.

Gospel ~ John 10:11-18

John tells the parable of the good shepherd.

[11]I am the good shepherd. The good shepherd is willing to die for the sheep. [12]A hireling who is not a shepherd, whose own the sheep are not, sees the wolf coming and leaves the sheep and flees; and the wolf snatches them and scatters them. [13]One who is a hireling flees, caring nothing for the sheep. [14]I am the good shepherd; I know my own and my own know me, [15]as God⊗ knows me and I know God;⊗ and I lay down my life for the sheep. [16]And I have other sheep, that are not of this fold; I must bring them also, and they will heed my voice. So there shall be one flock, one shepherd. [17]For this reason God⊗ loves me, because I lay down my life, that I may take it again. [18]No one takes it from me, but I lay it down of my own accord. I have power to lay it down, and I have power to take it again; this charge I have received from [God] my Father [and Mother*].

◇RSV *his Son.* See Appendix.
⊗RSV *the Father.*
*Addition to the text. See "Metaphor" and "God the Father and Mother" in the Appendix.

EASTER 5

Lesson 1 ~ Acts 8:26-40

Philip tells the good news of Jesus to an Ethiopian official.

²⁶An angel said to Philip, "Rise and go toward the south to the road that goes down from Jerusalem to Gaza." This is a desert road. ²⁷And Philip rose and went. And behold, an Ethiopian, a eunuch,ᵇ a minister of the Candace, queen of the Ethiopians, in charge of all her treasure, had come to Jerusalem to worship ²⁸and was returning; seated in his chariot, the Ethiopian was reading the prophet Isaiah. ²⁹And the Spirit said to Philip, "Go up and join this chariot." ³⁰So Philip hurried over to the Ethiopian, and heard him reading Isaiah the prophet, and asked, "Do you understand what you are reading?" ³¹And the Ethiopian replied, "How can I, unless some one guides me?" And he invited Philip to come up and sit with him. ³²Now the passage of the scripture which he was reading was this:

"As a sheep led to the slaughter

or a lamb before its shearer is dumb,

so this one does not say a word.

³³In the humiliation of the silent one, justice was denied.

Who can describe the generation

of the one whose life is taken up from the earth?"

³⁴And the Ethiopian eunuch said to Philip, "About whom, pray, does the prophet say this, about himself or about some one else?" ³⁵Then Philip opened his mouth, and beginning with this scripture, told the Ethiopian the good news of Jesus. ³⁶And as they went along the road they came to some water, and the eunuch said, "See, here is water! What is to prevent my being baptized?" ³⁸And he commanded the chariot to stop, and they both went down into the water, Philip and the eunuch, and Philip baptized him. ³⁹And when they came up out of the water, the Spirit of the Sovereign□ caught up Philip; and the Ethiopian eunuch saw him no more, and went on his way rejoicing. ⁴⁰But Philip was found at Azotus, and passing on he preached the gospel to all the towns till he came to Caesarea.

ᵇSee Notes, p. 249.
□RSV *Lord.* See Appendix.

[25]From you comes my praise in the great congregation;
    my vows I will pay before those who fear God.
[26]The afflicted shall eat and be satisfied;
    those who seek God shall praise GOD!
    May your hearts live for ever!
[27]All the ends of the earth shall remember
    and turn to GOD;
  and all the families of the nations
    shall worship before God.
[28]For dominion belongs to GOD,
    who rules over the nations.
[29]Indeed, to God shall all the proud of the earth bow down;
    before God shall bow all who go down to the dust,
    and those who cannot keep themselves alive.
[30]Posterity shall serve God;
    people shall tell of God to the coming generation,
[31]and proclaim God's deliverance to a people yet unborn,
    that God has wrought it.

Lesson 2 ~ 1 John 4:7-12

John unfolds the mystery and power of God's love.

[7]Beloved, let us love one another; for love is of God, and whoever loves is born of God and knows God. [8]Whoever does not love does not know God; for God is love. [9]In this the love of God was made manifest among us, that God sent God's only Child◇ into the world, so that we might live through that Child. [10]In this is love, not that we loved God but that God loved us and sent God's own Child◇ to be the expiation for our sins. [11]Beloved, if God so loved us, we also ought to love one another. [12]No one has ever seen God; if we love one another, God abides in us and God's love is perfected in us.

◇RSV v. 9 *his only Son;* v. 10 *his Son.* See Appendix.

Gospel ~ John 15:1-8

Jesus tells the parable of the true vine.

¹I am the true vine, and God⊗ is the vinedresser. ²Every branch of mine that bears no fruit, God takes away, and every branch that does bear fruit God prunes, that it may bear more fruit. ³You are already made clean by the word which I have spoken to you. ⁴Abide in me, and I in you. As the branch cannot bear fruit by itself, unless it abides in the vine, neither can you, unless you abide in me. ⁵I am the vine, you are the branches. All who abide in me, and I in them, they are the ones who bear much fruit, for apart from me you can do nothing. ⁶Any one who does not abide in me is cast forth as a branch and withers; and the branches are gathered, thrown into the fire and burned. ⁷If you abide in me, and my words abide in you, ask whatever you will, and it shall be done for you. ⁸By this [*God*] my Father [*and Mother**] is glorified, that you bear much fruit, and so prove to be my disciples.

⊗RSV *my Father.*

*Addition to the text. See "Metaphor" and "God the Father and Mother" in the Appendix.

EASTER 6

Lesson 1 ~ Acts 10:44-48

When Peter preaches at Caesarea, the Holy Spirit comes upon Jews and Gentiles alike.

⁴⁴While Peter was still saying this, the Holy Spirit fell on all who heard the word. ⁴⁵And the believers from among the Jews who came with Peter were amazed, because the gift of the Holy Spirit had been poured out even on the Gentiles. ⁴⁶For they heard the Gentiles speaking in tongues and extolling God. Then Peter declared, ⁴⁷"Can any one forbid water for baptizing these people who have received the Holy Spirit just as we have?" ⁴⁸And Peter commanded them to be baptized in the name of Jesus Christ. Then they asked Peter to remain for some days.

Psalm 98

¹O sing a new song to GOD,
    who has done marvelous things,
  whose right hand and holy arm
    have gained the victory.
²GOD has made known the victory,
    and has revealed God's vindication in the sight of the nations.
³God has remembered God's steadfast love and faithfulness
    to the house of Israel.
  All the ends of the earth have seen
    the victory of our God.
⁴Make a joyful noise to GOD, all the earth;
    break forth into joyous song and sing praises!
⁵Sing praises to GOD with the lyre,
    with the lyre and the sound of melody!
⁶With trumpets and the sound of the horn
    make a joyful noise before the Ruler,▢ the SOVEREIGN ONE!
⁷Let the sea roar, and all that fills it;
    the world and those who dwell in it!
⁸Let the floods clap their hands;
    let the hills sing for joy together
⁹before the SOVEREIGN ONE, for God comes
    to judge the earth,
  to judge the world with righteousness,
    and the peoples with equity.

▢RSV *King.* See Appendix.

Lesson 2 ~ 1 John 5:1-6

We are children of God by the gift of God's Child, Jesus Christ.

[1]Every one who believes that Jesus is the Christ is a child of God, and every one who loves the parent loves the child. [2]By this we know that we love the children of God, when we love God and obey God's commandments. [3]For this is the love of God, that we keep God's commandments, and they are not burdensome. [4]For whatever is born of God overcomes the world; and this is the victory that overcomes the world, our faith. [5]Who is it that overcomes the world but the person who believes that Jesus is the Child° of God?

[6]This is the one who came by water and blood, Jesus Christ, not with the water only but with the water and the blood.

Gospel ~ John 15:9-17

Jesus commands us to love one another.

[9]As [*God*] the Father [*and Mother**] has loved me, so have I loved you; abide in my love. [10]If you keep my commandments, you will abide in my love, just as I have kept God's⊗ commandments and abide in God's love. [11]These things I have spoken to you, that my joy may be in you, and that your joy may be full.

[12]This is my commandment, that you love one another as I have loved you. [13]Greater love has no one than this, that one lay down one's life for a friend. [14]You are my friends if you do what I command you. [15]No longer do I call you servants, for the servant does not know what the master is doing; but I have called you friends, for all that I have heard from God⊗ I have made known to you. [16]You did not choose me, but I chose you and appointed you that you should go and bear fruit and that your fruit should abide; so that whatever you ask [*God the Mother and**] Father in my name may be given to you. [17]This I command you, to love one another.

°RSV *Son.* See Appendix.
*Addition to the text. RSV vs. 9, 16 *the Father.* See "Metaphor" and "God the Father and Mother" in the Appendix.
⊗RSV v. 10 *my Father's;* v. 15 *my Father.*

ASCENSION
(Or on Easter 7)

Lesson 1 ~ Acts 1:1-11

The risen Jesus is taken up into heaven.

¹In the first book, O Theophilus, I have dealt with all that Jesus began to do and teach, ²until the day when Jesus was taken up, having given commandment through the Holy Spirit to the apostles whom Jesus had chosen. ³After the passion Jesus was seen alive by the apostles through many proofs, appearing to them during forty days, and speaking of the realm* of God. ⁴And while staying with the apostles Jesus charged them not to depart from Jerusalem, but to wait for the promise of God,⊗ which, Jesus said, "you heard from me, ⁵for John baptized with water, but before many days you shall be baptized with the Holy Spirit."

⁶So when the apostles had come together, they asked Jesus, "Our Sovereign,☐ will you at this time restore the realm* to Israel?" ⁷Jesus said, "It is not for you to know times or seasons which have been fixed by God's⊗ own authority. ⁸But you shall receive power when the Holy Spirit has come upon you; and you shall be my witnesses in Jerusalem and in all Judea and Samaria and to the end of the earth." ⁹And having said this, as the apostles were looking on, Jesus was lifted up and carried on a cloud out of their sight. ¹⁰And while they were gazing into heaven as Jesus went, two figures stood by them in white robes, ¹¹and said, "People of Galilee, why do you stand looking into heaven? This Jesus, who was taken up from you into heaven, will come in the same way as you saw Jesus go into heaven."

Psalm 47

¹Clap your hands, all peoples!
  Shout to God with loud songs of joy!
²For GOD, the Most High, is terrible,
  a great ruler▯ over all the earth,
³subduing peoples under us,
  and nations under our feet,
⁴choosing our heritage for us,
  the pride of Jacob whom God loves.

---

*RSV *kingdom*. See Appendix.
⊗RSV v. 4 *the Father;* v. 7 *the Father has fixed by his own authority.*
☐RSV *Lord*. See Appendix.
▯RSV *king*. See Appendix.

133

⁵God has gone up with a shout,
    the SOVEREIGN ONE with the sound of a trumpet.
⁶Sing praises to God, sing praises!
    Sing praises to our Ruler,[□] sing praises!
⁷For God is the ruler[□] of all the earth;
    sing praises with a psalm!
⁸God reigns over the nations,
    God sits on the holy throne.
⁹The nobles[◻] of the peoples gather
    as the people of the God of Abraham.
For the shields of the earth belong to God,
    who is highly exalted!

Lesson 2 ~ Ephesians 1:15-23

The risen Christ is exalted as head over all.

¹⁵For this reason, because I have heard of your faith in the Sovereign[◻] Jesus and your love toward all the saints, ¹⁶I do not cease to give thanks for you, remembering you in my prayers, ¹⁷that the God of our Sovereign[◻] Jesus Christ, the Father [*and Mother**] of glory, may give you a spirit of wisdom and of revelation in the knowledge of God, ¹⁸having the eyes of your hearts enlightened, that you may know what is the hope to which you have been called, what are the riches of God's glorious inheritance in the saints, ¹⁹and what is the immeasurable greatness of God's power in us who believe, according to the working of God's great might ²⁰which was accomplished in Christ when God raised Christ from the dead and made Christ sit at the right hand in the heavenly places, ²¹far above all rule and authority and power and dominion, and above every name that is named, not only in this age but also in that which is to come; ²²and God has put all things under Christ's feet and has made Christ the head over all things for the church, ²³which is the body of Christ, the fulness of the one who fills all in all.

□RSV v. 6 *King;* v. 7 *king.* See Appendix.
◻RSV *princes.*
□RSV *Lord.* See Appendix.
*Addition to the text. See "Metaphor" and "God the Father and Mother" in the Appendix.

Gospel ~ Luke 24:46-53

Jesus commissions the disciples and is parted from them.

⁴⁶And Jesus said to them, "Thus it is written, that the Christ should suffer and on the third day rise from the dead, ⁴⁷and that repentance and forgiveness of sins should be preached in Christ's name to all nations, beginning from Jerusalem. ⁴⁸You are witnesses of these things. ⁴⁹And behold, I send upon you the promise of [God] my Father [and Mother*]; but stay in the city, until you are clothed with power from on high."
⁵⁰Then Jesus led them out as far as Bethany, and with uplifted hands blessed them. ⁵¹While blessing them, Jesus parted from them, and was carried up into heaven. ⁵²And they returned to Jerusalem with great joy, ⁵³and were continually in the temple blessing God.

Gospel (alternate) ~ Mark 16:9-16, 19-20

The risen Jesus appears first to Mary Magdalene and then to others, sending the disciples to preach the gospel.

⁹Now having risen early on the first day of the week, Jesus appeared first to Mary Magdalene, from whom Jesus had cast out seven demons. ¹⁰She went and told those who had been with Jesus, as they mourned and wept. ¹¹But when they heard that Jesus was alive and had been seen by her, they would not believe it.
¹²After this Jesus appeared in another form to two of them, as they were walking into the country. ¹³And they went back and told the rest, but they did not believe them.
¹⁴Afterward Jesus appeared to the eleven themselves as they sat at table, and upbraided them for their unbelief and hardness of heart, because they had not believed those who saw Jesus who had been raised. ¹⁵And Jesus said to them, "Go into all the world and preach the gospel to the whole creation. ¹⁶Whoever believes and is baptized will be saved; but whoever does not believe will be condemned."
¹⁹So then the Sovereign⁰ Jesus, after speaking to them, was taken up into heaven, and sat down at the right hand of God. ²⁰And they went forth and preached everywhere, while the Sovereign⁰ worked with them and confirmed the message by the signs that attended it. Amen.

---

*Addition to the text. See "Metaphor" and "God the Father and Mother" in the Appendix.
⁰RSV *Lord.* See Appendix.

EASTER 7

Lesson 1 ~ Acts 1:15-17, 21-26

A new apostle is chosen to complete the number of the twelve.

¹⁵In those days Peter stood up in the midst of the community—the company of persons was in all about a hundred and twenty—and said, ¹⁶"Sisters and brothers, the scripture had to be fulfilled, which the Holy Spirit spoke beforehand by the mouth of David, concerning Judas who was guide to those who arrested Jesus. ¹⁷For Judas was numbered among us, and was allotted his share in this ministry. ²¹So one of those who have accompanied us during all the time that the Sovereign□ Jesus went in and out among us, ²²beginning from the baptism of John until the day when Jesus was taken up from us—one of those must become with us a witness of Jesus' resurrection." ²³And they put forward two, Joseph called Barsabbas, who was surnamed Justus, and Matthias. ²⁴And they prayed and said, "Our Sovereign,□ who knows the hearts of all, show which one of these two you have chosen ²⁵to take the place in this ministry and apostleship from which Judas turned aside, to go to his own place." ²⁶And they cast lots for the two, and the lot fell on Matthias, who was enrolled with the eleven apostles.

Psalm 1

¹Blessed is the one
   who walks not in the counsel of the wicked,
  nor stands in the way of sinners,
   nor sits in the seat of scoffers,
²but whose delight is in the law of GOD,
   and who meditates on that law day and night.
³That one is like a tree
   planted by streams of water,
  that yields its fruit in its season,
   and its leaf does not wither.
In every deed, that one prospers.
⁴The wicked are not so,
   but are like chaff which the wind drives away.
⁵Therefore the wicked will not stand in the judgment,
   nor sinners in the congregation of the righteous;
⁶for GOD knows the way of the righteous,
   but the way of the wicked will perish.

□RSV *Lord*. See Appendix.

Lesson 2 ~ 1 John 5:9-13

John reminds us of the testimony of God concerning God's own Child.

[9]If we receive human testimony, the testimony of God is greater; for this is the testimony of God that God has borne witness to God's own Child.° [10]Those who believe in the Child° of God have the testimony within themselves. Those who do not believe God have made God a liar, by not believing in the testimony that God has borne to God's own Child.° [11]And this is the testimony, that God gave us eternal life, and this life is in God's Child.° [12]Whoever has that Child° has life; whoever does not have the Child° of God does not have life.

[13]I write this to you who believe in the name of the Child° of God, that you may know that you have eternal life.

Gospel ~ John 17:11b-19

Jesus prays for the disciples.

[11]Holy [*God, my Mother and**] Father, keep them in your name, which you have given me, that they may be one, even as we are one. [12]While I was with them, I kept them in your name, which you have given me; I have guarded them, and none of them is lost but the son of perdition, that the scripture might be fulfilled. [13]But now I am coming to you; and these things I speak in the world, that they may have my joy fulfilled in themselves. [14]I have given them your word; and the world has hated them because they are not of the world, even as I am not of the world. [15]I do not pray that you should take them out of the world, but that you should keep them from the evil one. [16]They are not of the world, even as I am not of the world. [17]Sanctify them in the truth; your word is truth. [18]As you sent me into the world, so I have sent them into the world. [19]And for their sake I consecrate myself, that they also may be consecrated in truth.

°RSV vs. 9, 10b, 11 *his Son;* vs. 10a, 12b, 13 *Son;* v. 12a *the Son.* See Appendix.
*Addition to the text. See "Metaphor" and "God the Father and Mother" in the Appendix.

PENTECOST

(If the first lection is read from the Old Testament, the lection from Acts should be the second lection.)

Lesson 1 ~ Acts 2:1-21

Luke describes the day of Pentecost, when worshipers are filled with the Holy Spirit.

¹When the day of Pentecost had come, they were all together in one place. ²And suddenly a sound came from heaven like the rush of a mighty wind, and it filled all the house where they were sitting. ³And there appeared to them tongues as of fire, distributed and resting on each one of them. ⁴And they were all filled with the Holy Spirit and began to speak in other tongues, as the Spirit gave them utterance.

⁵Now there were dwelling in Jerusalem devout Jews from every nation under heaven. ⁶And at this sound the multitude came together, and they were bewildered, because they heard them speaking in their own language. ⁷And they were amazed and wondered, saying, "Are not all these who are speaking Galileans? ⁸And how is it that we hear, each of us in our own native language? ⁹Parthians and Medes and Elamites and residents of Mesopotamia, Judea and Cappadocia, Pontus and Asia, ¹⁰Phrygia and Pamphylia, Egypt and the parts of Libya belonging to Cyrene, and visitors from Rome, both Jews and proselytes, ¹¹Cretans and Arabians, we hear them telling in our own tongues the mighty works of God." ¹²And all were amazed and perplexed, saying to one another, "What does this mean?" ¹³But others mocking said, "They are filled with new wine."

¹⁴But Peter, standing with the eleven, lifted up his voice and addressed them, "People of Judea and all who dwell in Jerusalem, let this be known to you, and give ear to my words. ¹⁵For these people are not drunk, as you suppose, since it is only the third hour of the day; ¹⁶but this is what was spoken by the prophet Joel:
¹⁷'And in the last days it shall be, God declares,
that I will pour out my Spirit upon all flesh,
and your sons and your daughters shall prophesy,
and the young shall see visions,
and the old shall dream dreams;
¹⁸and on my menservants and my maidservants in those days
I will pour out my Spirit; and they shall prophesy.
¹⁹And I will show wonders in the heaven above
and signs on the earth beneath,
blood, and fire, and vapor of smoke;
²⁰the sun shall be turned into night
and the moon into blood,

before the day of the Sovereign□ comes,
the great and manifest day.
²¹And it shall be that whoever calls on the name of the
Sovereign□ shall be saved.' "

Lesson 1 (alternate) ~ Ezekiel 37:1-14

Ezekiel sees a vision of the glorification of Israel.

¹The hand of GOD was upon me, and brought me out by the Spirit of
GOD, and set me down in the midst of the valley; it was full of bones. ²And
God led me round among them; and behold, there were very many upon
the valley; and lo, they were very dry. ³And God said to me, "O mortal,°
can these bones live?" And I answered, "O Sovereign GOD, you know."
⁴Again God said to me, "Prophesy to these bones, and say to them, O dry
bones, hear the word of GOD. ⁵Thus says the Sovereign GOD to these bones:
Behold, I will cause breath to enter you, and you shall live. ⁶And I will lay
sinews upon you, and will cause flesh to come upon you, and cover you with
skin, and put breath in you, and you shall live; and you shall know that I am
the SOVEREIGN ONE."

⁷So I prophesied as I was commanded; and as I prophesied, there was a
noise, and behold, a rattling; and the bones came together, bone to its
bone. ⁸And as I looked, there were sinews on them, and flesh had come
upon them, and skin had covered them; but there was no breath in them.
⁹Then God said to me, "Prophesy to the breath, prophesy, O mortal,° and
say to the breath, Thus says the Sovereign GOD: Come from the four winds,
O breath, and breathe upon these slain, that they may live." ¹⁰So I
prophesied as God commanded me, and the breath came into them, and
they lived, and stood upon their feet, an exceedingly great host.

¹¹Then God said to me, "O mortal,° these bones are the whole house of
Israel. Behold, they say, 'Our bones are dried up, and our hope is lost; we
are clean cut off.' ¹²Therefore prophesy, and say to them, Thus says the
Sovereign GOD: Behold, I will open your graves, and raise you from your
graves, O my people; and I will bring you home into the land of Israel.
¹³And you shall know that I am the SOVEREIGN ONE, when I open your
graves, and raise you from your graves, O my people. ¹⁴And I will put my
Spirit within you, and you shall live, and I will place you in your own land;
then you shall know that I, the SOVEREIGN ONE, have spoken, and I have
done it, says GOD."

□RSV *Lord.* See Appendix.
°RSV vs. 3, 11 *Son of man;* v. 9 *son of man.*

24O GOD, how manifold are your works!
   In wisdom you have made them all;
   the earth is full of your creatures.
25Yonder is the sea, great and wide,
   which teems with things innumerable,
   living things both small and great.
26There go the ships,
   and Leviathan which you formed to sport in it.
27These all look to you,
   to give them their food in due season.
28When you give to them, they gather it up;
   when you open your hand, they are filled with good things.
29When you hide your face, they are dismayed;
   when you take away their breath, they die
   and return to their dust.
30When you send forth your Spirit, they are created;
   and you renew the face of the ground.
31May the glory of GOD endure for ever,
   may GOD rejoice in God's works,
32who looks on the earth and it trembles,
   who touches the mountains and they smoke!
33I will sing to GOD as long as I live;
   I will sing praise to my God while I have being.
34May my meditation be pleasing to God,
   in whom I rejoice.

Lesson 2 ~ Romans 8:22-27
(If Ezekiel 37:1-14 is read as the first lection, Acts 2:1-21 should be read as the second lection.)

Paul tells the Romans that the Spirit is constantly at work on their behalf.

22We know that the whole creation has been groaning in travail together until now; 23and not only the creation, but we ourselves, who have the first fruits of the Spirit, groan inwardly as we wait for adoption as children [*of God**], the redemption of our bodies. 24For in this hope we were saved. Now hope that is seen is not hope. For who hopes for what is already seen? 25But if we hope for what we do not see, we wait for it with patience.

---

*Addition to the text.

²⁶The Spirit helps us in our weakness; for we do not know how to pray as we ought, but that very Spirit intercedes for us with sighs too deep for words. ²⁷And the one who searches human hearts knows what is the mind of the Spirit, because the Spirit intercedes for the saints according to the will of God.

Gospel ~ John 15:26-27; 16:4b-15

Jesus promises to send the Spirit of truth, so we will not be alone.

²⁶But when the Counselor comes, whom I shall send to you from God⊛—even the Spirit of truth, who proceeds from [God] the Father [*and Mother**]—that Counselor will bear witness to me; ²⁷and you also are witnesses, because you have been with me from the beginning.

^{16:4}I did not say these things to you from the beginning, because I was with you. ⁵But now I am going to the one who sent me; yet none of you asks me, "Where are you going?" ⁶But because I have said these things to you, sorrow has filled your hearts. ⁷Nevertheless I tell you the truth: it is to your advantage that I go away, for if I do not go away, the Counselor will not come to you; but if I go, I will send the Counselor to you, ⁸who, having come, will convince the world of sin and of righteousness and of judgment: ⁹of sin, because they do not believe in me; ¹⁰of righteousness, because I go to God,⊛ and you will see me no more; ¹¹of judgment, because the ruler of this world is judged.

¹²I have yet many things to say to you, but you cannot bear them now. ¹³The Spirit of truth, having come, will guide you into all the truth; for the Spirit will not speak independently, but will speak only what that Spirit hears, and will declare to you the things that are to come. ¹⁴The Spirit will glorify me by taking what is mine and declaring it to you. ¹⁵All that [God] the [*Mother and**] Father has is mine; therefore I said that the Spirit will take what is mine and declare it to you.

⊛RSV *the Father.* See Appendix.
*Addition to the text. See "Metaphor" and "God the Father and Mother" in the Appendix.

TRINITY

Lesson 1 ~ Isaiah 6:1-8

Isaiah sees a vision.

¹In the year that King Uzziah died I saw God sitting upon a throne, high and lifted up, whose train filled the temple. ²Above God stood the seraphim; each had six wings: with two they covered their faces, and with two they covered their feet, and with two they flew. ³And one called to another and said:

"Holy, holy, holy is the GOD of hosts;
the whole earth is full of God's glory."
⁴And the foundations of the thresholds shook at the voice of the one who called, and the house was filled with smoke. ⁵And I said: "Woe is me! For I am lost; for I am a person of unclean lips, and I dwell in the midst of a people of unclean lips; for my eyes have seen the Sovereign,□ the GOD of hosts!"

⁶Then flew one of the seraphim to me, having in its hand a burning coal which it had taken with tongs from the altar. ⁷And the seraph touched my mouth, and said: "Behold, this has touched your lips; your guilt is taken away, and your sin forgiven." ⁸And I heard the voice of God saying, "Whom shall I send, and who will go for us?" Then I said, "Here am I! Send me."

Psalm 29

¹Ascribe to GOD, O heavenly beings,
    ascribe to GOD glory and strength.
²Ascribe to GOD the glory of God's name;
    worship GOD in holy array.
³The voice of GOD is upon the waters;
    the God of glory thunders,
    GOD, upon many waters.
⁴The voice of GOD is powerful,
    the voice of GOD is full of majesty.
⁵The voice of GOD breaks the cedars,
    GOD breaks the cedars of Lebanon,
⁶making Lebanon to skip like a calf,
    and Sirion like a young wild ox.
⁷The voice of GOD flashes forth flames of fire.

□RSV *King.* See Appendix.

⁸The voice of GOD shakes the wilderness,
   GOD shakes the wilderness of Kadesh.
⁹The voice of GOD makes the oaks to whirl,
   and strips the forests bare;
   and in God's temple all cry, "Glory!"
¹⁰GOD sits enthroned over the flood;
   GOD sits enthroned as ruler□ for ever.
¹¹May GOD give strength to God's people!
   May GOD bless the people with peace!

Lesson 2 ~ Romans 8:12-17

Paul exhorts the Romans to live in the Spirit.

¹²So then, brothers and sisters, we are debtors, not to the flesh, to live according to the flesh— ¹³for if you live according to the flesh you will die, but if by the Spirit you put to death the deeds of the body you will live. ¹⁴For all who are led by the Spirit of God are daughters and sons of God. ¹⁵For you did not receive the spirit of slavery to fall back into fear, but you have received the spirit of adoption as heirs. When we cry, "[*God! my Mother and*ᵃ] Father!" ¹⁶it is the Spirit bearing witness with our spirit that we are children of God, ¹⁷and if children, then heirs, heirs of God and joint heirs with Christ, provided we suffer with Christ in order that we may also be glorified with Christ.

Gospel ~ John 3:1-17

Jesus tells Nicodemus about being born of the Spirit.

¹Now there was a man of the Pharisees, named Nicodemus, a ruler of the Jews. ²Nicodemus came to Jesus by night and said, "Rabbi, we know that you are a teacher come from God; for no one can do these signs that you do, except by the power of God." ³Jesus answered Nicodemus, "Truly, truly, I say to you, unless one is born anew,* one cannot see the realm✶ of God." ⁴Nicodemus replied, "How can some one be born who is old? Can any one enter the womb of one's mother a second time and be born?" ⁵Jesus answered, "Truly, truly, I say to you, unless one is born of

---

□RSV *king.* See Appendix.
ᵃAddition to the text. RSV *Abba!* See Notes, p. 249.
*Or *from above.*
✶RSV *kingdom.* See Appendix.

water and the Spirit, one cannot enter the realm* of God. ⁶That which is born of the flesh is flesh, and that which is born of the Spirit is spirit. ⁷Do not marvel that I said to you, 'You must be born anew.*' ⁸The wind blows where it wills, and you hear the sound of it, but you do not know where it comes from or where it goes; so it is with every one who is born of the Spirit." ⁹Nicodemus said to Jesus, "How can this be?" ¹⁰Jesus answered, "Are you a teacher of Israel, and yet you do not understand this? ¹¹Truly, truly, I say to you, we speak of what we know, and bear witness to what we have seen; but you do not receive our testimony. ¹²If I have told you earthly things and you do not believe, how can you believe if I tell you heavenly things? ¹³No one has ascended into heaven but the one who descended from heaven, the Human One.° ¹⁴And as Moses lifted up the serpent in the wilderness, so must the Human One° be lifted up, ¹⁵that whoever believes in that one may have eternal life."

¹⁶For God so loved the world that God gave God's only Child,° that whoever believes in that Child should not perish but have eternal life. ¹⁷For God sent that Child° into the world, not to condemn the world, but that through that Child the world might be saved.

---

*RSV *kingdom.* See Appendix.
*Or *from above.*
°RSV *Son of man.* See Appendix.
°RSV v. 16 *Son;* v. 17 *the Son.* See Appendix.

PENTECOST 2

Lesson 1 ~ 1 Samuel 16:1-13

Samuel anoints David to be king over Israel.

¹GOD said to Samuel, "How long will you grieve over Saul, seeing I have rejected him from being king over Israel? Fill your horn with oil, and go; I will send you to Jesse the Bethlehemite, for I have provided for myself a king among Jesse's sons." ²And Samuel said, "How can I go? If Saul hears it, he will kill me." And GOD said, "Take a heifer with you, and say, 'I have come to sacrifice to GOD.' ³And invite Jesse to the sacrifice, and I will show you what you shall do; and you shall anoint for me the one whom I name to you." ⁴Samuel did what GOD commanded, and came to Bethlehem. The elders of the city came to meet Samuel trembling, and said, "Do you come peaceably?" ⁵And Samuel said, "Peaceably; I have come to sacrifice to GOD; consecrate yourselves, and come with me to the sacrifice." And he consecrated Jesse and his sons, and invited them to the sacrifice.

⁶When they came, Samuel looked on Eliab and thought, "Surely GOD's anointed is present." ⁷But GOD said to Samuel, "Do not look on Eliab's appearance or on the height of his stature, because I have rejected Eliab; for GOD sees not as people see; people look on the outward appearance, but GOD looks on the heart." ⁸Then Jesse called Abinadab, and made Abinadab pass before Samuel. And Samuel said, "Neither has GOD chosen this one." ⁹Then Jesse made Shammah pass by. And Samuel said, "Neither has GOD chosen this one." ¹⁰And Jesse made seven of his sons pass before Samuel. And Samuel said to Jesse, "GOD has not chosen these." ¹¹And Samuel said to Jesse, "Are all your sons here?" And Jesse said, "There remains yet the youngest, but behold, he is keeping the sheep." And Samuel said to Jesse, "Send and fetch him; for we will not sit down till he comes here." ¹²And Jesse sent, and brought David in. Now David was ruddy, and had beautiful eyes, and was handsome. And GOD said, "Arise, anoint David; for this is the one." ¹³Then Samuel took the horn of oil, and anointed David in the midst of his brothers; and the Spirit of GOD came mightily upon David from that day forward. And Samuel rose up, and went to Ramah.

Psalm 20

¹May GOD answer you in the day of trouble!
  The name of the God of Jacob protect you!
²May God send you help from the sanctuary,
  and give you support from Zion,
³remembering all your offerings,
  and regarding with favor your burnt sacrifices!
⁴May God grant you your heart's desire,
  and fulfil all your plans!
⁵May we shout for joy over your victory,
  and in the name of our God set up our banners!
 May GOD fulfil all your petitions!
⁶Now I know that GOD will help God's anointed,
  and will answer the anointed one from God's holy heaven
  with mighty victories by God's right hand.
⁷Some boast of chariots, and some of horses;
  but we boast of the name of the SOVEREIGN ONE our God.
⁸They will collapse and fall;
  but we shall rise and stand upright.
⁹Give victory to the ruler,□ O GOD;
  answer us when we call.

Lesson 2 ~ 2 Corinthians 4:5-12

Paul reveals to the Corinthians that eternal life is present even in their mortal bodies.

⁵For what we preach is not ourselves, but Jesus Christ as Sovereign,□ with ourselves as your servants for Jesus' sake. ⁶For it is the God who said, "Let light shine out of darkness," who has shone in our hearts to give the light of the knowledge of the glory of God in the face of Christ.

⁷But we have this treasure in earthen vessels, to show that the transcendent power belongs to God and not to us. ⁸We are afflicted in every way, but not crushed; perplexed, but not driven to despair; ⁹persecuted, but not forsaken; struck down, but not destroyed; ¹⁰always carrying in the body the death of Jesus, so that the life of Jesus may also be manifested in our bodies. ¹¹For while we live we are always being given up to death for Jesus' sake, so that the life of Jesus may be manifested in our mortal flesh. ¹²So death is at work in us, but life in you.

□RSV *king.* See Appendix.
□RSV *Lord.* See Appendix.

146

Gospel ~ Mark 2:23–3:6

Jesus heals on the sabbath.

²³One sabbath Jesus was going through the grainfields; and as they made their way the disciples began to pluck heads of grain. ²⁴And the Pharisees said to Jesus, "Look, why are they doing what is not lawful on the sabbath?" ²⁵And Jesus said to them, "Have you never read what David did, when needy and hungry, he and those who were with him: ²⁶how David entered the house of God, when Abiathar was high priest, and ate the bread of the Presence, which it is not lawful for any but the priests to eat, and also gave it to those who were with him?" ²⁷And Jesus said to them, "The sabbath was made for humankind, not humankind for the sabbath; ²⁸so the Human One° is sovereign□ even of the sabbath."

³:¹Again Jesus entered the synagogue, and a person was there who had a withered hand. ²And they watched, to see whether Jesus would heal on the sabbath, so that they might accuse him. ³And Jesus said to the one who had the withered hand, "Come here." ⁴And Jesus said to them, "Is it lawful on the sabbath to do good or to do harm, to save life or to kill?" But they were silent. ⁵And looking around at them with anger, grieved at their hardness of heart, Jesus said to the person, "Stretch out your hand." The one with the withered hand stretched it out, and it was restored. ⁶The Pharisees went out, and immediately held counsel with the Herodians against Jesus, how to destroy him.

°RSV *Son of man.* See Appendix.
□RSV *lord.* See Appendix.

PENTECOST 3

Lesson 1 ~ 1 Samuel 16:14-23

David becomes servant to Saul.

¹⁴Now the Spirit of God departed from Saul, and an evil spirit from God tormented Saul. ¹⁵And Saul's servants said to him, "Behold now, an evil spirit from God is tormenting you. ¹⁶Let our lord now command your servants, who are before you, to seek out some one who is skilful in playing the lyre; and when the evil spirit from God is upon you, that person will play it, and you will be well." ¹⁷So Saul said to the servants, "Provide for me some one who can play well, and bring that person to me." ¹⁸One of the young servants answered, "Behold, I have seen a son of Jesse the Bethlehemite, who is skilful in playing, brave, a warrior, prudent in speech, and of good presence; and God is with him." ¹⁹Therefore Saul sent messengers to Jesse, and said, "Send me David your son, who is with the sheep." ²⁰And Jesse took an ass laden with bread, and a skin of wine and a kid, and sent them by David his son to Saul. ²¹And David came to Saul, and entered his service. And Saul loved him greatly, and David became Saul's armor-bearer. ²²And Saul sent to Jesse, saying, "Let David remain in my service, for he has found favor in my sight." ²³And whenever the evil spirit from God was upon Saul, David took the lyre and played it with his hand; so Saul was refreshed, and was well, and the evil spirit departed from Saul.

Psalm 57

¹Be merciful to me, O God, be merciful to me,
   for in you my soul takes refuge;
 in the shadow of your wings I will take refuge,
   till the storms of destruction pass by.
²I cry to God Most High,
   to God who fulfils God's purpose for me.
³God will send from heaven and save me,
   putting to shame those who trample upon me.
 God will send forth God's steadfast love and faithfulness!
⁴I lie in the midst of lions
   that greedily devour their human prey;
 their teeth are spears and arrows,
   their tongues sharp swords.
⁵Be exalted, O God, above the heavens!
   Let your glory be over all the earth!

⁶They set a net for my steps;
    my soul was bowed down.
 They dug a pit in my way,
    but they have fallen into it themselves.
⁷My heart is steadfast, O God,
    my heart is steadfast!
 I will sing and make melody!
⁸ Awake, my soul!
  Awake, O harp and lyre!
    I will awake the dawn!
⁹I will give thanks to you, O God, among the peoples;
    I will sing praises to you among the nations.
¹⁰For your steadfast love is great to the heavens,
    your faithfulness to the clouds.
¹¹Be exalted, O God, above the heavens!
    Let your glory be over all the earth!

Lesson 2 ~ 2 Corinthians 4:13–5:1

Paul exhorts the Corinthians to have faith in what they cannot see.

¹³Since we have the same spirit of faith as the psalmist who wrote, "I believed, and so I spoke," we too believe, and so we speak, ¹⁴knowing that the one who raised the Sovereign□ Jesus will raise us also with Jesus and will present us with you. ¹⁵For it is all for your sake, so that as grace extends to more and more people it may increase thanksgiving, to the glory of God.

¹⁶So we do not lose heart. Though our outer nature is wasting away, our inner nature is being renewed every day. ¹⁷For this slight momentary affliction is preparing for us an eternal weight of glory beyond all comparison, ¹⁸because we look not to the things that are seen but to the things that are unseen; for the things that are seen are transient, but the things that are unseen are eternal.

⁵:¹For we know that if the earthly tent we live in is destroyed, we have a building from God, a house not made with hands, eternal in the heavens.

□RSV *Lord.* See Appendix.

Jesus teaches that a house divided cannot stand.

²⁰And the crowd came together again, so that they could not even eat. ²¹And when Jesus' family heard it, they went out to seize him, for people were saying, "He is beside himself." ²²And the scribes who came down from Jerusalem said, "He is possessed by Beelzebul, and casts out the demons by the prince of demons." ²³And Jesus called them, and said to them in parables, "How can Satan cast out Satan? ²⁴If a kingdom is divided against itself, that kingdom cannot stand. ²⁵And if a house is divided against itself, that house will not be able to stand. ²⁶And if Satan has risen up against Satan and is divided, Satan cannot stand, but is coming to an end. ²⁷But none can enter the house of the strong and plunder their goods, without first binding them; then indeed they may plunder the house.

²⁸"Truly, I say to you, all sins will be forgiven human beings, and whatever blasphemies they utter; ²⁹but whoever blasphemes against the Holy Spirit never has forgiveness, but is guilty of an eternal sin"—³⁰for they had said, "Jesus has an unclean spirit."

³¹And Jesus' mother and brothers came; and standing outside they sent to Jesus and called him. ³²And a crowd was sitting about Jesus; and they said, "Your mother and your brothers are outside, asking for you." ³³And Jesus replied, "Who are my mother and my brothers?" ³⁴And looking around on those who sat about him, Jesus said, "Here are my mother and my brothers! ³⁵Whoever does the will of God is my brother, and sister, and mother."

PENTECOST 4

Lesson 1 ~ 2 Samuel 1:1, 17-27

David grieves for Saul and Jonathan.

¹After the death of Saul, when David had returned from the slaughter of the Amalekites, David remained two days in Ziklag.

¹⁷And David lamented with this lamentation over Saul and Jonathan his son, ¹⁸and David said it should be taught to the people of Judah; behold, it is written in the Book of Jashar:
¹⁹"Your glory, O Israel, is slain upon your high places!
How are the mighty fallen!
²⁰Tell it not in Gath,
publish it not in the streets of Ashkelon;
lest the daughters of the Philistines rejoice,
lest the daughters of the Gentiles exult.
²¹You mountains of Gilboa,
let there be no dew or rain upon you,
nor upsurging of the deep!
For there the shield of the mighty was defiled,
the shield of Saul, not anointed with oil.
²²From the blood of the slain,
from the fat of the mighty,
the bow of Jonathan turned not back,
and the sword of Saul returned not empty.
²³Saul and Jonathan, beloved and lovely!
In life and in death they were not divided;
they were swifter than eagles,
they were stronger than lions.
²⁴You daughters of Israel, weep over Saul,
who clothed you daintily in scarlet,
who put ornaments of gold upon your apparel.
²⁵How are the mighty fallen
in the midst of the battle!
Jonathan lies slain upon your high places.
²⁶ I am distressed for you, my brother Jonathan;
very pleasant have you been to me;
your love to me was wonderful,
passing the love of women.
²⁷How are the mighty fallen,
and the weapons of war perished!"

¹God is our refuge and strength,
　　a very present help in trouble.
²Therefore we will not fear though the earth should change,
　　though the mountains shake in the heart of the sea;
³though its waters roar and foam,
　　though the mountains tremble with its tumult.
⁴There is a river whose streams make glad the city of God,
　　the holy habitation of the Most High.
⁵God is in the midst of it and it shall not be moved;
　　God will help it right early.
⁶The nations rage, the kingdoms totter;
　　God speaks, the earth melts.
⁷The GOD of hosts is with us;
　　the God of Jacob is our refuge.
⁸Come, behold the works of GOD.
　　who has wrought desolations in the earth,
⁹making wars cease to the end of the earth,
　　breaking the bow, shattering the spear,
　　and burning the chariots with fire!
¹⁰"Be still, and know that I am God.
　　I am exalted among the nations,
　　I am exalted in the earth!"
¹¹The GOD of hosts is with us;
　　the God of Jacob is our refuge.

Lesson 2 ~ 2 Corinthians 5:6-10, 14-17

Paul writes to the Corinthians that through Christ they are a new creation.

⁶So we are always of good courage; we know that while we are at home in the body we are away from the Sovereign,□ ⁷for we walk by faith, not by sight. ⁸We are of good courage, and we would rather be away from the body and at home with the Sovereign.□ ⁹So whether we are at home or away, we make it our aim to please the Sovereign.□ ¹⁰For we must all appear before the judgment seat of Christ, so that each one may receive good or evil, according to what each has done in the body.

¹⁴For the love of Christ controls us, because we are convinced that one has died for all; therefore all have died. ¹⁵And Christ died for all, that those

---

□RSV *Lord.* See Appendix.

who live might live no longer for themselves but for the one who for their sake died and was raised.

¹⁶From now on, therefore, we regard no one from a human point of view; even though we once regarded Christ from a human point of view, we regard Christ thus no longer. ¹⁷Therefore, if any one is in Christ, there is a new creation; the old has passed away, behold, the new has come.

Gospel ~ Mark 4:26-34

Jesus teaches in parables about the realm of God.

²⁶And Jesus said, "The realm* of God is as if some one should scatter seed upon the ground, ²⁷and should sleep and rise night and day, and the seed should sprout and grow, without the sower knowing how. ²⁸The earth produces of itself, first the blade, then the ear, then the full grain in the ear. ²⁹But when the grain is ripe, at once the one who has sown puts in the sickle, because the harvest has come."

³⁰And Jesus said, "With what can we compare the realm* of God, or what parable shall we use for it? ³¹It is like a grain of mustard seed, which, when sown upon the ground is the smallest of all the seeds on earth; ³²yet when it is sown it grows up and becomes the greatest of all shrubs, and puts forth large branches, so that the birds of the air can make nests in its shade."

³³With many such parables Jesus spoke the word to them, as they were able to hear it; ³⁴he did not speak to them without a parable, but privately to his own disciples Jesus explained everything.

---

*RSV *kingdom*. See Appendix.

PENTECOST 5

Lesson 1 ~ 2 Samuel 5:1-5[+]

David reigns over Israel and Judah.

¹Then all the tribes of Israel came to David at Hebron, and said, "Behold, we are your bone and flesh. ²In times past, when Saul was king over us, it was you that led out and brought in Israel; and GOD said to you, 'You shall be shepherd of my people Israel, and you shall be prince over Israel.' " ³So all the elders of Israel came to the king at Hebron; and King David made a covenant with them at Hebron before GOD, and they anointed David king over Israel. ⁴David was thirty years old when he began to reign, and he reigned forty years. ⁵At Hebron David reigned over Judah seven years and six months; and at Jerusalem he reigned over all Israel and Judah thirty-three years.

Psalm 48

¹Great is GOD and greatly to be praised
    in the city of our God!
God's holy mountain, ²beautiful in elevation,
    is the joy of all the earth,
Mount Zion, in the far north,
    the city of the great Ruler.▫
³Within its citadels God
    has proven to be a sure defense.
⁴For lo, the rulers▫ assembled,
    they came on together.
⁵As soon as they saw it, they were astounded,
    they were in panic, they took to flight;
⁶trembling took hold of them there,
    anguish as of a woman in travail.
⁷By the east wind you shattered the ships of Tarshish.
⁸As we have heard, so have we seen
    in the city of the GOD of hosts,
  in the city of our God,
    which God establishes for ever.

[+]The NACCL reads 2 Sam. 5:1-12. See Appendix, p. 248.
▫RSV Ps. 48:2 *King;* v. 4 *kings.* See Appendix.

154

⁹We have thought on your steadfast love, O God,
in the midst of your temple.
¹⁰As your name, O God,
so your praise reaches to the ends of the earth.
Your right hand is filled with victory;
¹¹ let Mount Zion be glad!
Let the daughters of Judah rejoice
because of your judgments!
¹²Walk about Zion, go round about it,
number its towers,
¹³consider well its ramparts,
go through its citadels;
that you may tell the next generation
¹⁴ that this is God,
our God for ever and ever,
who will be our guide for ever.

Lesson 2 ~ 2 Corinthians 5:18–6:2

Paul speaks of the reconciliation of the world to God through Christ.

¹⁸All this is from God, who through Christ reconciled us to God's self and gave us the ministry of reconciliation; ¹⁹that is, God was in Christ reconciling the world to God's self, not counting their trespasses against them, and entrusting to us the message of reconciliation. ²⁰So we are ambassadors for Christ, God making God's appeal through us. We beseech you on behalf of Christ, be reconciled to God. ²¹For our sake God made Christ to be sin who knew no sin, so that in Christ we might become the righteousness of God.

⁶:¹Working together with God, then, we entreat you not to accept the grace of God in vain. ²For God says,
"At the acceptable time I have listened to you,
and helped you on the day of salvation."
Behold, now is the acceptable time; behold, now is the day of salvation.

Mark tells of Jesus' calming the sea.

[35]On that day, when evening had come, Jesus said to the disciples, "Let us go across to the other side." [36]And leaving the crowd, they took Jesus with them, just as he was, in the boat. And other boats were there. [37]And a great storm of wind arose, and the waves beat into the boat, so that the boat was already filling. [38]And the disciples woke Jesus, who was asleep on a cushion in the stern, and they said, "Teacher, do you not care if we perish?" [39]And Jesus awoke and rebuked the wind, and said to the sea, "Peace! Be still!" And the wind ceased, and there was a great calm. [40]Jesus said to them, "Why are you afraid? Have you no faith?" [41]And they were filled with awe, and said to one another, "Who then is this, whom even the wind and the sea obey?"

PENTECOST 6

Lesson 1 ~ 2 Samuel 6:1-15

The ark of the covenant is brought to the city of David.

¹David again gathered all the chosen of Israel, thirty thousand. ²And David arose and went with all the people who were with him from Baale-judah, to bring up from there the ark of God, which is called by the name of the GOD of hosts who sits enthroned on the cherubim. ³And they carried the ark of God upon a new cart, and brought it out of the house of Abinadab which was on the hill; and Uzzah and Ahio, the sons of Abinadab, were driving the new cart ⁴with the ark of God; and Ahio went before the ark. ⁵And David and all the house of Israel were making merry before GOD with all their might, with songs and lyres and harps and tambourines and castanets and cymbals.

⁶And when they came to the threshing floor of Nacon, Uzzah put out his hand to the ark of God and took hold of it, for the oxen stumbled. ⁷And the anger of GOD was kindled against Uzzah; and God smote Uzzah there because he put forth his hand to the ark; and Uzzah died there beside the ark of God. ⁸And David was angry because GOD had broken forth upon Uzzah; and that place is called Perez-uzzah, to this day. ⁹And David was afraid of GOD that day; and David said, "How can the ark of GOD come to me?" ¹⁰So David was not willing to take the ark of GOD into the city of David; but David took it aside to the house of Obed-edom the Gittite. ¹¹And the ark of GOD remained in the house of Obed-edom the Gittite three months; and GOD blessed Obed-edom and all his household.

¹²And it was told King David, "GOD has blessed the household of Obed-edom and all that belongs to him, because of the ark of God." So David went and brought up the ark of God from the house of Obed-edom to the city of David with rejoicing; ¹³and when those who bore the ark of GOD had gone six paces, David sacrificed an ox and a fatling. ¹⁴And David danced before God with all his might; and David was girded with a linen ephod. ¹⁵So David and all the house of Israel brought up the ark of GOD with shouting, and with the sound of the horn.

Psalm 24

¹The earth is GOD's and the fulness thereof,
   the world and those who dwell therein;
²for God has founded it upon the seas,
   and established it upon the rivers.
³Who shall ascend the hill of GOD?
   And who shall stand in God's holy place?
⁴Those who have clean hands and a pure heart,
   who do not lift up their soul to what is false,
   and do not swear deceitfully.
⁵They will receive blessing from GOD,
   and vindication from the God of their salvation.
⁶Such is the generation of those who seek God,
   who seek the face of the God of Jacob.
⁷Lift up your heads, O gates!
   and be lifted up, O ancient doors!
   that the Glorious Ruler◻ may come in.
⁸Who is the Glorious Ruler?◻
   GOD, strong and mighty,
   GOD, mighty in battle!
⁹Lift up your heads, O gates!
   and be lifted up, O ancient doors!
   that the Glorious Ruler◻ may come in.
¹⁰Who is this Glorious Ruler?◻
   The GOD of hosts,
   that one is the Glorious Ruler!◻

Lesson 2 ~ 2 Corinthians 8:7-15

Paul urges the Corinthians to share out of their abundance.

⁷Now as you excel in everything—in faith, in utterance, in knowledge, in all earnestness, and in your love for us—see that you excel in this gracious work also.

⁸I say this not as a command, but to prove by the earnestness of others that your love also is genuine. ⁹For you know the grace of our Sovereign◻ Jesus Christ, who though rich, yet for your sake became poor, so that by the poverty of Christ you might become rich. ¹⁰And in this matter I give my advice: it is best for you now to complete what a year ago you began not only

---

◻RSV *King of glory.*
◻RSV *Lord.* See Appendix.

158

to do but to desire, [11]so that your readiness in desiring it may be matched by your completing it out of what you have. [12]For if the readiness is there, it is acceptable according to what one has, not according to what one has not. [13]I do not mean that others should be eased and you burdened, [14]but that as a matter of equality your abundance at the present time should supply their want, so that their abundance may supply your want, that there may be equality. [15]As it is written, "The one who gathered much had nothing over, and the one who gathered little had no lack."

Gospel ∼ Mark 5:21-43

Jesus heals Jairus' daughter and the woman with the flow of blood.

[21]And when Jesus had crossed again in the boat to the other side, a great crowd gathered around, and Jesus was beside the sea. [22]Then came one of the rulers of the synagogue, Jairus by name, who, seeing Jesus, fell at his feet, [23]and pleaded, "My little daughter is at the point of death. Come and lay your hands on her, so that she may be made well, and live." [24]And Jesus went with him.

And a great crowd followed and thronged about Jesus. [25]And there was a woman who had had a flow of blood for twelve years, [26]and who had suffered much under many physicians, and had spent all that she had, and was no better but rather grew worse. [27]Having heard the reports about Jesus, she came up in the crowd from behind, and touched Jesus' garment. [28]For she said, "If I touch even his garments, I shall be made well." [29]And immediately the hemorrhage ceased; and she felt in her body that she was healed of her disease. [30]And Jesus, perceiving in himself that power had gone forth from him, immediately turned about in the crowd, and said, "Who touched my garments?" [31]And the disciples said, "You see the crowd pressing around you, and yet you say 'Who touched me?' " [32]And Jesus looked around to see who had done it. [33]But the woman, knowing what had been done to her, came in fear and trembling and fell down before Jesus, and told the whole truth. [34]And Jesus said to her, "Daughter, your faith has made you well; go in peace, and be healed of your disease."

[35]While Jesus was still speaking, there came from the ruler's house some who said, "Your daughter is dead. Why trouble the Teacher any further?" [36]But ignoring what they said, Jesus said to the ruler of the synagogue, "Do not fear, only believe." [37]And Jesus allowed no one to follow him except Peter and James and John the brother of James. [38]When they came to the house of the ruler of the synagogue, Jesus saw a tumult, and people weeping and wailing loudly. [39]And having entered, Jesus said to them, "Why do you make a tumult and weep? The child is not dead but sleeping." [40]And they laughed at him. But Jesus put them all outside, and took the

child's father and mother and the disciples, and went in where the child was. ⁴¹ Taking her by the hand Jesus said to her, "Talitha cumi"; which means, "Little girl, I say to you, arise." ⁴²And immediately the girl got up and walked (for she was twelve years of age), and they were immediately overcome with amazement. ⁴³And Jesus strictly charged them that no one should know this, and told them to give her something to eat.

PENTECOST 7

Lesson 1 ~ 2 Samuel 7:1-17

David receives promises from God.

[1]Now when David the king dwelt in his house, and GOD had given him rest from all his enemies round about, [2]the king said to Nathan the prophet, "See now, I dwell in a house of cedar, but the ark of God dwells in a tent." [3]And Nathan said to the king, "Go, do all that is in your heart; for GOD is with you."

[4]But that same night the word of GOD came to Nathan, [5]"Go and tell my servant David, 'Thus says the SOVEREIGN ONE: Would you build me a house to dwell in? [6]I have not dwelt in a house since the day I brought up the people of Israel from Egypt to this day, but I have been moving about in a tent for my dwelling. [7]In all places where I have moved with all the people of Israel, did I speak a word with any of the judges of Israel, whom I commanded to shepherd my people Israel, saying, "Why have you not built me a house of cedar?" ' [8]Now therefore thus you shall say to my servant David, 'Thus says the GOD of hosts, I took you from the pasture, from following the sheep, that you should be prince over my people Israel; [9]and I have been with you wherever you went, and have cut off all your enemies from before you, and I will make for you a great name, like the name of the great ones of the earth. [10]And I will appoint a place for my people Israel, and will plant them, that they may dwell in their own place, and be disturbed no more; and the violent shall afflict them no more, as formerly, [11]from the time that I appointed judges over my people Israel; and I will give you rest from all your enemies. Moreover GOD declares to you that GOD will make you a house. [12]When your days are fulfilled and you lie down with your ancestors, I will raise up your offspring after you, who shall come forth from your body, and I will establish a kingdom for that offspring, [13]who shall build a house for my name, and I will establish the throne of that kingdom for ever. [14]I will be parent to your child, and your child shall be my child. When your child commits iniquity, I will chasten that one with a rod of human discipline, with stripes of human hands; [15]but I will not take away my steadfast love as I took it from Saul, whom I put away from before you. [16]And your house and your kingdom shall be made sure for ever before me; your throne shall be established for ever.' " [17]In accordance with all these words, and in accordance with all this vision, Nathan spoke to David.

²⁰I have found David, my servant;
   with my holy oil I have anointed him;
²¹so that my hand shall ever abide with David,
   my arm also shall strengthen him.
²²The enemy shall not outwit him,
   the wicked shall not humble him.
²³I will crush David's foes before him
   and strike down those who hate him.
²⁴My faithfulness and my steadfast love shall be with him,
   and in my name shall David's horn be exalted.
²⁵I will set his hand on the sea
   and his right hand on the rivers.
²⁶David shall cry to me, "You are my Father [*and my Mother**],
   my God, and the Rock of my salvation."
²⁷And I will make him the first-born,
   the highest of the kings of the earth.
²⁸My steadfast love I will keep for David for ever,
   and my covenant will stand firm for him.
²⁹I will establish David's line for ever
   and his throne as the days of the heavens.
³⁰If David's children forsake my law
   and do not walk according to my ordinances,
³¹if they violate my statutes
   and do not keep my commandments,
³²then I will punish their transgression with the rod
   and their iniquity with scourges;
³³but I will not remove from David my steadfast love,
   or be false to my faithfulness.
³⁴I will not violate my covenant,
   or alter the word that went forth from my lips.
³⁵Once for all I have sworn by my holiness;
   I will not lie to David,
³⁶whose line shall endure for ever,
   whose throne as long as the sun before me.
³⁷Like the moon it shall be established for ever;
   it shall stand firm while the skies endure.

---

*Addition to the text. See "Metaphor" and "God the Father and Mother" in the Appendix.

Lesson 2 ~ 2 Corinthians 12:1-10

Paul writes of God's all-sufficient grace.

[1]I must boast; there is nothing to be gained by it, but I will go on to visions and revelations of the Sovereign.□ [2]I know some one in Christ who fourteen years ago was caught up to the third heaven—whether in the body or out of the body I do not know, God knows. [3]And I know that this person was caught up into Paradise—whether in the body or out of the body I do not know, God knows—[4]and there heard things that cannot be told, which may not be uttered. [5]On behalf of this one I will boast, but on my own behalf I will not boast, except of my weaknesses. [6]Though if I wish to boast, I shall not be a fool, for I shall be speaking the truth. But I refrain from it, so that no one may think more of me than can be seen in me or heard from me. [7]And to keep me from being too elated by the abundance of revelations, a thorn was given me in the flesh, a messenger of Satan, to harass me, to keep me from being too elated. [8]Three times I besought the Sovereign□ about this, that it should leave me; [9]but the Sovereign said to me, "My grace is sufficient for you, for my power is made perfect in weakness." I will all the more gladly boast of my weaknesses, that the power of Christ may rest upon me. [10]For the sake of Christ, then, I am content with weaknesses, insults, hardships, persecutions, and calamities; for when I am weak, then I am strong.

Gospel ~ Mark 6:1-6

Jesus' neighbors are astonished and take offense at him.

[1]Jesus went away from there and came to his own country; and the disciples followed. [2]And on the sabbath Jesus began to teach in the synagogue; and many who heard were astonished, saying, "Where did this man get all this? What is the wisdom given to him? What mighty works are wrought by his hands! [3]Is not this the carpenter, the son of Mary and brother of James and Joses and Judas and Simon, and are not his sisters here with us?" And they took offense at Jesus. [4]And Jesus said to them, "A prophet is not without honor, except in the prophet's own country, and among the prophet's own kin, and in the prophet's own house." [5]And Jesus could do no mighty work there, except to lay hands upon a few sick people and heal them. [6]And Jesus marveled because of their unbelief.

□RSV *Lord.* See Appendix.

PENTECOST 8

Lesson 1 ~ 2 Samuel 7:18-29

David responds to promises from God.

¹⁸Then King David went in and sat before GOD, and said, "Who am I, O Sovereign GOD, and what is my house, that you have brought me thus far? ¹⁹And yet this was a small thing in your eyes, O Sovereign GOD; you have spoken also of your servant's house for a great while to come, and have shown me future generations, O Sovereign GOD! ²⁰And what more can David say to you? For you know your servant, O Sovereign GOD! ²¹Because of your promise, and according to your own heart, you have wrought all this greatness, to make your servant know it. ²²Therefore you are great, O SOVEREIGN God; for there is none like you, and there is no God besides you, according to all that we have heard with our ears. ²³What other nation on earth is like your people Israel, whom God went to redeem to be God's people, making for God a name, and doing for them great and terrible things, by driving out before God's people a nation and its gods? ²⁴And you established for yourself your people Israel to be your people for ever; and you, O GOD, became their God. ²⁵And now, O SOVEREIGN God, confirm for ever the word which you have spoken concerning your servant and concerning his house, and do as you have spoken; ²⁶and your name will be magnified for ever, saying, 'The GOD of hosts is God over Israel,' and the house of your servant David will be established before you. ²⁷For you, O GOD of hosts, the God of Israel, have made this revelation to your servant, saying, 'I will build you a house'; therefore your servant has found courage to pray this prayer to you. ²⁸And now, O Sovereign GOD, you are God, and your words are true, and you have promised this good thing to your servant; ²⁹now therefore may it please you to bless the house of your servant, that it may continue for ever before you; for you, O Sovereign GOD, have spoken, and with your blessing shall the house of your servant be blessed for ever."

Psalm 132:11-18

¹¹GOD swore to David a sure oath
  and will not turn back from it:
"One from the fruit of your body
  I will set on your throne.
¹²If your children keep my covenant
  and my testimonies which I shall teach them,
their children also for ever
  shall sit upon your throne."

¹³For GOD has chosen Zion,
    and has desired it for a habitation:
¹⁴"This is my resting place for ever;
    here I will dwell, for I have desired it.
¹⁵I will abundantly bless its provisions;
    I will satisfy its poor with bread.
¹⁶Its priests I will clothe with salvation,
    and its saints will shout for joy.
¹⁷There I will make a horn to sprout for David;
    I have prepared a lamp for my anointed,
¹⁸whose enemies I will clothe with shame;
    but upon my anointed the crown will shed its luster."

Lesson 2 ~ Ephesians 1:1-10

The writer greets the saints who are faithful in Christ Jesus.

¹Paul, an apostle of Christ Jesus by the will of God,
    To the saints who are also faithful in Christ Jesus:
²Grace to you and peace from God our Father [*and Mother**] and from the Sovereign□ Jesus Christ.
³Blessed be God, Father [*and Mother**] of our Sovereign□ Jesus Christ, who has blessed us in Christ with every spiritual blessing in the heavenly places, ⁴even as God chose us in Christ before the foundation of the world, that we should be holy and blameless before God, ⁵who destined us in love to be adopted children through Jesus Christ, according to the purpose of God's will, ⁶to the praise of God's glorious grace freely bestowed on us in the Beloved, ⁷in whom we have redemption by blood, the forgiveness of our trespasses, according to the riches of God's grace ⁸lavished upon us. ⁹For God has made known to us in all wisdom and insight the mystery of God's will, according to God's purpose set forth in Christ ¹⁰as a plan for the fulness of time, to unite all things in Christ, things in heaven and things on earth.

---

*Addition to the text. RSV v. 2 *God our Father;* v. 3 *the God and Father.* See "Metaphor" and "God the Father and Mother" in the Appendix.
□RSV *Lord.* See Appendix.

Gospel ~ Mark 6:7-13

Jesus sends out the twelve.

⁷Jesus called the twelve, and began to send them out two by two, and gave them authority over the unclean spirits. ⁸He charged them to take nothing for their journey except a staff; no bread, no bag, no money in their belts; ⁹but to wear sandals and not put on two tunics. ¹⁰And Jesus said to them, "Where you enter a house, stay there until you leave the place. ¹¹And if any place will not receive you and they refuse to hear you, when you leave, shake off the dust that is on your feet for a testimony against them." ¹²So they went out and preached that people should repent. ¹³And they cast out many demons, and anointed with oil many that were sick and healed them.

PENTECOST 9

Lesson 1 ~ 2 Samuel 11:1-15

David takes Bathsheba and plots against her husband, Uriah.

[1]In the spring of the year, the time when kings go forth to battle, David sent Joab, and his servants with him, and all Israel; and they ravaged the Ammonites, and besieged Rabbah. But David remained at Jerusalem.

[2]It happened, late one afternoon, when David arose from his couch and was walking upon the roof of the king's house, that he saw from the roof a woman bathing; and the woman was very beautiful. [3]And David sent and inquired about the woman. And one said, "Is not this Bathsheba, the daughter of Eliam, the wife of Uriah the Hittite?" [4]So David sent messengers, and took her; and she came to him, and he lay with her. (Now she was carrying out her ritual purification.) Then she returned to her house. [5]And the woman conceived; and she sent and told David, "I am with child."

[6]So David sent word to Joab, "Send me Uriah the Hittite." And Joab sent Uriah to David. [7]When Uriah came to him, David asked how Joab was doing, and how the people fared, and how the war prospered. [8]Then David said to Uriah, "Go down to your house, and wash your feet." And Uriah went out of the king's house, and there followed him a present from the king. [9]But Uriah slept at the door of the king's house with all the servants of his lord, and did not go down to his house. [10]When they told David, "Uriah did not go down to his house," David said to Uriah, "Have you not come from a journey? Why did you not go down to your house?" [11]Uriah said to David, "The ark and Israel and Judah dwell in booths; and my lord Joab and the servants of my lord are camping in the open field; shall I then go to my house, to eat and to drink, and to lie with my wife? As you live, and as your soul lives, I will not do this thing." [12]Then David said to Uriah, "Remain here today also, and tomorrow I will let you depart." So Uriah remained in Jerusalem that day, and the next. [13]And David invited Uriah, who ate in his presence and drank, so that David made him drunk; and in the evening Uriah went out to lie on his couch with the servants of his lord, but did not go down to his house.

[14]In the morning David wrote a letter to Joab, and sent it by the hand of Uriah. [15]In the letter he wrote, "Set Uriah in the forefront of the hardest fighting, and then draw back from him, that he may be struck down, and die."

Psalm 53

[1]Fools say in their heart,
  "There is no God."
They are corrupt, doing abominable iniquity;
  there is none that does good.
[2]God looks down from heaven
  upon humankind
to see if there are any that are wise,
  that seek after God.
[3]They have all fallen away;
  they are all alike depraved;
there is none that does good,
  no, not one.
[4]Have those who work evil no understanding,
  who eat up my people as they eat bread,
  and do not call upon God?
[5]There they are, in great terror,
  in terror such as has not been!
For God will scatter the bones of the ungodly;
  they will be put to shame, for God has rejected them.
[6]O that deliverance for Israel would come from Zion!
  When God restores the fortunes of God's people,
  Jacob will rejoice and Israel be glad.

Lesson 2 ~ Ephesians 2:11-22

The unity and peace of the household of God is in Christ.

[11]Therefore remember that at one time you Gentiles in the flesh, called the uncircumcision by what is called the circumcision, which is made in the flesh by hands—[c] [12]remember that you were at that time separated from Christ, alienated from the commonwealth of Israel, and strangers to the covenants of promise, having no hope and without God in the world. [13]But now in Christ Jesus you who once were far off have been brought near in the blood of Christ. [14]For Christ is our peace, who has made us both one, and has broken down the dividing wall of hostility, [15]by abolishing in Christ's own flesh the law of commandments and ordinances, in order to create in Christ one new humanity in place of the two, so making peace, [16]and in order to reconcile us both to God in one body through the cross, thereby bringing the hostility to an end. [17]And Christ came and preached peace to

---

[c]See Notes, p. 249.

you who were far off and peace to those who were near; [18]for through Christ we both have access in one Spirit to [God] the [*Mother and**] Father. [19]So then you are no longer strangers and sojourners, but you are citizens together with the saints and members of the household of God, [20]built upon the foundation of the apostles and prophets, Christ Jesus being the cornerstone, [21]in whom the whole structure is joined together and grows into a holy temple in the Sovereign;□ [22]in whom you also are built into it for a dwelling place of God in the Spirit.

Gospel ~ Mark 6:30-34

Large crowds keep following Jesus, who has compassion on them.

[30]The apostles returned to Jesus, and reported all that they had done and taught. [31]And Jesus said to them, "Come away by yourselves to a lonely place, and rest a while." For many were coming and going, and they had no leisure even to eat. [32]And they went away in the boat to a lonely place by themselves. [33]Now many saw them going and knew them, and they ran there on foot from all the towns, and got there ahead of them. [34]Going ashore, Jesus saw a great throng and had compassion on them, because they were like sheep without a shepherd; and Jesus began to teach them many things.

---

*Addition to the text. See "Metaphor" and "God the Father and Mother" in the Appendix.
□RSV *Lord*. See Appendix.

PENTECOST 10

Lesson 1 ~ 2 Samuel 12:1-14

David is judged for taking Bathsheba and betraying Uriah.

¹And GOD sent Nathan to David. Nathan came to him and said, "There were two men in a certain city, the one rich and the other poor. ²The rich man had very many flocks and herds; ³but the poor man had nothing but one little ewe lamb, which he had bought. And he brought it up, and it grew up with him and with his children; it used to eat of his morsel, and drink from his cup, and lie in his bosom, and it was like a daughter to him. ⁴Now there came a traveler to the rich man, and he was unwilling to take one of his own flock or herd to prepare for the wayfarer who had come to him, but he took the poor man's lamb, and prepared it for the man who had come to him." ⁵Then David's anger was greatly kindled against the man; and he said to Nathan, "As GOD lives, the man who has done this deserves to die; ⁶and he shall restore the lamb fourfold, because he did this thing, and because he had no pity."

⁷Nathan said to David, "You are the man. Thus says the SOVEREIGN ONE, the God of Israel, 'I anointed you king over Israel, and I delivered you out of the hand of Saul; ⁸and I gave you your master's house, and your master's wives into your bosom, and gave you the house of Israel and of Judah; and if this were too little, I would add to you as much more. ⁹Why have you despised the word of GOD, to do what is evil in God's sight? You have smitten Uriah the Hittite with the sword, and have taken his wife to be your wife, and have slain him with the sword of the Ammonites. ¹⁰Now therefore the sword shall never depart from your house, because you have despised me, and have taken the wife of Uriah the Hittite to be your wife.' ¹¹Thus says the SOVEREIGN ONE, 'Behold, I will raise up evil against you out of your own house; and I will take your wives before your eyes, and give them to your neighbor, and he shall lie with your wives in the sight of this sun. ¹²For you did it secretly; but I will do this thing before all Israel, and before the sun.' " ¹³David said to Nathan, "I have sinned against GOD." And Nathan said to David, "GOD also has put away your sin; you shall not die. ¹⁴Nevertheless, because by this deed you have utterly scorned GOD, the child that is born to you shall die."

Psalm 32

¹Blessed is the one whose transgression is forgiven,
  whose sin is covered.
²Blessed is the person to whom GOD imputes no iniquity,
  and in whose spirit there is no deceit.
³When I declared not my sin, my body wasted away
  through my groaning all day long.
⁴For day and night your hand was heavy upon me;
  my strength was dried up as by the heat of summer.
⁵I acknowledged my sin to you,
  and I did not hide my iniquity;
 I said, "I will confess my transgressions to GOD";
  then you forgave the guilt of my sin.
⁶Therefore let all who are godly
  offer prayer to you;
 at a time of distress, the rush of great waters
  shall not reach them.
⁷You are a hiding place for me,
  you preserve me from trouble;
  you encompass me with deliverance.
⁸I will instruct you and teach you
  the way you should go;
 I will counsel you with my eye upon you.
⁹Be not like a horse or a mule, without understanding,
  which must be curbed with bit and bridle,
  else it will not keep with you.
¹⁰Many are the pangs of the wicked;
  but steadfast love surrounds the one who trusts in GOD.
¹¹Be glad in GOD, and rejoice, O righteous,
  and shout for joy, all you upright in heart!

Lesson 2 ~ Ephesians 3:14-21

The apostle prays for the church.

¹⁴For this reason I bow my knees before [God] the Father [and Mother*], ¹⁵from whom every family in heaven and on earth is named, ¹⁶that according to the riches of God's glory God may grant you to be strengthened with might through God's Spirit in the inner person, ¹⁷and that Christ may dwell in your hearts through faith; that you, being rooted

---

*Addition to the text. See "Metaphor" and "God the Father and Mother" in the Appendix.

171

and grounded in love, [18]may have power to comprehend with all the saints what is the breadth and length and height and depth, [19]and to know the love of Christ which surpasses knowledge, that you may be filled with all the fulness of God.

[20]Now to the one who by the power at work within us is able to do far more abundantly than all that we ask or think, [21]to God be glory in the church and in Christ Jesus to all generations, for ever and ever. Amen.

Gospel ~ John 6:1-15

Jesus feeds the multitude.

[1]After this Jesus went to the other side of the Sea of Galilee, which is the Sea of Tiberias. [2]And a multitude followed, because they saw the signs which he did on those who were diseased. [3]Jesus went up on the mountain, and there sat down with the disciples. [4]Now the Passover, the Jewish feast, was at hand. [5]Looking up, then, and seeing that a multitude was approaching, Jesus said to Philip, "How are we to buy bread, so that these people may eat?" [6]This Jesus said to test Philip, for Jesus knew what he would do. [7]Philip answered, "Two hundred denarii would not buy enough bread for each of them to get a little." [8]One of the disciples, Andrew, Simon Peter's brother, said to Jesus, [9]"There is a child here who has five barley loaves and two fish; but what are they among so many?" [10]Jesus said, "Make the people sit down." Now there was much grass in the place; so the people sat down, in number about five thousand. [11]Jesus then took the loaves, and having given thanks, distributed them to those who were seated; so also the fish, as much as they wanted. [12]And when they had eaten their fill, Jesus told the disciples, "Gather up the fragments left over, that nothing may be lost." [13]So they gathered them up and filled twelve baskets with fragments from the five barley loaves, left by those who had eaten. [14]When the people saw the sign which Jesus had done, they said, "This is indeed the prophet who is to come into the world!"

[15]Perceiving then that they were about to come and take him by force to make him king, Jesus withdrew again to the mountain alone.

PENTECOST 11

Lesson 1 ~ 2 Samuel 12:15b-24

Bathsheba gives birth to Solomon.

¹⁵And GOD struck the child that Uriah's wife bore to David, and it became sick. ¹⁶David therefore besought God for the child; and David fasted, and went in and lay all night upon the ground. ¹⁷And the elders of his house stood beside him, to raise him from the ground; but he would not, nor did he eat food with them. ¹⁸On the seventh day the child died. And the servants of David feared to tell him that the child was dead; for they said, "Behold, while the child was yet alive, we spoke to the king, and he did not listen to us; how then can we say to him the child is dead? He may do himself some harm." ¹⁹But when David saw that his servants were whispering together, David perceived that the child was dead; and David said to the servants, "Is the child dead?" They said, "It is dead." ²⁰Then David arose from the earth, and washed, and anointed himself, and changed his clothes, and went into the house of GOD, and worshiped; David then went home; and when he asked, they set food before him, and he ate. ²¹Then his servants said to him, "What is this thing that you have done? You fasted and wept for the child while it was alive; but when the child died, you arose and ate food." ²²David said, "While the child was still alive, I fasted and wept; for I said, 'Who knows whether GOD will be gracious to me, that the child may live?' ²³But now the child is dead; why should I fast? Can I bring it back again? I shall go to the child, but the child will not return to me."

²⁴Then David comforted his wife, Bathsheba, and went in to her, and lay with her; and she bore a son, and David called his name Solomon. And GOD loved Solomon.

Psalm 34:11-22

¹¹Come, O children, listen to me,
    I will teach you the fear of GOD.
¹²Which of you desires life,
    and covets many days to enjoy good?
¹³Keep your tongue from evil,
    and your lips from speaking deceit.
¹⁴Depart from evil, and do good;
    seek peace, and pursue it.
¹⁵The eyes of GOD are toward the righteous,
    and God's ears toward their cry.

¹⁶The face of God is against evildoers,
     to cut off the remembrance of them from the earth.
¹⁷When the righteous cry for help, God hears,
     and delivers them out of all their troubles.
¹⁸God is near to the brokenhearted,
     and saves the crushed in spirit.
¹⁹Many are the afflictions of the righteous,
     but God delivers them from their pain.
²⁰God keeps all their bones;
     not one of them is broken.
²¹Evil shall slay the wicked;
     and those who hate the righteous will be condemned.
²²God redeems the life of God's servants;
     none of those who take refuge in God will be condemned.

Lesson 2 ~ Ephesians 4:1-6

The apostle urges the unity of the Spirit in the bond of peace.

¹I therefore, a prisoner for the Sovereign,[□] beg you to lead a life worthy of the calling to which you have been called, ²with all lowliness and meekness, with patience, forbearing one another in love, ³eager to maintain the unity of the Spirit in the bond of peace. ⁴There is one body and one Spirit, just as you were called to the one hope that belongs to your call, ⁵one Sovereign,[□] one faith, one baptism, ⁶one God, [*Mother**] and Father of us all, who is above all and through all and in all.

Gospel ~ John 6:24-35

Jesus says that he is the bread of life.

²⁴So when the people saw that Jesus was not there, nor the disciples, they themselves got into the boats and went to Capernaum, seeking Jesus.
     ²⁵When they found Jesus on the other side of the sea, they said to him, "Rabbi, when did you come here?" ²⁶Jesus answered them, "Truly, truly, I say to you, you seek me, not because you saw signs, but because you ate your fill of the loaves. ²⁷Do not labor for the food which perishes, but for the food which endures to eternal life, which the Human One[○] will give to you; for on that one has God the Father [*and Mother**] set God's seal." ²⁸Then

---

□RSV *Lord.* See Appendix.
*Addition to the text. See "Metaphor" and "God the Father and Mother" in the Appendix.
○RSV *Son of man.* See Appendix.

they said to Jesus, "What must we do to be doing the works of God?" [29]Jesus answered them, "This is the work of God, that you believe in the one whom God has sent." [30]So they said to Jesus, "Then what sign do you do, that we may see, and believe you? What work do you perform? [31]Our ancestors ate the manna in the wilderness; as it is written, 'God gave them bread from heaven to eat.' " [32]Jesus then said to them, "Truly, truly, I say to you, it was not Moses who gave you the bread from heaven; God gives you the true bread from heaven. [33]For the bread of God is that which comes down from heaven, and gives life to the world." [34]They said to Jesus, "Give us this bread always."

[35]Jesus said to them, "I am the bread of life; whoever comes to me shall not hunger, and whoever believes in me shall never thirst."

PENTECOST 12

Lesson 1 (alternate) ~ 2 Samuel 14:4-17[+]

The woman of Tekoa argues with David on Absalom's behalf.

[4]When the woman of Tekoa came to David, she fell on her face to the ground, and did obeisance, and said, "Help, O king." [5]And the king said to her, "What is your trouble?" She answered, "Alas, I am a widow; my husband is dead. [6]And your handmaid had two sons, and they quarreled with one another in the field; there was no one to part them, and one struck the other and killed him. [7]And now the whole family has risen against your handmaid, and they say, 'Give up the man who struck his brother, that we may kill him for the life of his brother whom he slew'; and so they would destroy the heir also. Thus they would quench my coal which is left, and leave to my husband neither name nor remnant upon the face of the earth."

[8]Then the king said to the woman, "Go to your house, and I will give orders concerning you." [9]And the woman of Tekoa said to the king, "On me be the guilt, my lord the king, and on my father's house; let the king and his throne be guiltless." [10]The king said, "Let whoever says anything to you be brought to me, and that person shall never touch you again." [11]Then she said, "Pray let the king invoke the Sovereign One your God, that the avenger of blood slay no more, and my son be not destroyed." David said, "As God lives, not one hair of your son shall fall to the ground."

[12]Then the woman said, "Pray let your handmaid speak a word to my lord the king." David said, "Speak." [13]And the woman said, "Why then have you planned such a thing against the people of God? For in giving this decison the king convicts himself, inasmuch as the king does not bring Absalom, his banished one, home again. [14]We must all die, we are like water spilt on the ground, which cannot be gathered up again; but God will not take away the life of the one who devises means not to keep his banished one an outcast. [15]Now I have come to say this to my lord the king because the people have made me afraid; and your handmaid thought, 'I will speak to the king; it may be that the king will perform the request of his servant. [16]For the king will hear, and deliver his servant from the hand of the one who would destroy me and my son together from the heritage of God.' [17]And your handmaid thought, 'The word of my lord the king will set me at rest'; for my lord the king is like the angel of God to discern good and evil. The Sovereign One your God be with you!"

[+]Lection added. See Appendix, p. 248.

Lesson 1 ~ 2 Samuel 18:1, 5, 9-15

David's son Absalom is killed.

[1]Then David mustered the men who were with him, and set over them commanders of thousands and commanders of hundreds. [5]And the king ordered Joab and Abishai and Ittai, "Deal gently for my sake with the young Absalom." And all the people heard when the king gave orders to all the commanders about Absalom.

[9]And Absalom chanced to meet the servants of David. Absalom was riding upon his mule, and the mule went under the thick branches of a great oak, and Absalom's head caught fast in the oak, and he was left hanging between heaven and earth, while the mule that was under him went on. [10]And some one saw it, and told Joab, "Behold, I saw Absalom hanging in an oak." [11]Joab said to the one who told him, "What, you saw Absalom! Why then did you not strike him there to the ground? I would have been glad to give you ten pieces of silver and a belt." [12]But the man said to Joab, "Even if I felt in my hand the weight of a thousand pieces of silver, I would not put forth my hand against the king's son; for in our hearing the king commanded you and Abishai and Ittai, 'For my sake protect the young Absalom.' [13]On the other hand, if I had dealt treacherously against Absalom's life (and there is nothing hidden from the king), then you yourself would have stood aloof." [14]Joab said, "I will not waste time like this with you." And Joab took three darts in his hand, and thrust them into the heart of Absalom, while he was still alive in the oak. [15]And ten young men, Joab's armor-bearers, surrounded Absalom and struck him, and killed Absalom.

Psalm 143:1-8

[1]Hear my prayer, O GOD; give ear to my supplications!
  In your faithfulness, answer me, in your righteousness!
[2]Enter not into judgment with your servant;
  for no one living is righteous before you.
[3]For the enemy has pursued me,
  has crushed my life to the ground,
  and has made me sit in darkness like those long dead.
[4]Therefore my spirit faints within me;
  my heart within me is appalled.
[5]I remember the days of old,
  I meditate on all that you have done;
  I muse on what your hands have wrought.

⁶I stretch out my hands to you;
  my soul thirsts for you like a parched land.
⁷Make haste to answer me, O GOD!
  My spirit fails!
Hide not your face from me,
  lest I be like those who go down to the Pit.
⁸Let me hear in the morning of your steadfast love,
  for in you I put my trust.
Teach me the way I should go,
  for to you I lift up my soul.

Lesson 2 ~ Ephesians 4:25–5:2

The apostle gives ethical instructions to the Ephesians.

²⁵Therefore, putting away falsehood, let every one speak the truth with their neighbor, for we are members one of another. ²⁶Be angry but do not sin; do not let the sun go down on your anger, ²⁷and give no opportunity to the devil. ²⁸Let the thief no longer steal, but rather labor, doing honest manual work, in order to be able to give to those in need. ²⁹Let no evil talk come out of your mouths, but only such as is good for edifying, as fits the occasion, that it may impart grace to those who hear. ³⁰And do not grieve the Holy Spirit of God, in whom you were sealed for the day of redemption. ³¹Let all bitterness and wrath and anger and clamor and slander be put away from you, with all malice, ³²and be kind to one another, tenderhearted, forgiving one another, as God in Christ forgave you.

⁵:¹Therefore be imitators of God, as beloved children. ²And walk in love, as Christ loved us and gave up Christ's self for us, a fragrant offering and sacrifice to God.

Gospel (alternate) ~ John 8:2-11⁺

Jesus defends a woman who has been abused.

²Early in the morning Jesus came again to the temple; all the people came to him, and he sat down and taught them. ³The scribes and the Pharisees brought a woman who had been caught in adultery, and placing her in the midst ⁴they said, "Teacher, this woman has been caught in the act of adultery. ⁵Now in the law Moses commanded us to stone such. What do you say about her?" ⁶This they said to test Jesus, that they might have

---

⁺Lection added. See Appendix, p. 248.

some charge to bring against him. Jesus bent down and wrote with his finger on the ground. [7]And as they continued to ask Jesus, he stood up and said to them, "Let one who is without sin among you be the first to throw a stone at her." [8]And once more Jesus bent down and wrote with his finger on the ground. [9]But when they heard it, they went away, one by one, beginning with the eldest, and Jesus was left alone with the woman standing before him. [10]Jesus looked up and said to her, "Woman, where are they? Has no one condemned you?" [11]She said, "No one, Sir." And Jesus said, "Neither do I condemn you; go, and do not sin again."

Gospel ~ John 6:35, 41-51

Jesus is the bread of life.

[35]Jesus said to them, "I am the bread of life; whoever comes to me shall not hunger, and whoever believes in me shall never thirst."

[41]The religious authorities[∇] then murmured at Jesus for saying, "I am the bread which came down from heaven." [42]They said, "Is not this Jesus, the son of Joseph, whose father and mother we know? How does he now say, 'I have come down from heaven'?" [43]Jesus answered them, "Do not murmur among yourselves. [44]No one can come to me unless drawn by [God] the Father [and Mother*] who sent me; and I will raise up that one at the last day. [45]It is written in the prophets, 'And they shall all be taught by God.' Every one who has heard and learned from God[⊗] comes to me. [46]Not that any one has seen God[⊗] except the one who is from God; that one has seen God.[⊗] [47]Truly, truly, I say to you, whoever believes has eternal life. [48]I am the bread of life. [49]Your ancestors ate the manna in the wilderness, and they died. [50]This is the bread which comes down from heaven, that people may eat of it and not die. [51]I am the living bread which came down from heaven; any one who eats of this bread will live for ever; and the bread which I shall give for the life of the world is my flesh."

[∇]RSV *The Jews*. See Appendix.
*Addition to the text. See "Metaphor" and "God the Father and Mother" in the Appendix.
[⊗]RSV *the Father*.

PENTECOST 13

Lesson 1 ~ 2 Samuel 18:24-33

David receives the report of the death of Absalom.

²⁴Now David was sitting between the two gates; and the sentry went up to the roof of the gate by the wall, and looking up, the sentry saw some one running alone. ²⁵And the sentry called out and told the king. And the king said, "If the runner is alone, there are tidings." And the runner came apace, and drew near. ²⁶And the sentry saw another runner, and the sentry called to the gate and said, "See, another runner who is alone!" The king said, "That runner also brings tidings." ²⁷And the sentry said, "I think the running of the foremost is like the running of Ahimaaz the son of Zadok." And the king said, "He is a good man, and comes with good tidings."

²⁸Then Ahimaaz cried out to the king, "All is well." And he bowed before the king with his face to the earth, and said, "Blessed be the Sovereign One your God, who has delivered up those who raised their hand against my lord the king." ²⁹And the king said, "Is it well with the young Absalom?" Ahimaaz answered, "When Joab sent your servant, I saw a great tumult, but I do not know what it was." ³⁰And the king said, "Turn aside, and stand here." So Ahimaaz turned aside, and stood still.

³¹And behold, the Cushite came; and the Cushite said, "Good tidings for my lord the king! For God has delivered you this day from the power of all who rose up against you." ³²The king said to the Cushite, "Is it well with the young Absalom?" And the Cushite answered, "May the enemies of my lord the king, and all who rise up against you for evil, be like Absalom." ³³And the king was deeply moved, and went up to the chamber over the gate, and wept; and as he went, David said, "O my son Absalom, my son, my son Absalom! Would I had died instead of you, O Absalom, my son, my son!"

Psalm 102:1-12

¹Hear my prayer, O God;
   let my cry come to you!
²Do not hide your face from me
   in the day of my distress!
  Incline your ear to me;
   answer me speedily in the day when I call!
³For my days pass away like smoke,
   and my bones burn like a furnace.
⁴My heart is smitten like grass, and withered;
   I forget to eat my bread.

⁵Because of my loud groaning
   my bones cleave to my flesh.
⁶I am like a vulture of the wilderness,
   like an owl of the waste places;
⁷I lie awake,
   I am like a lonely bird on the housetop.
⁸All the day my enemies taunt me,
   those who deride me use my name for a curse.
⁹For I eat ashes like bread,
   and mingle tears with my drink,
¹⁰because of your indignation and anger;
   for you have taken me up and thrown me away.
¹¹My days are like an evening shadow;
   I wither away like grass.
¹²But you, O GOD, are enthroned for ever;
   your name endures to all generations.

Lesson 2 ~ Ephesians 5:15-20

The apostle exhorts the Ephesians always to give thanks.

¹⁵Look carefully then how you walk, not unwisely but wisely, ¹⁶making the most of the time, because the days are evil. ¹⁷Therefore do not be foolish, but understand what the will of the Sovereign□ is. ¹⁸And do not get drunk with wine, for that is debauchery; but be filled with the Spirit, ¹⁹addressing one another in psalms and hymns and spiritual songs, singing and making melody to the Sovereign□ with all your heart, ²⁰always and for everything giving thanks in the name of our Sovereign□ Jesus Christ to God the Father [*and Mother**].

□RSV *Lord.* See Appendix.
*Addition to the text. See "Metaphor" and "God the Father and Mother" in the Appendix.

Gospel ~ John 6:51-58

Jesus teaches about the living bread.

[51]"I am the living bread which came down from heaven; any one who eats of this bread will live for ever; and the bread which I shall give for the life of the world is my flesh."

[52]The religious authorities[v] then disputed among themselves, saying, "How can this man give us his flesh to eat?" [53]So Jesus said to them, "Truly, truly, I say to you, unless you eat the flesh and drink the blood of the Human One,[o] you have no life in you; [54]those who eat my flesh and drink my blood have eternal life, and I will raise them up at the last day. [55]For my flesh is food indeed, and my blood is drink indeed. [56]Those who eat of my flesh and drink of my blood abide in me, and I in them. [57]As the living God[⊛] sent me, and I live because of God,[⊛] so whoever partakes of me will live because of me. [58]This is the bread which came down from heaven, not such as our ancestors ate and died; whoever eats this bread will live for ever."

---

[v]RSV *The Jews.* See Appendix.
[o]RSV *Son of man.* See Appendix.
[⊛]RSV v. 57a *Father;* v. 57b *the Father.*

PENTECOST 14

Lesson 1 ~ 2 Samuel 23:1-7

David speaks a final word about the everlasting covenant with God.

¹Now these are the last words of David:
The oracle of David, the son of Jesse,
  the oracle of the one who was raised on high,
the anointed of the God of Jacob,
  the sweet psalmist of Israel:
²"The Spirit of GOD speaks by me,
  God's word is upon my tongue.
³The God of Israel has spoken,
  the Rock of Israel has said to me:
When one rules justly over others,
  ruling in the fear of God,
⁴God dawns on them like the morning light,
  like the sun shining forth upon a cloudless morning,
  like rain that makes grass to sprout from the earth.
⁵Indeed, does not my house stand so with God?
  For God has made with me an everlasting covenant,
  ordered in all things and secure.
For will God not cause to prosper
  all my help and my desire?
⁶But the godless are all like thorns that are thrown away;
  for they cannot be taken with the hand;
⁷but the one who touches them
  is armed with iron and the shaft of a spear,
  and they are utterly consumed with fire."

Psalm 67

[1]May God be gracious to us and bless us
   and make God's face to shine upon us,
[2]that your way may be known upon earth,
   your saving power among all nations.
[3]Let the peoples praise you, O God;
   let all the peoples praise you!
[4]Let the nations be glad and sing for joy,
   for you judge the peoples with equity
   and guide the nations upon earth.
[5]Let the peoples praise you, O God;
   let all the peoples praise you!
[6]The earth has yielded its increase;
   God, our God, has blessed us.
[7]God has blessed us;
   let all the ends of the earth fear God!

Lesson 2 ~ Ephesians 6:1-4[+]

Paul writes about the responsibilities of parents and children to each other.

[1]Children, obey your parents in the Sovereign,[□] for this is right. [2]"Honor your father and mother" (this is the first commandment with a promise), [3]"that it may be well with you and that you may live long on the earth." [4]Parents, do not provoke your children to anger, but bring them up in the guidance and instruction of the Sovereign.[□]

[+]Substitute lection. The NAACL reads Eph. 5:21-33. See Appendix, p. 248.
[□]RSV *Lord.* See Appendix.

Gospel ~ John 6:55-69

The author of the Gospel of John speaks about Jesus, the bread of life.

[55]"For my flesh is food indeed, and my blood is drink indeed. [56]Those who eat of my flesh and drink of my blood abide in me, and I in them. [57]As the living God® sent me, and I live because of God,® so whoever partakes of me will live because of me. [58]This is the bread which came down from heaven, not such as our ancestors ate and died; whoever eats this bread will live for ever." [59]This Jesus said in the synagogue, while teaching at Capernaum.

[60]Many of the disciples, when they heard it, said, "This is a hard saying; who can listen to it?" [61]But Jesus, knowing that the disciples murmured at it, said to them, "Do you take offense at this? [62]Then what if you were to see the Human One° ascending back to heaven? [63]It is the spirit that gives life, the flesh is of no avail; the words that I have spoken to you are spirit and life. [64]But there are some of you that do not believe." For Jesus knew from the first who those were that did not believe, and who it was that would betray him. [65]And Jesus said, "This is why I told you that no one can come to me unless it is granted by [God] the Father [and Mother*]."

[66]After this many of the disciples drew back and no longer went about with him. [67]Jesus said to the twelve, "Do you also wish to go away?" [68]Simon Peter answered Jesus, "To whom shall we go? You have the words of eternal life; [69]and we have believed, and have come to know, that you are the Holy One of God."

®RSV v. 57a *Father;* v. 57b *the Father.*
°RSV *Son of man.* See Appendix.
*Addition to the text. See "Metaphor" and "God the Father and Mother" in the Appendix.

PENTECOST 15

Lesson 1 ~ 1 Kings 2:1-4, 10-12

After David's death Solomon becomes king.

[1]When David's time to die drew near, he charged Solomon his son, saying, [2]"I am about to go the way of all the earth. Be strong, and show yourself courageous, [3]and keep the charge of the Sovereign One your God, walking in God's ways and keeping God's statutes, commandments, ordinances, and testimonies, as it is written in the law of Moses, that you may prosper in all that you do and wherever you turn; [4]that the word which God spoke concerning me may be established: 'If your descendants take heed to their way, to walk before me in faithfulness with all their heart and with all their soul, you shall not be without a descendant on the throne of Israel.' "

[10]Then David slept with his ancestors, and was buried in the city of David. [11]And the time that David reigned over Israel was forty years—seven years in Hebron, and thirty-three years in Jerusalem. [12]So Solomon sat upon the throne of David his father; and Solomon's kingdom was firmly established.

Psalm 121

[1]I lift up my eyes to the hills.
From whence does my help come?
[2]My help comes from God,
who made heaven and earth.
[3]God will not let your foot be moved;
the one who keeps you will not slumber;
[4]behold, the one who keeps Israel
will neither slumber nor sleep.
[5]God is your keeper;
God is your shade
on your right hand.
[6]The sun shall not smite you by day,
nor the moon by night.
[7]God will keep you from all evil,
and will keep your life.
[8]God will keep
your going out and your coming in
from this time forth and for evermore.

Lesson 2 ~ Ephesians 6:10-20

The armor of God is sufficient for the struggle.

[10]Finally, be strong in the Sovereign□ and in the strength of the Sovereign's might. [11]Put on the whole armor of God, that you may be able to stand against the wiles of the devil. [12]For we are not contending against flesh and blood, but against the principalities, against the powers, against the world rulers of this present evil age, against the spiritual hosts of wickedness in the heavenly places. [13]Therefore take the whole armor of God, that you may be able to withstand in the evil day, and having done all, to stand. [14]Stand therefore, having girded your loins with truth, and having put on the breastplate of righteousness, [15]and having shod your feet with the equipment of the gospel of peace; [16]besides all these, taking the shield of faith, with which you can quench all the flaming darts of the evil one. [17]And take the helmet of salvation, and the sword of the Spirit, which is the word of God. [18]Pray at all times in the Spirit, with all prayer and supplication. To that end keep alert with all perseverance, making supplications for all the saints, [19]and also for me, that utterance may be given me in opening my mouth boldly to proclaim the mystery of the gospel, [20]for which I am an ambassador in chains; that I may declare it boldly, as I ought to speak.

□RSV *Lord.* See Appendix.

Gospel ~ Mark 7:1-8, 14-15, 21-23

Jesus teaches about the sources of defilement.

[1]Now when the Pharisees gathered together to Jesus, with some of the scribes, who had come from Jerusalem, [2]they saw that some of Jesus' disciples ate with hands defiled, that is, unwashed. [3](For the Pharisees, and all the Jews, do not eat unless they wash their hands, observing the tradition of the elders; [4]and when they come from the market place, they do not eat unless they purify themselves; and there are many other traditions which they observe, the washing of cups and pots and vessels of bronze.) [5]And the Pharisees and the scribes asked Jesus, "Why do your disciples not live according to the tradition of the elders, but eat with hands defiled?" [6]And Jesus said to them, "Well did Isaiah prophesy of you hypocrites, as it is written,

'This people honors me with their lips,
but their heart is far from me;
[7]in vain do they worship me,
teaching human precepts as doctrines.'
[8]You leave the commandment of God, and hold fast human tradition."

[14]And Jesus called the people to him again, and said to them, "Hear me, all of you, and understand: [15]there is nothing outside a person which by going in can defile; but the things which come out are what defile. [21]For from within, out of the human heart, come evil thoughts, fornication, theft, murder, adultery, [22]coveting, wickedness, deceit, licentiousness, envy, slander, pride, foolishness. [23]All these evil things come from within, and these are what defile."

PENTECOST 16

Lesson 1 ~ Ecclesiasticus 5:8-15

Sirach teaches that every facet of life must be lived attentively.

⁸Do not depend on dishonest wealth,
    for it will not benefit you in the day of calamity.
⁹Do not winnow with every wind,
    nor follow every path:
    the double-tongued sinner does that.
¹⁰Be steadfast in your understanding,
    and let your speech be consistent.
¹¹Be quick to hear,
    and be deliberate in answering.
¹²If you have understanding, answer your neighbor;
    but if not, put your hand on your mouth.
¹³Glory and dishonor come from speaking,
    and the tongue is a person's downfall.
¹⁴Do not be called a slanderer,
    and do not lie in ambush with your tongue;
for shame comes to the thief,
    and severe condemnation to the double-tongued.
¹⁵In great or small matters do not act amiss,
    and do not become an enemy instead of a friend.

Lesson 1 (alternate) ~ Proverbs 2:1-8

Knowledge and fear of God are reflected in the way one lives, according to Proverbs.

¹My child, if you receive my words
    and treasure up my commandments with you,
²making your ear attentive to wisdom
    and inclining your heart to understanding;
³yes, if you cry out for insight
    and raise your voice for understanding,
⁴if you seek it like silver
    and search for it as for hidden treasures;
⁵then you will understand the fear of God
    and find the knowledge of God.

⁶For God gives wisdom;
 from God's mouth come knowledge and understanding;
⁷God stores up sound wisdom for the upright
 and is a shield to those who walk in integrity,
⁸guarding the paths of justice
 and preserving the way of God's saints.

Psalm 119:129-136

¹²⁹Your testimonies are wonderful;
 therefore my soul keeps them.
¹³⁰The unfolding of your words gives light;
 it imparts understanding to those who are simple.
¹³¹With open mouth I pant,
 because I long for your commandments.
¹³²Turn to me and be gracious to me,
 as is your wont toward those who love your name.
¹³³Keep steady my steps according to your promise,
 and let no iniquity get dominion over me.
¹³⁴Redeem me from human oppression,
 that I may keep your precepts.
¹³⁵Make your face shine upon your servant,
 and teach me your statutes.
¹³⁶My eyes shed streams of tears,
 because people do not keep your law.

Lesson 2 ~ James 1:17-27

James urges the church to be hearers and doers of the word.

¹⁷Every good endowment and every perfect gift is from above, coming down from the God[⊗] of lights with whom there is no variation or shadow due to change. ¹⁸Of God's own will were we brought forth by the word of truth that we should be a kind of first fruits of God's creatures.

¹⁹Know this, my beloved brothers and sisters. Let every one be quick to hear, slow to speak, slow to anger, ²⁰for human anger does not work the righteousness of God. ²¹Therefore put away all filthiness and rank growth of wickedness and receive with meekness the implanted word, which is able to save your souls.

⊗RSV *Father.*

190

²²But be doers of the word, and not hearers only, deceiving yourselves. ²³For if any are hearers of the word and not doers, they are like those who observe their natural face in a mirror; ²⁴for they observe themselves and go away and at once forget what they were like. ²⁵But those who look into the perfect law, the law of liberty, and persevere, being no hearers that forget but doers that act, they shall be blessed in their doing.

²⁶If any think they are religious, and do not bridle their tongue but deceive their heart, their religion is vain. ²⁷Religion that is pure and undefiled before God⊗ is this: to visit orphans and widows in their affliction, and to keep oneself unstained from the world.

Gospel ~ Mark 7:31-37

Jesus heals a person who is deaf and has a speech impediment.

³¹Then Jesus returned from the region of Tyre, and went through Sidon to the Sea of Galilee, through the region of the Decapolis. ³²And they brought to him one who was deaf and had a speech impediment; and they besought Jesus to lay his hand upon that person. ³³And taking the person aside from the multitude privately, Jesus put his fingers into the person's ears, and spat and touched the person's tongue; ³⁴and looking up to heaven, Jesus sighed, and said, "Ephphatha," that is, "Be opened." ³⁵And the ears were opened, the tongue was released, and the person spoke plainly. ³⁶And Jesus charged them to tell no one; but the more he charged them, the more zealously they proclaimed it. ³⁷And they were astonished beyond measure, saying, "He has done all things well, even making those who are deaf to hear and those who are mute to speak."

⊗RSV *God and the Father.*

PENTECOST 17

Lesson 1 ~ Proverbs 22:1-2, 8-9

The just and the unjust are repaid in kind, according to Proverbs.

¹A good name is to be chosen rather than great riches,
and favor is better than silver or gold.
²The rich and the poor meet together;
GOD is the maker of them all.
⁸Those who sow injustice will reap calamity,
and the rod of their fury will fail.
⁹Those who have a bountiful eye will be blessed,
for they share their bread with the poor.

Psalm 125

¹Those who trust in GOD are like Mount Zion,
which cannot be moved, but abides for ever.
²As the mountains are round about Jerusalem,
so GOD is round about God's people,
from this time forth and for evermore.
³For the scepter of wickedness shall not rest
upon the land allotted to the righteous,
lest the righteous put forth
their hands to do wrong.
⁴Do good, O GOD, to those who are good,
and to those who are upright in their hearts!
⁵But those who turn aside upon their crooked ways
GOD will lead away with evildoers!
Peace be in Israel!

Lesson 2 ~ James 2:1-5, 8-10, 14-17

James teaches that faith is expressed in one's works.

¹My brothers and sisters, show no partiality as you hold the faith of our Sovereign☐ Jesus Christ, the Sovereign☐ of glory. ²For if some one with gold rings and in fine clothing comes into your assembly, and a poor person in shabby clothing also comes in, ³and you pay attention to the one who wears the fine clothing and say, "Have a seat here, please," while you say to the poor person, "Stand there," or, "Sit at my feet," ⁴have you not made distinctions among yourselves, and become judges with evil thoughts? ⁵Listen, my beloved sisters and brothers. Has not God chosen those who are poor in the world to be rich in faith and heirs of the realm* which God has promised to those who love God?

⁸If you really fulfil the royal law, according to the scripture, "You shall love your neighbor as yourself," you do well. ⁹But if you show partiality, you commit sin, and are convicted by the law as transgressors. ¹⁰For whoever keeps the whole law but fails in one point has become guilty of all of it.

¹⁴What does it profit, my brothers and sisters, if some one claims to have faith but has not works? Can such faith save? ¹⁵If a brother or sister is ill-clad and in lack of daily food, ¹⁶and one of you says to them, "Go in peace, be warmed and filled," without giving them the things needed for the body, what does it profit? ¹⁷So faith by itself, if it has no works, is dead.

☐RSV *Lord.* See Appendix.
*RSV *kingdom.* See Appendix.

Jesus is recognized as the Christ, and then teaches about discipleship.

²⁷And Jesus went on with the disciples, to the villages of Caesarea Philippi; and on the way he asked them, "Who do people say that I am?" ²⁸And they said, "John the Baptist; and others say, Elijah; and others one of the prophets." ²⁹And Jesus asked them, "But who do you say that I am?" Peter answered, "You are the Christ." ³⁰And Jesus charged them to tell no one.

³¹And Jesus began to teach them that the Human One° must suffer many things, and be rejected by the elders and the chief priests and the scribes, and be killed, and after three days rise again. ³²And Jesus said this plainly. And Peter took Jesus, and began to rebuke him. ³³But turning and seeing the disciples, Jesus rebuked Peter, and said, "Get behind me, Satan! For you are not on God's side, but on the human side."

³⁴And Jesus called the multitude with the disciples, and said to them, "If any would come after me, let them deny themselves and take up their cross and follow me. ³⁵For those who would save their life will lose it; and those who lose their life for my sake and the gospel's will save it. ³⁶For what does it profit them, to gain the whole world and forfeit their life? ³⁷For what can they give in return for their life? ³⁸For any who are ashamed of me and of my words in this adulterous and sinful generation, of them will the Human One° also be ashamed, when coming in the glory of God[⊛] with the holy angels."

°RSV *Son of man.* See Appendix.
[⊛]RSV *his Father.*

PENTECOST 18

Lesson 1 ~ Job 28:20-28

God is the source of all wisdom.

20Whence then comes wisdom?
    And where is the place of understanding?
21It is hid from the eyes of all living,
    and concealed from the birds of the air.
22Abaddon and Death say,
    "We have heard a rumor of it with our ears."
23God understands the way to it,
    and knows its place.
24For God looks to the ends of the earth,
    and sees everything under the heavens.
25When God gave to the wind its weight,
    and meted out the waters by measure,
26and made a decree for the rain,
    and a way for the lightning of the thunder;
27then God saw it and declared it,
    established it, and searched it out.
28And God said to every human being,
    "Behold, the fear of God, that is wisdom;
    and to depart from evil is understanding."

Psalm 27:1-6

1GOD is my light and my salvation;
    whom shall I fear?
GOD is the stronghold of my life;
    of whom shall I be afraid?
2When evildoers assail me,
    uttering slanders against me,
my adversaries and foes,
    they shall stumble and fall.
3Though a host encamp against me,
    my heart shall not fear;
though war arise against me,
    yet I will be confident.

⁴One thing have I asked of GOD,
    that will I seek after;
  that I may dwell in the house of GOD
    all the days of my life,
  to behold GOD's beauty,
    and to inquire in God's temple.
⁵For God will hide me in a shelter
    in the day of trouble,
  and will conceal me under the cover of God's tent.
    God will set me high upon a rock.
⁶And now my head shall be lifted up
    above my enemies round about me;
  and I will offer in God's tent
    sacrifices with shouts of joy;
  I will sing and make melody to GOD.

Lesson 2 ~ James 3:13-18

James writes of the nature of wisdom.

¹³Who is wise and understanding among you? By a good life show your works in the meekness of wisdom. ¹⁴But if you have bitter jealousy and selfish ambition in your hearts, do not boast and be false to the truth. ¹⁵This wisdom is not such as comes down from above, but is earthly, unspiritual, devilish. ¹⁶For where jealousy and selfish ambition exist, there will be disorder and every vile practice. ¹⁷But the wisdom from above is first pure, then peaceable, gentle, open to reason, full of mercy and good fruits, without uncertainty or insincerity. ¹⁸And the harvest of righteousness is sown in peace by those who make peace.

Jesus teaches about the meaning of discipleship.

[30]They went on from there and passed through Galilee. And Jesus would not have any one know it; [31]for Jesus was teaching the disciples, saying to them, "The Human One° will be delivered into the hands of human beings, and will be killed by them; and having been killed, the Human One will rise after three days." [32]But they did not understand the saying, and they were afraid to ask Jesus.

[33]And they came to Capernaum; and having entered the house, Jesus asked them, "What were you discussing on the way?" [34]But they were silent; for on the way they had discussed with one another who was the greatest. [35]And Jesus sat down and called the twelve and said to them, "Any one who would be first must be last of all and servant of all." [36]And Jesus took a child, and put the child in the midst of them; and taking the child in his arms, Jesus said to them, [37]"Whoever receives one such child in my name receives me; and whoever receives me, receives not me but the one who sent me."

°RSV *Son of man.* See Appendix.

PENTECOST 19

Lesson 1 ~ Job 42:1-6

Job repents in the presence of God.

¹Then Job answered GOD:
²"I know that you can do all things,
    and that no purpose of yours can be thwarted.
³'Who is this that hides counsel without knowledge?'
Therefore I have uttered what I did not understand,
    things too wonderful for me, which I did not know.
⁴'Hear, and I will speak;
    I will question you, and you declare to me.'
⁵I had heard of you by the hearing of the ear,
    but now my eye sees you;
⁶therefore I despise myself,
    and repent in dust and ashes."

Psalm 27:7-14

⁷Hear, O GOD, when I cry aloud,
    be gracious to me and answer me!
⁸You have said, "Seek my face."
    My heart says to you,
"Your face, O GOD, do I seek."
⁹ Hide not your face from me.
Turn not your servant away in anger,
    you who have been my help.
Cast me not off, forsake me not,
    O God of my salvation!
¹⁰For my father and my mother have forsaken me,
    but GOD will take me up.
¹¹Teach me your way, O GOD;
    and lead me on a level path
    because of my enemies.
¹²Give me not up to the will of my adversaries;
    for false witnesses have risen against me,
    and they breathe out violence.
¹³I believe that I shall see the goodness of GOD
    in the land of the living!
¹⁴Wait for GOD;
    be strong, and let your heart take courage;
    yes, wait for GOD!

Lesson 2 ~ James 4:13-17; 5:7-11

James instructs all believers to be patient and faithful.

¹³Come now, you who say, "Today or tomorrow we will go into such and such a town and spend a year there and trade and get gain"; ¹⁴whereas you do not know about tomorrow. What is your life? For you are a mist that appears for a little time and then vanishes. ¹⁵Instead you ought to say, "If the Sovereign□ wills, we shall live and we shall do this or that." ¹⁶As it is, you boast in your arrogance. All such boasting is evil. ¹⁷It is sin for a person who knows what is right to fail to do it.

⁵:⁷Be patient, therefore, sisters and brothers, until the coming of the Sovereign.□ Behold, the farmer waits for the precious fruit of the earth, being patient over it until it receives the early and the late rain. ⁸You also be patient. Establish your hearts, for the coming of the Sovereign□ is at hand. ⁹Do not grumble, brothers and sisters, against one another, that you may not be judged; behold, the Judge is standing at the doors. ¹⁰As an example of suffering and patience, sisters and brothers, take the prophets who spoke in the name of the Sovereign.□ ¹¹Behold, we call those happy who were steadfast. You have heard of the steadfastness of Job, and you have seen the purpose of the Sovereign,□ how the Sovereign□ is compassionate and merciful.

□RSV *Lord.* See Appendix.

Jesus speaks of the inclusiveness of the gospel.

[38]John said to Jesus, "Teacher, we saw some one casting out demons in your name, and we forbade it, because the one who did it was not following us." [39]But Jesus said, "Do not forbid such a person; for no one who does a mighty work in my name will be able soon after to speak evil of me. [40]For whoever is not against us is for us. [41]For truly, I say to you, whoever gives you a cup of water to drink because you bear the name of Christ will by no means go unrewarded.

[42]"Whoever causes one of these little ones who believe in me to sin, it would be better to have a great millstone hung around the neck and to be thrown into the sea. [43]And if your hand causes you to sin, cut it off; it is better for you to enter life maimed than with two hands to go to hell, to the unquenchable fire. [45]And if your foot causes you to sin, cut it off; it is better for you to enter life lame than with two feet to be thrown into hell. [47]And if your eye causes you to sin, pluck it out; it is better for you to enter the realm* of God with one eye than with two eyes to be thrown into hell, [48]where their worm does not die, and the fire is not quenched. [49]For every one will be salted with fire. [50]Salt is good; but if the salt has lost its saltness, how will you season it? Have salt in yourselves, and be at peace with one another."

---

*RSV *kingdom.* See Appendix.

PENTECOST 20

Lesson 1 ~ Genesis 2:18-24

God creates humankind.

[18]Then God the SOVEREIGN ONE said, "It is not good that the human being should be alone; I will make a companion corresponding to the human being." [19]So out of the ground God the SOVEREIGN ONE formed every beast of the field and every bird of the air, and brought them to the human being to see what they would be called; and whatever the human being called every living creature, that was its name. [20]The human being gave names to all cattle, and to the birds of the air, and to every beast of the field; but a companion corresponding to the human being was not found. [21]So God the SOVEREIGN ONE caused a deep sleep to fall upon the human being, and took a rib out of the human being and closed up the place with flesh; [22]and God the SOVEREIGN ONE made the rib taken from that human being into a woman and brought her to the man. [23]Then the man said,

"This at last is bone of my bones
   and flesh of my flesh;
she shall be called Woman,
   because she was taken out of Man."[d]
[24]Therefore a man leaves his father and mother and cleaves to his wife, and they become one flesh.

Psalm 128

[1]Blessed is every one who fears GOD,
   who walks in God's ways!
[2]You shall eat the fruit of the labor of your hands;
   you shall be happy, and it shall be well with you.
[3]Your beloved will be like a fruitful vine
   within your house;
your children will be like olive shoots
   around your table.
[4]Thus shall the one be blessed
   who fears GOD.
[5]GOD bless you from Zion!
   May you see the prosperity of Jerusalem
   all the days of your life!
[6]May you see your children's children!
   Peace be upon Israel!

---

[d]See Notes, p. 249.

God speaks to us by the one through whom God created the world.

¹In many and various ways God spoke of old to our ancestors by the prophets; ²but in these last days God has spoken to us by a Child,° whom God appointed the heir of all things, through whom also God created the world. ³This Child, by whose word of power the universe is upheld, reflects the glory of God and bears the very stamp of God's nature. Having made purification for sins, the Child sat down at the right hand of the Majesty on high, ⁴having become as much superior to angels as the name the Child has obtained is more excellent than theirs.

²:⁹But we see Jesus, who for a little while was made lower than the angels, crowned with glory and honor because of the suffering of death, so that by the grace of God Jesus might taste death for every one.

¹⁰For it was fitting that God, for whom and by whom all things exist, in bringing many to glory, should make the pioneer of their salvation perfect through suffering. ¹¹For the one who sanctifies and those who are sanctified have all one origin. That is why Jesus is not ashamed to call them brothers and sisters.

°RSV *Son.* See Appendix.

After teaching about marriage and divorce, Jesus receives and blesses the children.

²And Pharisees came up and in order to test Jesus asked, "Is it lawful for a husband to divorce his wife?" ³He answered them, "What did Moses command you?" ⁴They said, "Moses allowed a husband to write a certificate of divorce, and to put her away." ⁵But Jesus said to them, "For your hardness of heart Moses wrote you this commandment. ⁶But from the beginning of creation, 'God made them male and female.' ⁷'For this reason a man shall leave his father and mother and be joined to his wife, ⁸and the two shall become one flesh.' So they are no longer two but one flesh. ⁹What therefore God has joined together, let no one put asunder."

¹⁰And in the house the disciples asked Jesus again about this matter. ¹¹And Jesus said to them, "Whoever divorces his wife and marries another, commits adultery against her; ¹²and if she divorces her husband and marries another, she commits adultery."

¹³And they were bringing children to Jesus, that he might touch them; and the disciples rebuked them. ¹⁴But when Jesus saw it he was indignant, and said to them, "Let the children come to me, do not hinder them; for to such belongs the realm* of God. ¹⁵Truly, I say to you, whoever does not receive the realm* of God like a child shall not enter it." ¹⁶And Jesus took the children in his arms and blessed them, laying his hands upon them.

---

*RSV *kingdom*. See Appendix.

PENTECOST 21

Lesson 1 ~ Genesis 3:8-19

The woman and the man learn the consequences of eating the forbidden fruit.

⁸And they heard the sound of God the SOVEREIGN ONE walking in the garden in the cool of the day, and the man and the woman hid themselves from the presence of God the SOVEREIGN ONE among the trees of the garden. ⁹But God the SOVEREIGN ONE called to the man, and said to him, "Where are you?" ¹⁰And he said, "I heard the sound of you in the garden, and I was afraid, because I was naked; and I hid myself." ¹¹God said, "Who told you that you were naked? Have you eaten of the tree of which I commanded you not to eat?" ¹²The man said, "The woman whom you gave to be with me, she gave me fruit of the tree, and I ate." ¹³Then God the SOVEREIGN ONE said to the woman, "What is this that you have done?" The woman said, "The serpent beguiled me, and I ate." ¹⁴God the SOVEREIGN ONE said to the serpent,

"Because you have done this,
cursed are you above all cattle,
and above all wild animals;
upon your belly you will go,
and dust you will eat
all the days of your life.
¹⁵I will put enmity between you and the woman,
and between your seed and her seed;
they will bruise your head,
and you will bruise their heel."
¹⁶To the woman God said,
"I will greatly multiply your labor in childbearing;
in labor you will bring forth children,
yet your desire will be for your husband,
and he will rule over you."
¹⁷And to Adam God said,
"Because you have listened to the voice of your mate,
and have eaten of the tree
of which I commanded you,
'You shall not eat of it,'
cursed is the ground because of you;
in labor you will eat of it all the days of your life;
¹⁸thorns and thistles it will bring forth to you;
and you will eat the plants of the field.

[19]In the sweat of your face
    you will eat bread
till you return to the ground,
    for out of it you were taken;
you are dust;
    and to dust you shall return."

Psalm 90:1-12

[1]O God, you have been our dwelling place
    in all generations.
[2]Before the mountains were brought forth,
    or ever you had formed the earth and the world,
    from everlasting to everlasting you are God.
[3]You turn people back to the dust,
    and say, "Turn back, O mortals!"
[4]For a thousand years in your sight
    are but as yesterday when it is past,
    or as a watch in the night.
[5]You sweep people away; they are like a dream,
    like grass which is renewed in the morning:
[6]in the morning it flourishes and is renewed;
    in the evening it fades and withers.
[7]For we are consumed by your anger;
    by your wrath we are overwhelmed.
[8]You have set our iniquities before you,
    our secret sins in the light of your countenance.
[9]For all our days pass away under your wrath,
    our years come to an end like a sigh.
[10]The years of our life are threescore and ten,
    or even by reason of strength fourscore;
yet their span is but toil and trouble;
    they are soon gone, and we fly away.
[11]Who considers the power of your anger,
    and your wrath according to the fear of you?
[12]So teach us to number our days
    that we may get a heart of wisdom.

Lesson 2 ~ Hebrews 4:1-3, 9-13

The sabbath rest which God has prepared is not easily attained.

[1]Therefore, while the promise of entering God's rest remains, let us fear lest any of you be judged to have failed to reach it. [2]For good news came to us just as to them; but the message which they heard did not benefit them, because it did not meet with faith in the hearers. [3]For we who have believed enter that rest, as God has said,

"As I swore in my wrath,
'They shall never enter my rest,' "

although God's works were finished from the foundation of the world. [9]So then, there remains a sabbath rest for the people of God; [10]for those who enter God's rest cease from their labors as God also did.

[11]Let us therefore strive to enter that rest, that no one fall by the same sort of disobedience. [12]For the word of God is living and active, sharper than any two-edged sword, piercing to the division of soul and spirit, of joints and marrow, and discerning the thoughts and intentions of the heart. [13]And before God no creature is hidden, but all are open and laid bare to the eyes of the one with whom we have to do.

Gospel ~ Mark 10:17-30

Jesus teaches about wealth and eternal life.

[17]And as Jesus was setting out on a journey, some one ran up and knelt before him, and asked, "Good Teacher, what must I do to inherit eternal life?" [18]And Jesus said, "Why do you call me good? No one is good but God alone. [19]You know the commandments: 'Do not kill, Do not commit adultery, Do not steal, Do not bear false witness, Do not defraud, Honor your father and mother.' " [20]And the questioner said to Jesus, "Teacher, all these I have observed from my youth." [21]And Jesus looked upon the questioner with love and said, "You lack one thing; go, sell what you have, and give to the poor, and you will have treasure in heaven; and come, follow me." [22]Dismayed by this word, the person went away sorrowful because of having great possessions.

[23]And Jesus looked around and said to the disciples, "How hard it will be for those who have riches to enter the realm* of God!" [24]And the disciples were amazed at Jesus' words. But Jesus said to them again, "Children, how hard it is to enter the realm* of God! [25]It is easier for a camel to go through the eye of a needle than for a rich person to enter the realm* of God." [26]And

---

*RSV *kingdom.* See Appendix.

they were exceedingly astonished, and said to Jesus, "Then who can be saved?" ²⁷Jesus looked at the disciples and said, "With human beings it is impossible, but not with God; for all things are possible with God." ²⁸Peter began to say to Jesus, "Lo, we have left everything and followed you." ²⁹Jesus said, "Truly, I say to you, there is no one who has left house or brothers or sisters or mother or father or children or lands, for my sake and for the gospel, ³⁰who will not receive a hundredfold now in this time, houses and brothers and sisters and mothers and children and lands, with persecutions, and in the age to come eternal life."

PENTECOST 22

Lesson 1 ~ Isaiah 53:7-12

Isaiah writes of the Suffering Servant.

⁷The servant was oppressed, and was afflicted,
  yet did not say a word;
 like a lamb that is led to the slaughter,
  and like a ewe that before her shearers is dumb,
  the servant did not say a word.
⁸By oppression and judgment the servant was taken away;
  and as for that one's generation, who considered
 that the servant was cut off out of the land of the living,
  stricken for the transgression of my people?
⁹Although the servant had done no violence
  and spoken no deceit,
 the servant was buried with the wicked,
  and with the rich in death.
¹⁰Yet it was the will of GOD to bruise
  and put to grief this one;
 who, after choosing to become an offering for sin,
  shall see offspring, and enjoy long life;
 the will of GOD shall prosper in the servant's hand;
¹¹ my servant shall see the fruit of the soul's travail and be satisfied;
 by knowledge shall the righteous one, my servant,
  make many to be accounted righteous,
  and shall bear their iniquities.
¹²Therefore I will divide for this one a portion with the great,
  and my servant shall divide the spoil with the strong;
 because my servant poured out self unto death,
  and was numbered with the transgressors;
 yet bore the sin of many,
  and made intercession for the transgressors.

17How long, O God, will you look on?
 Rescue me from their ravages,
  my life from the lions!
18Then I will thank you in the great congregation;
 in the mighty throng I will praise you.
19Let not those rejoice over me
 who are wrongfully my foes,
 and let not those wink the eye
 who hate me without cause.
20For they do not speak peace,
 but against those who are quiet in the land
 they conceive words of deceit.
21They open wide their mouths against me;
 they say, "Aha, Aha!
 our eyes have seen it!"
22You have seen, O GOD; be not silent!
 O God, be not far from me!
23Bestir yourself, and awake for my right,
 for my cause, my God and my Sovereign!
24Vindicate me, O SOVEREIGN ONE, my God,
  according to your righteousness;
 and let them not rejoice over me!
25Let them not say to themselves,
 "Aha, we have our heart's desire!"
 Let them not say, "We have swallowed that one up."
26Let them be put to shame and confusion altogether
 who rejoice at my calamity!
 Let them be clothed with shame and dishonor
 who magnify themselves against me!
27Let those who desire my vindication
 shout for joy and be glad,
 and say evermore,
 "Great is GOD,
 who delights in the welfare of God's servant!"
28Then my tongue shall tell of your righteousness
 and of your praise all the day long.

Lesson 2 ~ Hebrews 4:14-16

Jesus, the great high priest, is one who knows our human nature.

[14]Since then we have a great high priest who has passed through the heavens, Jesus, the Child° of God, let us hold fast our confession. [15]For we have not a high priest who is unable to sympathize with our weaknesses, but one who in every respect has been tempted as we are, yet without sin. [16]Let us then with confidence draw near to the throne of grace, that we may receive mercy and find grace to help in time of need.

Gospel ~ Mark 10:35-45

Jesus answers James and John about greatness in the realm of God.

[35]And James and John, the sons of Zebedee, came forward to Jesus, and said, "Teacher, we want you to do for us whatever we ask of you." [36]And Jesus said to them, "What do you want me to do for you?" [37]And they said, "Grant us to sit, one at your right hand and one at your left, in your glory." [38]But Jesus said to them, "You do not know what you are asking. Are you able to drink the cup that I drink, or to be baptized with the baptism with which I am baptized?" [39]And they said to Jesus, "We are able." And Jesus said to them, "The cup that I drink you will drink; and with the baptism with which I am baptized, you will be baptized; [40]but to sit at my right hand or at my left is not mine to grant, but it is for those for whom it has been prepared." [41]And when the ten heard it, they began to be indignant at James and John. [42]And Jesus called them to him and said, "You know that those who are supposed to rule over the Gentiles lord it over them, and their great leaders exercise authority over them. [43]But it shall not be so among you; but whoever would be great among you must be your servant, [44]and whoever would be first among you must be slave of all. [45]For the Human One° also came not to be served but to serve, and to give up life as a ransom for many."

°RSV *Son.* See Appendix.
°RSV *Son of man.* See Appendix.

PENTECOST 23

Lesson 1 ~ Jeremiah 31:7-9

Jeremiah announces God's redemption of the remnant of Israel.

⁷For thus says the SOVEREIGN ONE:
"Sing aloud with gladness for Jacob,
    and raise shouts for the chief of the nations;
proclaim, give praise, and say,
    'GOD has saved God's people,
    the remnant of Israel.'
⁸Behold, I will bring them from the north country,
    and gather them from the farthest parts of the earth,
among them those who are blind and those who are lame,
    the woman with child and her who is in travail, together;
    a great company, they shall return here.
⁹With weeping they shall come,
    and with consolations I will lead them back,
I will make them walk by brooks of water,
    in a straight path in which they shall not stumble;
for I am a parent to Israel,
    and Ephraim is my first-born."

Psalm 126

¹When GOD restored the fortunes of Zion,
    we were like those who dream.
²Then our mouth was filled with laughter,
    and our tongue with shouts of joy;
then they said among the nations,
    "GOD has done great things for them."
³GOD has done great things for us;
    we are glad.
⁴Restore our fortunes, O GOD,
    like the watercourses in the Negeb!
⁵May those who sow in tears
    reap with shouts of joy!
⁶Those who go forth weeping,
    bearing the seed for sowing,
shall come home with shouts of joy,
    bearing their sheaves of grain.

Lesson 2 ~ Hebrews 5:1-6

The author interprets the meaning of Jesus' high priesthood.

[1]For every high priest chosen from among human beings is appointed to act on their behalf in relation to God, to offer gifts and sacrifices for sins. [2]A high priest can deal gently with the ignorant and wayward, since a high priest is also beset with weakness. [3]Because of this, high priests are bound to offer sacrifice for their own sins as well as for those of the people. [4]And one does not take the honor upon one's self, but is called by God, just as Aaron was.

[5]So also Christ did not claim the exalted office of high priest, but was appointed to it by the one who said,

"You are my Child,◊

today I have begotten you";

[6]as is said also in another place,

"You are a priest for ever,

after the order of Melchizedek."

Gospel ~ Mark 10:46-52

Jesus heals Bartimaeus.

[46]And they came to Jericho; and as Jesus was leaving Jericho with the disciples and a great multitude, Bartimaeus, a blind beggar, the son of Timaeus, was sitting by the roadside. [47]And hearing that it was Jesus of Nazareth, Bartimaeus began to cry out and say, "Jesus, Son of David, have mercy on me!" [48]And many rebuked Bartimaeus, telling him to be silent; but he cried out all the more, "Son of David, have mercy on me!" [49]And Jesus stopped and said, "Call him." And they called him, saying, "Take heart; rise, Jesus is calling you." [50]And throwing off his mantle, Bartimaeus sprang up and came to Jesus. [51]And Jesus said to him, "What do you want me to do for you?" And he replied, "Teacher, let me receive my sight." [52]And Jesus said, "Go your way; your faith has made you well." And immediately Bartimaeus received his sight and followed Jesus on the way.

◊RSV *Son.* See Appendix.

PENTECOST 24

Lesson 1 ~ Deuteronomy 6:1-9

Moses teaches Israel the commandments of God.

[1]Now this is the commandment, the statutes and the ordinances which the SOVEREIGN ONE your God commanded me to teach you, that you may do them in the land to which you are going over, to possess it; [2]that you may fear the SOVEREIGN ONE your God, you and your children and your children's children, by keeping all God's statutes and commandments, which I command you, all the days of your life; and that your days may be prolonged. [3]Hear therefore, O Israel, and be careful to do them; that it may go well with you, and that you may multiply greatly, as the SOVEREIGN ONE, the God of your ancestors, has promised you, in a land flowing with milk and honey.

[4]Hear, O Israel: The SOVEREIGN ONE is our God, the SOVEREIGN ONE alone; [5]and you shall love the SOVEREIGN ONE your God with all your heart, and with all your soul, and with all your might. [6]And these words which I command you this day shall be upon your heart; [7]and you shall teach them diligently to your children, and shall talk of them when you sit in your house, and when you walk by the way, and when you lie down, and when you rise. [8]And you shall bind them as a sign upon your hand, and they shall be as frontlets between your eyes. [9]And you shall write them on the doorposts of your house and on your gates.

Psalm 119:33-48

[33]Teach me, O GOD, the way of your statutes;
  and I will keep it to the end.
[34]Give me understanding, that I may keep your law
  and observe it with my whole heart.
[35]Lead me in the path of your commandments,
  for I delight in it.
[36]Incline my heart to your testimonies,
  and not to gain!
[37]Turn my eyes from looking at vanities;
  and give me life in your ways.
[38]Confirm to your servant your promise,
  which is for those who fear you.
[39]Turn away the reproach which I dread;
  for your ordinances are good.

⁴⁰Behold, I long for your precepts;
    in your righteousness give me life!
⁴¹Let your steadfast love come to me, O God,
    your salvation according to your promise;
⁴²then I shall have an answer for those who taunt me,
    for I trust in your word.
⁴³And take not the word of truth utterly out of my mouth,
    for my hope is in your ordinances.
⁴⁴I will keep your law continually,
    for ever and ever;
⁴⁵and I shall walk at liberty,
    for I have sought your precepts.
⁴⁶I will also speak of your testimonies before rulers,□
    and shall not be put to shame;
⁴⁷for I find my delight in your commandments,
    which I love.
⁴⁸I revere your commandments, which I love,
    and I will meditate on your statutes.

Lesson 2 ~ Hebrews 7:23-28

Jesus' sacrifice is contrasted with sacrifices made by human high priests.

²³The former priests were many in number, because they were prevented by death from continuing in office; ²⁴but Jesus, who continues for ever, holds the priesthood permanently, ²⁵and so is able for all time to save those who draw near to God through Jesus, who always lives to make intercession for them.

²⁶For it was fitting that we should have such a high priest, holy, blameless, unstained, separated from sinners, exalted above the heavens. ²⁷Jesus has no need, like those high priests, to offer sacrifices daily, first for their own sins and then for those of the people; Jesus did this once for all, having offered up Jesus' own self. ²⁸Indeed, the law appoints human beings in their weakness as high priests, but the word of the oath, which came later than the law, appoints a Child◇ who has been made perfect for ever.

□RSV *kings*. See Appendix.
◇RSV *Son*. See Appendix.

Jesus interprets the great commandment.

²⁸One of the scribes came up and heard them disputing with one another, and seeing that Jesus answered them well, asked, "Which commandment is the first of all?" ²⁹Jesus answered, "The first is, 'Hear, O Israel: The Sovereign□ our God, the Sovereign□ is one; ³⁰and you shall love the Sovereign□ your God with all your heart, and with all your soul, and with all your mind, and with all your strength.' ³¹The second is this, 'You shall love your neighbor as yourself.' There is no other commandment greater than these." ³²And the scribe said to Jesus, "You are right, Teacher; you have truly said that God is one, and there is no other but God; ³³and to love God with all the heart, and with all the understanding, and with all the strength, and to love one's neighbor as oneself, is much more than all whole burnt offerings and sacrifices." ³⁴And when Jesus saw that the scribe answered wisely, Jesus said to him, "You are not far from the realm* of God." And after that no one dared to ask Jesus any question.

□RSV *Lord.* See Appendix.
*RSV *kingdom.* See Appendix.

PENTECOST 25

Lesson 1 ~ 1 Kings 17:8-16

The widow from Zarephath ministers to Elijah.

⁸Then the word of GOD came to Elijah, ⁹"Arise, go to Zarephath, which belongs to Sidon, and dwell there. Behold, I have commanded a widow there to feed you." ¹⁰So Elijah arose and went to Zarephath; and when he came to the gate of the city, behold, a widow was there gathering sticks; and Elijah called to her and said, "Bring me a little water in a vessel, that I may drink." ¹¹And as she was going to bring it, he called to her and said, "Bring me a morsel of bread in your hand." ¹²And she said, "As the SOVEREIGN ONE your God lives, I have nothing baked, only a handful of meal in a jar and a little oil in a cruse; and now, I am gathering a couple of sticks, that I may go in and prepare it for myself and my child, that we may eat it, and die." ¹³And Elijah said to her, "Fear not; go and do as you have said; but first make me a little cake of it and bring it to me, and afterward make for yourself and your child. ¹⁴For thus says the SOVEREIGN ONE the God of Israel, 'The jar of meal shall not be spent, and the cruse of oil shall not fail, until the day that GOD sends rain upon the earth.' " ¹⁵And she went and did as Elijah said; and she, and he, and her household ate for many days. ¹⁶The jar of meal was not spent, neither did the cruse of oil fail, according to the word of GOD which God spoke by Elijah.

Psalm 146

¹Praise GOD!
  Praise GOD, O my soul!
²I will praise GOD as long as I live;
  I will sing praises to my God while I have being.
³Put not your trust in rulers,▯
  in mortals, in whom there is no help.
⁴When their breath departs they return to their earth;
  on that very day their plans perish.
⁵Happy is the one whose help is the God of Jacob,
  whose hope is in God, the SOVEREIGN ONE,
⁶who made heaven and earth,
  the sea, and all that is in them;
  who keeps faith for ever;

▯RSV *princes.*

7   who executes justice for the oppressed;
    who gives food to the hungry.
 GOD sets the prisoners free,
8   GOD opens the eyes of the blind.
 GOD lifts up those who are bowed down,
    GOD loves the righteous.
9GOD watches over the sojourners,
    and upholds the widow and the orphan,
    but brings the way of the wicked to ruin.
10GOD will reign for ever,
    your God, O Zion, to all generations.
 Praise GOD!

Lesson 2 ~ Hebrews 9:24-28

Christ, who will appear a second time, has offered a single sacrifice for sin.

24For Christ has entered, not into a sanctuary made with hands, a copy of the true one, but into heaven itself, now to appear in the presence of God on our behalf. 25Nor was it to offer Christ's self repeatedly, as the high priest enters the Holy Place yearly with the blood of another; 26for then Christ would have had to suffer repeatedly since the foundation of the world. But as it is, Christ has appeared once for all at the end of the age to put away sin through Christ's sacrifice. 27And just as it is appointed for human beings to die once, and after that comes judgment, 28so Christ, having been offered once to bear the sins of many, will appear a second time, not to deal with sin but to save those who are eagerly waiting for Christ.

Jesus praises a poor widow for her offering.

[38]And in his teaching Jesus said, "Beware of the scribes, who like to go about in long robes, and to have salutations in the market places [39]and the best seats in the synagogues and the places of honor at feasts, [40]who devour widows' houses and for a pretense make long prayers. They will receive the greater condemnation."

[41]And Jesus sat down opposite the treasury, and watched the multitude putting money into the treasury. Many rich people put in large sums. [42]And a poor widow came, and put in two copper coins, which make a penny. [43]And Jesus called the disciples, and said to them, "Truly, I say to you, this poor widow has put in more than all those who are contributing to the treasury. [44]For they all contributed out of their abundance; but she out of her poverty has put in everything she had, her whole living."

PENTECOST 26

Lesson 1 ~ Daniel 7:9-14

One like a human one comes to the Ancient of Days.

⁹As I looked,
  thrones were placed
    and one that was ancient of days sat down,
  whose raiment was white as snow,
    and whose hair was like pure wool;
  whose throne was fiery flames,
    its wheels were burning fire.
¹⁰A stream of fire issued
    and came forth from before the ancient of days,
  who was served by a thousand thousands,
    and before whom stood ten thousand times ten thousand;
  the court sat in judgment,
    and the books were opened.
¹¹I looked then because of the sound of the great words which the horn was speaking. And as I looked, the beast was slain, and its body destroyed and given over to be burned with fire. ¹²As for the rest of the beasts, their dominion was taken away, but their lives were prolonged for a season and a time.
¹³I saw in the night visions,
  and behold, with the clouds of heaven
    there came one like a human one,°
  who came to the Ancient of Days
    and was presented before the Ancient of Days.
¹⁴And to that one was given dominion
    and glory and sovereignty,*
  that all peoples, nations, and languages
    should serve that one,
  whose dominion is an everlasting dominion,
    which shall not pass away,
  and whose realm* is one
    that shall not be destroyed.

°RSV *son of man.* See Appendix.
*RSV *kingdom.* See Appendix.

Psalm 145:8-13

[8]GOD is gracious and merciful,
   slow to anger and abounding in steadfast love.
[9]GOD is good to all,
   and has compassion over all that God has made.
[10]All your works shall give thanks to you, O GOD,
   and all your saints shall bless you!
[11]They shall speak of the glory of your realm,*
   and tell of your power,
[12]to make known to humankind your mighty deeds,
   and the glorious splendor of your realm.*
[13]Your realm* is an everlasting realm,*
   and your dominion endures throughout all generations.

Lesson 2 ~ Hebrews 10:11-18

Jesus the high priest offered a single sacrifice for sins.

[11]And every priest stands daily at services, offering repeatedly the same sacrifices, which can never take away sins. [12]But this one, having offered for all time a single sacrifice for sins, sat down at the right hand of God, [13]then to wait until all enemies should be made a stool for Christ's feet. [14]For by a single offering Christ has perfected for all time those who are sanctified. [15]And the Holy Spirit also bears witness to us; for after saying,
[16]"This is the covenant that I will make with them
   after those days, says the Sovereign:□
I will put my laws on their hearts, and write them on their minds,"
[17]then it is added,
   "I will remember their sins and their misdeeds no more."
[18]Where there is forgiveness of these, there is no longer any offering for sin.

---

*RSV *kingdom.* See Appendix.
□RSV *Lord.* See Appendix.

Jesus speaks of the day when the Human One will come.

²⁴But in those days, after that tribulation, the sun will be darkened, and the moon will not give its light, ²⁵and the stars will be falling from heaven, and the powers in the heavens will be shaken. ²⁶And then they will see the Human One° coming in clouds with great power and glory. ²⁷And then the Human One will send out the angels, and gather the elect from the four winds, from the ends of the earth to the ends of heaven.

²⁸From the fig tree learn its lesson: as soon as its branch becomes tender and puts forth its leaves, you know that summer is near. ²⁹So also, when you see these things taking place, you know that the Human One is near, at the very gates. ³⁰Truly, I say to you, this generation will not pass away before all these things take place. ³¹Heaven and earth will pass away, but my words will not pass away.

³²But of that day or that hour no one knows, not even the angels in heaven, nor the Child,° but only God.⊗

°RSV *Son of man.* See Appendix.
◇RSV *Son.* See Appendix.
⊗RSV *the Father.* See Appendix.

PENTECOST 27

Lesson 1 ~ Jeremiah 23:1-6

Jeremiah announces God's promise of a righteous ruler.

¹"Woe to the shepherds who destroy and scatter the sheep of my pasture!" says the SOVEREIGN ONE. ²Therefore thus says the SOVEREIGN ONE, the God of Israel, concerning the shepherds who care for my people: "You have scattered my flock, and have driven them away, and you have not attended to them. Behold, I will attend to you for your evil doings, says the SOVEREIGN ONE. ³Then I will gather the remnant of my flock out of all the countries where I have driven them, and I will bring them back to their fold, and they shall be fruitful and multiply. ⁴I will set shepherds over them who will care for them, and they shall fear no more, nor be dismayed, neither shall any be missing, says the SOVEREIGN ONE.

⁵"Behold, the days are coming, says the SOVEREIGN ONE, when I will raise up for David a righteous Branch, who shall reign as ruler□ and deal wisely, and shall execute justice and righteousness in the land. ⁶In those days Judah will be saved, and Israel will dwell securely. And this is the name by which the Branch will be called: 'GOD is our righteousness.' "

Psalm 93

¹GOD reigns, robed in majesty;
   GOD is robed, and girded with strength.
 The world is established; it shall never be moved;
²   your throne is established from of old;
   you are from everlasting.
³The floods have lifted up, O GOD,
   the floods have lifted up their voice,
   the floods lift up their roaring.
⁴Mightier than the thunders of many waters,
   mightier than the waves of the sea,
   GOD on high is mighty!
⁵Your decrees are very sure;
   holiness befits your house,
   O GOD, for evermore.

□RSV *king*. See Appendix.

Lesson 2 ~ Revelation 1:4b-8

John addresses the seven churches in Asia.

⁴Grace to you and peace from the one who is and who was and who is to come, and from the seven spirits who are before the throne, ⁵and from Jesus Christ the faithful witness, the first-born of the dead, and the ruler of kings on earth.

To the one who loves us and has freed us from our sins by a blood sacrifice ⁶and made us a nation,* priests to God, Jesus' Father [*and Mother**], to whom be glory and dominion for ever and ever. Amen. ⁷Behold, that one is coming with the clouds, and will be seen by every eye, by all who pierced that one, and on account of whom all tribes of the earth will wail. Even so. Amen.

⁸"I am the Alpha and the Omega," says the Sovereign□ God, who is and who was and who is to come, the Almighty.

Gospel ~ John 18:33-37

Pilate learns the nature of Jesus' authority.

³³Pilate entered the praetorium again and called Jesus, and said, "Are you the King of the Jews?" ³⁴Jesus answered, "Do you say this of your own accord, or did others say it to you about me?" ³⁵Pilate answered, "Am I one of you?⊕ Your own nation and the chief priests have handed you over to me; what have you done?" ³⁶Jesus answered, "My realm* is not of this world; if my realm* were of this world, my servants would fight, that I might not be handed over to the religious authorities;▽ but my realm* is not from the world." ³⁷Pilate said to Jesus, "So you are a king?" Jesus answered, "You say that I am a king. For this I was born, and for this I have come into the world, to bear witness to the truth. Every one who is of the truth hears my voice."

---

*RSV v. 6 *kingdom;* v. 36 *kingship.* See Appendix.
*Addition to the text. RSV *to his God and Father.* See "Metaphor" and "God the Father and Mother" in the Appendix.
□RSV *Lord.* See Appendix.
⊕RSV *"Am I a Jew?"*
▽RSV *the Jews.* See Appendix.

PRESENTATION—FEBRUARY 2

Lesson 1 ~ Malachi 3:1-4

The messenger goes before God to bring judgment to the people.

¹Behold, I send my messenger to prepare the way before me, and God whom you seek will suddenly come to the temple; the messenger of the covenant in whom you delight, behold, that one is coming, says the GOD of hosts. ²But who can endure the day of that coming, and who can stand when the messenger appears?

For my messenger is like a refiner's fire and like fullers' soap, ³who will sit as a refiner and purifier of silver, and will purify the tribe of Levi and refine them like gold and silver, till they present right offerings to GOD. ⁴Then the offering of Judah and Jerusalem will be pleasing to GOD as in the days of old and as in former years.

Psalm 84

¹How lovely is your dwelling place,
   O GOD of hosts!
²My soul longs, yea, faints
   for the courts of GOD;
 my heart and flesh sing for joy
   to the living God.
³Even the sparrow finds a home,
   and the swallow a nest for herself,
   where she may lay her young,
 at your altars, O GOD of hosts,
   my Sovereign⊡ and my God.
⁴Blessed are those who dwell in your house,
   ever singing your praise!
⁵Blessed are those whose strength is in you,
   in whose heart are the highways to Zion.
⁶As they go through the valley of Baca
   they make it a place of springs;
   the early rain also covers it with pools.
⁷They go from strength to strength;
   the God of gods will be seen in Zion.
⁸O SOVEREIGN ONE, God of hosts, hear my prayer;
   give ear, O God of Jacob!

⊡RSV *King.* See Appendix.

224

⁹Behold our shield, O God;
   look upon the face of your anointed!
¹⁰For a day in your courts is better than a thousand elsewhere.
  I would rather be a doorkeeper in the house of my God
      than dwell in the tents of wickedness.
¹¹For God, the Sovereign One, is a sun and shield,
      who bestows favor and honor.
  No good thing does God withhold
      from those who walk uprightly.
¹²O God of hosts,
      blessed is the one who trusts in you!

Psalm 24:7-10 (alternate)

⁷Lift up your heads, O gates!
   and be lifted up, O ancient doors!
   that the Glorious Ruler□ may come in.
⁸Who is the Glorious Ruler?□
   God, strong and mighty,
   God, mighty in battle!
⁹Lift up your heads, O gates!
   and be lifted up, O ancient doors!
   that the Glorious Ruler□ may come in.
¹⁰Who is this Glorious Ruler?□
   The God of hosts,
   that one is the Glorious Ruler!□

□RSV *King of glory.*

Lesson 2 ~ Hebrews 2:14-18

Jesus came to save the people.

[14]Since therefore the children share in flesh and blood, Jesus likewise partook of the same nature, in order to destroy through death the one who has the power of death, that is, the devil, [15]and to deliver all those who through fear of death were subject to lifelong bondage. [16]For surely it is not with angels that Jesus is concerned but with the descendants of Abraham [*and Sarah**]. [17]Therefore Jesus had to be made like human beings in every respect, in order to become a merciful and faithful high priest in the service of God, to make expiation for the sins of the people. [18]For because Jesus also has suffered and been tempted, Jesus is able to help those who are tempted.

Gospel ~ Luke 2:22-40

Mary and Joseph take the infant Jesus to the temple in Jerusalem and the child is met there by Simeon and Anna.

[22]And when the time came for their purification according to the law of Moses, they brought the child Jesus up to Jerusalem to be presented to God,□ [23](as it is written in the law of God,□ "Every male that opens the womb shall be called holy to God□") [24]and to offer a sacrifice according to what is said in the law of God,□ "a pair of turtledoves, or two young pigeons." [25]Now there was a man in Jerusalem, whose name was Simeon, who was righteous and devout, looking for the consolation of Israel, and the Holy Spirit was upon him. [26]And it had been revealed to Simeon by the Holy Spirit that he should not see death before he had seen the Christ of God.□ [27]And inspired by the Spirit Simeon came into the temple; and when the parents brought in the child Jesus, to do for him according to the custom of the law, [28]Simeon took the child in his arms and blessed God and said,
[29]"O God,□ now let your servant depart in peace,
   according to your word;
[30]for my eyes have seen your salvation
[31]which you have prepared in the presence of all peoples,
[32]a light for revelation to the Gentiles,
   and for glory to your people Israel."

---

*Addition to the text. See Appendix.
□RSV vs. 22, 23, 24 *the Lord;* v. 26 *Lord's Christ;* v. 29 *Lord. See* Appendix.

[33]And Jesus' father and mother marveled at what was said about their child; [34]and Simeon blessed them and said to Mary, Jesus' mother,

"Behold, this child is set for the fall and rising of many in Israel,
and for a sign that is spoken against

[35](and a sword will pierce through your own soul also),
that thoughts out of many hearts may be revealed."

[36]And there was a prophet, Anna, the daughter of Phanuel, of the tribe of Asher; she was of a great age, having lived with her husband seven years, [37]and as a widow till she was eighty-four. She did not depart from the temple, worshiping with fasting and prayer night and day. [38]And coming up at that very hour she gave thanks to God, and spoke about the child to all who were looking for the redemption of Jerusalem.

[39]And when Mary and Joseph had performed everything according to the law of God,□ they returned into Galilee, to their own city, Nazareth. [40]And the child grew and became strong, filled with wisdom; and the favor of God was upon the child.

□RSV *the Lord.* See Appendix.

ANNUNCIATION—MARCH 25

Lesson 1 ~ Isaiah 7:10-14

Isaiah brings a word of assurance from God to Ahaz, ruler of Judah, in the face of a threat from the rulers of Syria.

[10]Again GOD spoke to Ahaz, [11]"Ask a sign of the SOVEREIGN ONE your God; let it be deep as Sheol or high as heaven." [12]But Ahaz said, "I will not ask, and I will not put GOD to the test." [13]And Isaiah said, "Hear then, O house of David! Is it too little for you to weary human beings, that you weary my God also? [14]Therefore God will give you a sign. Behold, a young woman shall conceive and bear a child, whom she shall call Immanuel."

Psalm 40:6-10[+]

[6]Sacrifice and offering you do not desire;
  but you have given me an open ear.
Burnt offering and sin offering
  you have not required.
[7]Then I said, "Lo, I come;
  in the roll of the book it is written of me;
[8]I delight to do your will, O my God;
  your law is within my heart."
[9]I have told the glad news of deliverance
  in the great congregation;
lo, I have not restrained my lips,
  as you know, O GOD.
[10]I have not hid your saving help within my heart,
  I have spoken of your faithfulness and your salvation;
I have not concealed your steadfast love and your faithfulness
  from the great congregation.

Lesson 2 ~ Hebrews 10:4-10

Jesus the high priest offered a single sacrifice for sins.

[4]For it is impossible that the blood of bulls and goats should take away sins.
  [5]Consequently, Christ, having come into the world, said,
  "Sacrifices and offerings you have not desired,
  but a body you have prepared for me;

[+]Alternate Ps. 45 not included. See Appendix, p. 248.

⁶in burnt offerings and sin offerings you have taken no pleasure.
⁷Then I said, 'Lo, I have come to do your will, O God,'
  as it is written of me in the roll of the book."
⁸When Christ said above, "You have neither desired nor taken pleasure in sacrifices and offerings and burnt offerings and sin offerings" (these are offered according to the law), ⁹then Christ added, "Lo, I have come to do your will." Christ abolishes the first in order to establish the second. ¹⁰And by that will we have been sanctified through the offering of the body of Jesus Christ once for all.

Gospel ~ Luke 1:26-38

The angel Gabriel announces to Mary that she will bear the holy child of God.

²⁶In the sixth month the angel Gabriel was sent from God to a city of Galilee named Nazareth, ²⁷to a virgin betrothed to a man whose name was Joseph, of the house of David; and her name was Mary. ²⁸And the angel came to her and said, "Hail, O favored one, God□ is with you!" ²⁹But she was greatly troubled at the saying, and considered in her mind what sort of greeting this might be. ³⁰And the angel said to her, "Do not be afraid, Mary, for you have found favor with God. ³¹And behold, you will conceive in your womb and bear a child, whose name you shall call Jesus.
³²This one will be great,and will be called the Child◇ of the Most High;
  and the Sovereign□ God will give to that Child the throne of David, the
    ancestor of the Child,
³³to reign over the house of Jacob for ever;
  and of that reign* there will be no end."
³⁴And Mary said to the angel, "How can this be, since I have no husband?"
³⁵And the angel said to her,
  "The Holy Spirit will come upon you,
  and the power of the Most High will overshadow you;
  therefore the child to be born will be called holy,
  the Child◇ of God.
³⁶And behold, your kinswoman Elizabeth in her old age has also conceived a child; and this is the sixth month with her who was called barren. ³⁷For with God nothing will be impossible." ³⁸And Mary said, "Behold, I am the handmaid of God;□ let it be to me according to your word." And the angel departed from her.

□RSV vs. 28, 38 *the Lord;* v. 32 *Lord.* See Appendix.
◇RSV *Son.* See Appendix.
*RSV *kingdom.* See Appendix.

Lesson 1 ~ 1 Samuel 2:1-10

Hannah offers a prayer to God.

¹Hannah also prayed and said,
"My heart exults in GOD;
  my strength is exalted in GOD.
My mouth derides my enemies,
  because I rejoice in your salvation.
²There is none holy like GOD,
  there is none besides you;
  there is no rock like our God.
³Talk no more so very proudly,
  let not arrogance come from your mouth;
for GOD is a God of knowledge,
  by whom actions are weighed.
⁴The bows of the mighty are broken,
  but the feeble gird on strength.
⁵Those who were full have hired themselves out for bread,
  but those who were hungry have ceased to hunger.
The barren has borne seven,
  but she who has many children is forlorn.
⁶It is GOD who kills and brings to life,
  who brings down to Sheol and raises up,
⁷who makes poor and makes rich,
  who brings low and also exalts.
⁸It is God who raises up the poor from the dust,
  and lifts the needy from the ash heap,
to make them sit with royalty[□]
  and inherit a seat of honor.
For the pillars of the earth belong to GOD,
  and on them God has set the world.
⁹God will guard the feet of the faithful ones;
  but the wicked shall be removed from sight;
  for not by might shall any one prevail.
¹⁰The adversaries of GOD shall be broken to pieces;
  against them God will thunder in heaven.
GOD will judge the ends of the earth;
  giving strength to God's ruler,[□]
  and exalting the power of the anointed one."

[□]RSV *princes.*
[□]RSV *king.* See Appendix.

Psalm 113

¹Praise GOD!
 Praise, O servants of GOD,
  praise the name of the SOVEREIGN ONE!
²Blessed be the name of the SOVEREIGN ONE
  from this time forth and for evermore!
³From the rising of the sun to its setting
  the name of the SOVEREIGN ONE is to be praised!
⁴GOD is high above all nations,
  and God's glory above the heavens!
⁵Who is like the SOVEREIGN ONE our God,
  who is seated on high,
⁶who looks far down
  upon the heavens and the earth?
⁷God raises the poor from the dust,
  and lifts the needy from the ash heap,
⁸to make them sit with nobles,◻
  with the nobles◻ of God's people.
⁹God gives the barren woman a home,
  making her the joyous mother of children.
 Praise GOD!

Lesson 2 ～ Romans 12:9-16b

Paul exhorts believers about their relationships to one another.

⁹Let love be genuine; hate what is evil, hold fast to what is good; ¹⁰be affectionately devoted to one another; outdo one another in showing honor. ¹¹Never flag in zeal, be aglow with the Spirit, serve the Sovereign.◻ ¹²Rejoice in your hope, be patient in tribulation, be constant in prayer. ¹³Contribute to the needs of the saints, practice hospitality.

¹⁴Bless those who persecute you; bless and do not curse them. ¹⁵Rejoice with those who rejoice, weep with those who weep. ¹⁶Live in harmony with one another; do not be haughty, but associate with the lowly.

◻RSV *princes.*
◻RSV *Lord.* See Appendix.

Mary greets Elizabeth, singing a song of praise to God.

[39]In those days Mary arose and went with haste into the hill country, to a city of Judah, [40]and she entered the house of Zechariah and greeted Elizabeth. [41]And when Elizabeth heard the greeting of Mary, the babe leaped in her womb; and Elizabeth was filled with the Holy Spirit [42]and she exclaimed with a loud cry, "Blessed are you among women, and blessed is the fruit of your womb! [43]And why is this granted me, that the mother of my Sovereign□ should come to me? [44]For behold, when the voice of your greeting came to my ears, the babe in my womb leaped for joy. [45]And blessed is she who believed that there would be a fulfilment of what was spoken to her from God."□ [46]And Mary said,

"My soul magnifies the Sovereign,□

[47]and my spirit rejoices in God my Savior,

[48]who has regarded the low estate of God's handmaiden.

For behold, henceforth all generations will call me blessed;

[49]for the one who is mighty has done great things for me,

and holy is God's name.

[50]And God's mercy is on those who fear God

from generation to generation.

[51]God has shown strength with God's arm,

and has scattered the proud in the imagination of their hearts,

[52]God has put down the mighty from their thrones,

and exalted those of low degree;

[53]God has filled the hungry with good things,

and has sent the rich empty away.

[54]God has helped God's servant Israel,

in remembrance of God's mercy,

[55]as God spoke to our ancestors,

to Abraham, [*Sarah**,] and their posterity for ever."

[56]And Mary remained with Elizabeth about three months, and returned to her home.

[57]Now the time came for Elizabeth to be delivered, and she gave birth to a son.

□RSV vs. 43, 46 *Lord;* v. 45 *the Lord.* See Appendix.

*Addition to the text. RSV *Abraham and his.* See Appendix.

HOLY CROSS—SEPTEMBER 14

Lesson 1 ~ Numbers 21:4b-9

Moses makes a bronze serpent to heal victims of the plague of fiery serpents.

⁴The people became impatient on the way, ⁵and they spoke against God and against Moses, "Why have you brought us up out of Egypt to die in the wilderness? For there is no food and no water, and we loathe this worthless food." ⁶Then GOD sent fiery serpents among the people, and they bit the people, so that many people of Israel died. ⁷And the people came to Moses, and said, "We have sinned, for we have spoken against GOD and against you; pray to GOD to take away the serpents from us." So Moses prayed for the people. ⁸And GOD said to Moses, "Make a fiery serpent, and set it on a pole; and all who are bitten, when they see it, shall live." ⁹So Moses made a bronze serpent, and set it on a pole; and any one whom a serpent bit would look at the bronze serpent and live.

Psalm 98:1-5

¹O sing a new song to GOD,
    who has done marvelous things,
  whose right hand and holy arm
    have gained the victory!
²GOD has made known the victory,
    has revealed God's vindication in the sight of the nations.
³God has remembered God's steadfast love and faithfulness
    to the house of Israel.
All the ends of the earth have seen
    the victory of our God.
⁴Make a joyful noise to GOD, all the earth;
    break forth into joyous song and sing praises!
⁵Sing praises to GOD with the lyre,
    with the lyre and the sound of melody!

Psalm 78:1-2, 34-38 (alternate)

¹Give ear, O my people, to my teaching;
   incline your ears to the words of my mouth!
²I will open my mouth in a parable;
   I will utter mysterious sayings from of old.
³⁴When God slew them, they sought for God;
   they repented and sought God earnestly.
³⁵They remembered that God was their rock,
   the Most High God their redeemer.
³⁶But they flattered God with their mouths;
   they lied to God with their tongues.
³⁷Their heart was not steadfast toward God;
   they were not true to God's covenant.
³⁸Yet God, being compassionate,
   forgave their iniquity,
   and did not destroy them,
restraining God's anger often,
   and not arousing all God's wrath.

Lesson 2 ~ 1 Corinthians 1:18-24

Paul writes to the Corinthian church about the wisdom of God.

¹⁸For the word of the cross is folly to those who are perishing, but to us who are being saved it is the power of God. ¹⁹For it is written,
   "I will destroy the wisdom of the wise,
   and the cleverness of the clever I will thwart."
²⁰Where is the wise one? Where is the scribe? Where is the debater of this age? Has not God made foolish the wisdom of the world? ²¹For since, in the wisdom of God, the world did not know God through wisdom, it pleased God through the folly of what we preach to save those who believe. ²²For Jews demand signs and Greeks seek wisdom, ²³but we preach Christ crucified, a stumbling block to Jews and folly to Gentiles, ²⁴but to those who are called, both Jews and Greeks, Christ the power of God and the wisdom of God.

Those who believe in the Child of God will have eternal life.

¹³"No one has ascended into heaven but the one who descended from heaven, the Human One.° ¹⁴And as Moses lifted up the serpent in the wilderness, so must the Human One° be lifted up, ¹⁵that whoever believes in that one may have eternal life."

¹⁶For God so loved the world that God gave God's only Child,◇ that whoever believes in that Child should not perish but have eternal life. ¹⁷For God sent that Child◇ into the world, not to condemn the world, but that through that Child the world might be saved.

°RSV *Son of man.* See Appendix.
◇RSV v. 16 *his only Son;* v. 17 *the Son.* See Appendix.

ALL SAINTS—NOVEMBER 1

(Or the first Sunday in November)

Lesson 1 ~ Revelation 21:1-6a

The seer envisions a new heaven and a new earth.

[1]Then I saw a new heaven and a new earth; for the first heaven and the first earth had passed away, and the sea was no more. [2]And I saw the holy city, new Jerusalem, coming down out of heaven from God, prepared as a bride adorned for her husband; [3]and I heard a loud voice from the throne saying, "Behold, the dwelling of God is with human beings. God will dwell with them, and they shall be God's people, and God will indeed be with them, [4]and will wipe away every tear from their eyes, and death shall be no more, neither shall there be mourning nor crying nor pain any more, for the former things have passed away."

[5]And the one who sat upon the throne said, "Behold, I make all things new," to which was added, "Write this, for these words are trustworthy and true." [6]And the one who sat upon the throne said to me, "It is done! I am the Alpha and the Omega, the beginning and the end."

Psalm 24:1-6

[1]The earth is GOD's and the fulness thereof,
   the world and those who dwell therein;
[2]for God has founded it upon the seas,
   and established it upon the rivers.
[3]Who shall ascend the hill of GOD?
   And who shall stand in God's holy place?
[4]Those who have clean hands and a pure heart,
   who do not lift up their soul to what is false,
   and do not swear deceitfully.
[5]They will receive blessing from GOD,
   and vindication from the God of their salvation.
[6]Such is the generation of those who seek God,
   who seek the face of the God of Jacob.

Lesson 2 ~ Colossians 1:9-14

The apostle prays for the Christians at Colossae.

⁹And so, from the day we heard of it, we have not ceased to pray for you, asking that you be filled with the knowledge of God's will in all spiritual wisdom and understanding, ¹⁰to lead a life worthy of the Sovereign,□ pleasing in everything, bearing fruit in every good work and increasing in the knowledge of God. ¹¹May you be strengthened with all power, according to God's glorious might, for all endurance and patience with joy, ¹²giving thanks to God,⊗ who has qualified us to share in the inheritance of the saints in light. ¹³God has delivered us from the dominion of evil and transferred us to the realm* of God's beloved Child,◇ ¹⁴in whom we have redemption, the forgiveness of sins.

Gospel ~ John 11:32-44

Jesus raises Lazarus from the dead.

³²Then Mary came and saw Jesus, fell at Jesus' feet, and said, "If you had been here, my brother would not have died." ³³When Jesus saw her weeping, and the Jews who came with her also weeping, Jesus was deeply disturbed in spirit and troubled, ³⁴and said, "Where have you laid Lazarus?" They answered, "Come and see." ³⁵Jesus wept. ³⁶So the Jews said, "See how Jesus loved Lazarus!" ³⁷But some of them said, "Could not the one who opened the eyes of the blind person have kept Lazarus from dying?"

³⁸Then Jesus, deeply moved again, came to the tomb; it was a cave, and a stone lay upon it. ³⁹Jesus said, "Take away the stone." Martha, the sister of the dead Lazarus, said to Jesus, "By this time there will be an odor, for my brother has been dead four days." ⁴⁰Jesus said to her, "Did I not tell you that if you would believe you would see the glory of God?" ⁴¹So they took away the stone. And Jesus looked up and said, "[*God, my Mother and**] Father, I thank you that you have heard me. ⁴²I knew that you hear me always, but I have said this on account of the people standing by, that they may believe that you sent me." ⁴³Having said this, Jesus cried with a loud voice, "Lazarus, come out." ⁴⁴The dead man came out, hands and feet bound with bandages, and face wrapped with a cloth. Jesus said to them, "Unbind Lazarus, and let him go."

□RSV *Lord.* See Appendix.
⊗RSV *the Father.*
*RSV *kingdom.* See Appendix.
◇RSV *Son.* See Appendix.
*Addition to the text. See "Metaphor" and "God the Father and Mother" in the Appendix.

THANKSGIVING DAY

(Lection may also be used in Series A and C)

Lesson 1 ~ Joel 2:21-27

The prophet Joel praises God for the promise of an abundant harvest.

²¹Fear not, O land;
  be glad and rejoice,
  for GOD has done great things!
²²Fear not, you beasts of the field,
  for the pastures of the wilderness are green;
the tree bears its fruit,
  the fig tree and vine give their full yield.
²³Be glad, O children of Zion,
  and rejoice in the SOVEREIGN ONE, your God,
who has given the early rain for your vindication,
  and has poured down for you abundant rain,
  the early and the latter rain, as before.
²⁴The threshing floors shall be full of grain,
  the vats shall overflow with wine and oil.
²⁵I will restore to you the years
  which the swarming locust has eaten,
the hopper, the destroyer, and the cutter,
  my great army, which I sent among you.
²⁶You shall eat in plenty and be satisfied,
  and praise the name of the SOVEREIGN ONE your God,
  who has dealt wondrously with you.
And my people shall never again be put to shame.
²⁷You shall know that I am in the midst of Israel,
  and that I, the SOVEREIGN ONE, am your God and there is none else.
And my people shall never again be put to shame.

Psalm 126

[1]When GOD restored the fortunes of Zion,
　we were like those who dream.
[2]Then our mouth was filled with laughter,
　and our tongue with shouts of joy;
then they said among the nations,
　"GOD has done great things for them."
[3]GOD has done great things for us;
　we are glad.
[4]Restore our fortunes, O GOD,
　like the watercourses in the Negeb!
[5]May those who sow in tears
　reap with shouts of joy!
[6]Those who go forth weeping,
　bearing the seed for sowing,
shall come home with shouts of joy,
　bearing their sheaves of grain.

Lesson 2 ~ 1 Timothy 2:1-7

The writer urges prayer for people in high places, in the name of God and the one mediator Christ Jesus.

[1]First of all, then, I urge that supplications, prayers, intercessions, and thanksgivings be made for all people, [2]for rulers[□] and all who are in high positions, that we may lead a quiet and peaceable life, godly and respectful in every way. [3]This is good, and it is acceptable in the sight of God our Savior, [4]who desires all people to be saved and to come to the knowledge of the truth. [5]For there is one God, and there is one mediator between God and humankind, Christ Jesus, [6]who sacrificed self as a ransom for all, the testimony to which was borne at the proper time. [7]For this I was appointed a preacher and apostle (I am telling the truth, I am not lying), a teacher of the Gentiles in faith and truth.

[□]RSV *kings*. See Appendix.

Jesus teaches the disciples to trust in God.

²⁵Therefore I tell you, do not be anxious about your life, what you shall eat or what you shall drink, nor about your body, what you shall put on. Is not life more than food, and the body more than clothing? ²⁶Look at the birds of the air: they neither sow nor reap nor gather into barns, and yet [*God*] your heavenly Father [*and Mother**] feeds them. Are you not of more value than they? ²⁷And which of you by being anxious can add one cubit to your span of life? ²⁸And why are you anxious about clothing? Consider the lilies of the field, how they grow; they neither toil nor spin; ²⁹yet I tell you, even Solomon in all his glory was not arrayed like one of these. ³⁰But if God so clothes the grass of the field, which today is alive and tomorrow is thrown into the oven, will God not much more clothe you, O you of little faith? ³¹Therefore do not be anxious, saying, "What shall we eat?" or "What shall we drink?" or "What shall we wear?" ³²For the Gentiles seek all these things; and [*God*] your heavenly [*Mother and**] Father knows that you need them all. ³³But seek first God's realm* and God's righteousness, and all these things shall be yours as well.

---

*Addition to the text. See "Metaphor" and "God the Father and Mother" in the Appendix.
*RSV *kingdom.* See Appendix.

Appendix

Metaphor

A metaphor is a figure of speech used to extend meaning through comparison of dissimilars. For example, "Life is a dream" is a metaphor. The character of dreams is ascribed to life, and the meaning of "life" is thus extended. "Dream" is used as a screen through which to view "life." Two dissimilars are juxtaposed.

The statement "God is Father" is also a metaphor. Two dissimilars, "Father" and "God," are juxtaposed, and so the meaning of "God" is extended. Although "God the Father" has been a powerful metaphor for communicating the nature of God, like any metaphor it can become worn. It may even be interpreted literally, that is, as describing exactly. The dissimilars become similar. The metaphor becomes a proposition.

Now, if one were to say "God is Mother," the power of the metaphor would be apparent. To offer the image "God the Mother and Father" as a lens through which to view God elicits the response of a true metaphor, just as the statement "God is Father" once did. In this lectionary, "God the Father and Mother" is used as a formal equivalent of "the Father" or "God the Father." "God the Father" is clearly a metaphor, just as "God the Mother" is. God *is* not a father any more than God *is* a mother or than life *is* a dream. By reading and hearing "God the Father and Mother" we provide a metaphor for God that balances the more familiar *male* imagery for God with *female* imagery.

There are many female images for God in the scriptures. For example, God as mother is found in the Old Testament: "Now I will cry out like a woman in travail" (Isa. 42:14) and "As one whom his mother comforts, so I will comfort you" (Isa. 66:13); and God is compared to a nurse carrying a suckling child (Num. 11:12). In the New Testament, the parable of the woman seeking the lost coin (Luke 15:8-10) functions as a female image for God. Metaphors are figurative and open-ended. Their meanings vary from hearer to hearer, but they are not dispensable, for there is no other way by which to say directly what the metaphor communicates. A metaphor provides a new way of seeing.

(*) [*God*] the Father [*and Mother*] (RSV the Father; God the Father, God our Father)

One of the outstanding characteristics of the Christian faith is its emphasis on the personal nature of God. While God is also described in impersonal terms (Rock, Light, Love), personal imagery prevails.

"Father" is one such personal term. The Gospels record that when Jesus prayed he called God "Father" (see Mark 14:36), and frequently, especially in the Gospel of John, Jesus refers to God as Father. To refer to God as Father has little precedent in the Old Testament. For Jesus, *Abba* ("Father") was a sacred word, pointing to the mysterious intimacy Jesus had with God ("No one knows the Son except the Father, and no one knows the Father except the Son," Matt. 11:27), and pointing to the intimate relationship his disciples also had with God ("Call no man your father on earth, for you have one Father, who is in heaven," Matt. 23:9). Jesus' own use of the word "Father" in addressing God supported the church's claim that Jesus was the "Son."

That Jesus called God "Father" is the basis for our thinking about Jesus Christ as one of the three Persons of the Trinity. As the words of the Nicene Creed state, Jesus Christ is "begotten, not made, being of one substance with the Father," a relationship that cannot be claimed by any created being. The relationship that the Father/Son imagery of the New Testament seeks to describe is that of Jesus being of the same substance as God. But if God the Son proceeded from God the Father alone, this procession is both a male and a female action, a begetting *and* a birth. God is the motherly father of the child who comes forth. It was the orthodox dogmatic tradition which most dramatically defended Trinitarian language about God, and it is this tradition which speaks most boldly of God in images of both genders. According to the Third Council of Toledo, "it must be held that the Son was created, neither out of nothingness nor yet out of any substance, but that He was begotten or born out of the Father's womb *(de utero Patris)*, that is, out of His very essence."

The phrase used in this lectionary, "God the Father and Mother," is an attempt to express in a fresh way the same intimacy, caring, and freedom as is found in Jesus' identification of God as *Abba*. It is also an attempt to hold on to the important Christian belief that Jesus is the Child of God. Just as we do not create our children, but give them birth out of our very selves, we believe that God did not create Jesus, but that God gave birth to Jesus.

It is also the case that Christians rejected as pagan the view that God is father of the world. For Christians, God is Father in relation to the Son. Christians are brought into this relationship because they are adopted as "sons," or heirs (Rom. 8:15, 23; Gal. 4:5; Eph. 1:5).

God, the Almighty Father, considered as the author of all things, is a Zeus-like figure, sitting on Mt. Olympus, a remote and solitary power. Such an authoritarian God causes earthly authorities to take their cues from "Him." God as Almighty Father legitimates the authority of the fathers of the church, the father of the country or of the family. This is not the way Jesus spoke of God as Father. *Abba* is an accessible, caring, revered figure.

The image of God as Father has been used to support the excessive authority of earthly fathers in a patriarchal social structure. The metaphor "God the Father and Mother" points to the close relationship between language about God and language about the human community. The mutuality and coequality of the persons of the Trinity is a model for human community and especially appropriate, therefore, for readings prepared for worship. Those who worship in the Christian church are struggling to bring about a community where there is no longer male or female, but where all are one in Christ Jesus and joint heirs according to the promise (Gal. 3:28). (See Metaphor.)

(⊗) God (RSV my Father, the Father)

In the Gospel of John, and occasionally elsewhere, RSV "Father" is rendered "God."

(◻) Sovereign, God the Sovereign One, etc. (RSV Lord, Lord, etc.)

According to Hebrew tradition, the personal name for God, *Yahweh,* was introduced by Moses at the time of the exodus. Sometime after 538 B.C. the name was no longer pronounced for fear that it would be profaned, even though it continued to be written in the text of the scriptures. From that time on, the chief word read in place of the divine name was *adonai*—an honorific title translated "my lord." In those places in the RSV where the underlying Hebrew text contains the divine name, and not simply the word *adonai*, the typography is changed to Lord. Where the divine name *(Yahweh)* is found in the original text (RSV "the Lord"), this lectionary renders it as "God" or "the Sovereign One." The latter equivalent is used especially where the name is emphasized or where literary concerns seem to make that wording preferable. Occasionally the divine name is found in combination with the word for God *(Yahweh elohim)* or with the word for Lord *(adonai Yahweh)*. These are rendered in the RSV as "the Lord God" and "the Lord God," respectively. In this lectionary, the former is rendered as "God the Sovereign One" and the latter as "the Sovereign God." In this lectionary, the Hebrew word *elohim* is rendered "God," as in the RSV.

When the Old Testament was translated into Greek, *elohim* was usually translated by *theos*, meaning "God." Both the name *Yahweh* and the title *adonai* were usually rendered by the word *kyrios*, meaning

"Lord." It was the Greek translation of the Hebrew Old Testament which the New Testament authors read. In the New Testament, therefore, the primary terms used to designate God are *theos* ("God") and *kyrios* ("Lord"); and the word *kyrios* was also taken over by the church as a primary way of designating Jesus: "Jesus is Lord."

Kyrios has a wide range of other meanings. It is used for the *owner* of possessions, for the *head* of a family, or for the *master* of a house or of slaves. In the vocative it often means "Sir." *Kyrios* is usually translated into English by "Lord" (in reference to God or Jesus) or "lord" (in reference to a man), a word that in common usage means a man with power and authority, such as a titled nobleman.

Because it is a gender-specific word, "Lord," when used of either God or Christ, connotes a male being. However, since the church believes that God transcends gender and that the risen Christ is one with God, in this lectionary *kyrios*, occasionally rendered "God" or "Christ," generally has been translated as "Sovereign," a word which, like "Lord," also means one who is supreme in power and authority. No theological difference is intended by the change, but "Sovereign" is free of purely male connotations. Women as well as men are sovereigns. Elizabeth II is currently sovereign of England.

"Sovereign" thus has another advantage for the translator over "Lord." It is a word in contemporary usage in the political arena, and is not confined to religious usage as is virtually the case with the word "Lord" in the United States. Not only are there living sovereigns in monarchical societies but nations as well are said to exercise sovereignty. The designation of Jesus Christ as *kyrios* by the early church carried precisely such a political meaning: Jesus, not Caesar, was *kyrios*. Christians believed that Jesus Christ is supreme over all earthly authorities. Hence, the status of the authority of the *Sovereign Jesus Christ* in relation to any national sovereignty is expressed in a contemporary idiom which brings to the fore the revolutionary significance of the statement *Kyrios Iēsous* (Jesus is Lord [Sovereign]) for the history of the church.

Hebrew	RSV	Inclusive-Language Lectionary
Elohim	God	God
Adonai	Lord	God
Yahweh	LORD	GOD, or the SOVEREIGN ONE
Yahweh Elohim, or *Elohim Yahweh*	the LORD God	God the SOVEREIGN ONE
Adonai Yahweh, or *Yahweh Adonai*	the Lord GOD	the Sovereign GOD

(°) Child, Child of God (RSV Son, Son of God)

"Son" is used as a designation of Jesus as the Messiah (Matt. 1:1; 9:27). At Jesus' baptism there was a voice from heaven: "This is my beloved Son" (Matt. 3:17). Jesus also refers to himself as "Son," though seldom except in the Gospel of John, where the self-designation is common.

A son is male, and of course the historical person Jesus was a man. As the Gospels depict Jesus, his maleness is not said to have any significance for salvation. It is the fact that Jesus was *human* that is crucial, both for Jesus' designation as the Christ and for Jesus' work of salvation.

If the fact that Jesus was a male has no Christological significance, then neither has the fact that Jesus was a *son* and not a *daughter*. Therefore, in this lectionary the formal equivalent "Child" or "Child of God" is used for "Son" when the latter has Christological significance, and the masculine pronouns that refer to "Child" ("Son") are rendered as "Child." Thus, all hearers of the lectionary readings will be enabled to identify themselves with Jesus' *humanity*.

In traditional language, Jesus as "the Son" makes believers "sons" and therefore heirs. In this lectionary, Jesus as the Child of God makes believers—men and women—children of God and therefore heirs. When Jesus is called "Son of God" it is not Jesus' male character that is of primary importance but Jesus' intimate relationship with God (see Matt. 11:25-27). Other connotations of "sonship" are divine authority (see Matt. 28:18-20), eschatological revelation, and freedom (see Rom. 8:21).

(°) The Human One (RSV the Son of man)

The term "the Son of man" is found frequently in the Gospels and almost nowhere else in the New Testament. Only Jesus uses the term (with a single exception), and the Gospel writers always intended the term to refer to Jesus. How do the Gospel authors interpret its meaning?

Much light would be shed on the meaning of the term if there were clear antecedents to its use in the Gospels, but any such antecedents are now impossible to demonstrate. It cannot be shown that Jewish use of the term "Son (son) of man" has influenced its use in the Gospels; in fact, the term does not appear to have functioned as a title prior to its application to Jesus by the church. Its meaning varies in different contexts, but one basic connotation is hard to miss: it speaks about a male human being, a "son" of a "man." In this lectionary, the term "the Human One" is used as a formal equivalent for "the Son of man." That formal equivalent is not derived from or dependent on any particular judgment as to the background of "the Son of man" in Judaism, and is not intended to prejudice in any way the ongoing discussion of that question. We believe, however, that the title "the Human One" is open to the same nuances of interpretation allowed by the title "the Son of man."

(*) Realm of God (RSV Kingdom, Kingdom of God)

The Greek word used frequently in the New Testament and usually translated by the male-specific word "kingdom" has generally been rendered in this lectionary as "realm." The Greek word refers either to the activity or God (i.e., God's "kingship" or "reign" or "rule") or to the state of affairs brought about by God (i.e., God's "kingdom" or "realm"). In this lectionary, the word "realm" has been used rather than the word "reign." "Realm" is closer in meaning to "kingdom," which is the customary English rendering, and is preferred to the word "reign" because of the possible confusion of that word with the homonyms "rain" or "rein." The Hebrew word usually translated "kingdom" in the RSV is occasionally rendered "kingdom" in this lectionary but is also rendered as "sovereignty" or "realm."

(□) Ruler, Monarch (RSV King)

The word "king" is used in the Bible both in reference to earthly royal figures and as a metaphor for God. In this lectionary "King" as a metaphor for God is rendered as "Ruler," "Sovereign," or occasionally as "Monarch." The word "king" is retained in reference to specific earthly kings, such as David, and in stories and parables about kings.

Sisters and Brothers, Friends, Neighbors, Followers (RSV Brethren)

The contemporary use of such phrases as "sisters and brothers in Christ" to address members of the church is helpful in clarifying how the words "brother" and "brethren" are used in the Bible. In Hebrew usage, the same word could refer to a sibling, a more distant relative, a neighbor, or a member of one's community or race. Paul appears to reflect such a broad use of the word "brethren" in Rom. 9:3, where "my brethren" (translated in this lectionary as "my own people") is the same as "my kinsmen by race." In Greek, "brother" was often used to refer to a friend, or to a person with whom one shares a common purpose, but not necessarily a blood relative.

In the New Testament, the plural form of the word "brother" appears to have been intended to include both women and men. For example, in Luke 21:16 "brothers" is certainly intended to mean "sisters and brothers"; and when Paul addressed Christians as "brethren" (see Rom. 8:12; 1 Cor. 2:1) he was surely including women as well as men. In such cases of direct address, "brethren" has been rendered in this lectionary either as "sisters and brothers" ("brothers and sisters") or as "friends." In postresurrection sayings attributed to Jesus, "brethren" is translated as "followers" (Matt. 28:10) or "friends" (John 20:17), to make clear that the reference is to the nascent church and not to Jesus' siblings.

(*) Addition of Women's Names to the Text

In several instances, women's names have been added to the text in this lectionary. These names are offered where generation or origin of the people is a major concern. The additional names therefore make explicit what was formerly implicit, namely, women's obvious role in childbearing. An example is, "As God spoke to our ancestors, to Abraham, [*Sarah,*] and their posterity for ever" (Luke 1:55). Other passages in Series B are Ps. 105:6; Isa. 63:16; Acts 3:13; Rom. 4:16; Heb. 2:16. The addition to the text is placed in brackets and is italicized to make clear that it is an addition. If the additional words involve a change in the verb form, the RSV rendering is in the footnote.

(ᵛ) The Jews

The term "the Jews" occurs very frequently in the Gospel of John. Sometimes it refers in a straightforward, historical way to the ethnic people of whom Jesus was one and among whom Jesus lived out his life. Sometimes, however, it is used almost as a code word for religious leaders who misunderstand the true identity of Christ. When "the Jews" is used in the former sense in the lections from the Gospel of John, it remains unchanged in this lectionary. When it is used in the latter sense, it is rendered "the religious authorities" so as to minimize what could be perceived as anti-Semitism in the Gospel of John.

Other Exclusive Imagery: Darkness

The New Testament imagery of light versus darkness (John 1:5; Rom. 13:12) is used to contrast good with evil. The equation of darkness with evil, or that which is done in secret and out of the light, has unfortunately led some persons and groups to condemn and reject anything that is black or any dark-hued person as evil or somehow condemned by God. This color symbolism has its equally inaccurate and unfortunate correlative in the equation of light with white—with what is true, good, and loved of God. For example, the William Bright hymn "And Now, O Father" has the line, "From tainting mischief keep them white and clear . . . ," and in the Bible "Wash me, and I shall be whiter than snow" (Ps. 51:7). While the biblical context may be free from racist intent, the too-easy misconception that dark people are also condemned and to be avoided has led to the use in this lectionary of terminology other than "darkness" as a metaphor for sin and evil.

Use of "They," "Them," "Themselves" and "Their" as Singular Pronouns

In some cases, indefinite singular pronouns are rendered in this lectionary by "they," "them," "themselves," or "their." This usage is recognized as appropriate by the National Council of Teachers of English in its *Guidelines for Nonsexist Use of Language in NCTE Publications*. The *Oxford English Dictionary* says that "they" is "often used in reference to a singular noun made universal by *every, any,* or *no,* etc., or is applied to one of either sex (= 'he or she')." Those grammarians who oppose this usage follow common practice established by an 1850 Act of Parliament declaring that "he" is generic and legally includes "she." That declaration in turn was based on a rule invented in 1746 by John Kirby: the male gender is "more comprehensive" than the female. This lectionary follows the precedent of St. John Fisher (1535), who wrote that God "never forsaketh any creature unlesse they before have forsaken themselves," and William Shakespeare, who urged "everyone to rest themselves." See Thomas Emswiler and Sharon Neufer, *Women and Worship,* revised and expanded edition (Harper & Row, 1984).

(⁺) Changes in the Table of Readings and Psalms

The mandate of the Inclusive-Language Lectionary Committee is to recast the language of the RSV in those places where male-biased or other exclusive language could be modified to reflect an inclusiveness of all persons. Consistent with the goal of this mandate the Committee has determined that it is also appropriate to add certain alternative lections about women that have not been included in the listing recommended by the North American Committee on Calendar and Lectionary. These alternate readings are:

Epiphany 2, Lesson 2	Rom. 16:1-7
Lent 4, Lesson 1	Judg. 4:4-9
Pentecost 12, Lesson 1	2 Sam. 14:4-17
Pentecost 12, Gospel	John 8:2-11

Furthermore, the Committee has occasionally shortened a lection or substituted a reading where consistent with our mandate. These alterations and substitutions are:

Epiphany 2, Lesson 2	1 Cor. 6:12-15a, 19-20 (prescribed reading: 6:12-20)
Pentecost 5, Lesson 1	2 Sam. 5:1-5 (prescribed reading: 5:1-12)
Pentecost 14, Lesson 2	Eph. 6:1-4 substituted for Eph. 5:21-33
Annunciation, Lesson 1	Ps. 45 not included

Notes

[a]The word *Abba!* is an intimate form, and Jesus' use of this term to refer to God was radically nontraditional. This warrants the use of nontraditional intimate language in contemporary reference to God. See Gal. 4:6 (Christmas 1, Lesson 2, p. 32, and January 1 [Holy Name of Jesus; Solemnity of Mary, Mother of God], Lesson 2, p. 37); Mark 14:36 (Lent 6, Passion Sunday, Gospel, p. 88); Rom. 8:15 (Trinity, Lesson 2, p. 143).

[b]The term for eunuch (*saris* O.T.; *eunouchos* N.T.) more regularly refers to a high government official than to one who is excluded from the covenant because of castration. The term is used of Potiphar (Gen. 39:1) and of the chief butler and the chief baker in the Joseph story (Gen. 40:2, 7), but it is translated as "officer" of Pharaoh. It is also used of royal officials in the Kingdom of Judah (2 Kings 8:6; 24:12, 15). References to religious exclusion because of physical impairment (e.g., Deut. 23:1) reflect ancient ritual law which is to be evaluated in relation to God's promise to honor the faithful eunuch (Isa. 56:4-5). Jesus is said to use the term "eunuch" not only to refer to those who are eunuchs from birth or by castration, but also to refer metaphorically to those who remain celibate (Matt. 19:12). Page 128.

[c]The labels "the circumcision" and "the uncircumcision" refer to the external mark of the deep divisions between Jews and Gentiles, and thus also of people's participation in or exclusion from the covenant with God. These labels are inherently exclusive, not only in their designation of the ethnic and religious division but also in their reflection of the assumption that only males could be counted as members of the covenant community. The author's point is precisely that such religious criteria no longer determine one's relationship to God. Rather, "now in Christ Jesus you who once were far off have been brought near" (Eph. 2:13). In Christ such "dividing walls of hostility" are superseded, and the new covenant is open to Gentiles as well as to Jews, to women as well as to men. Page 168.

[d]This literary pun on "man" (*ish*) and "woman" (*ishshah*) intends to show relationship rather than biological origin. The relationship is one of equality: "bone of my bones and flesh of my flesh" (Gen. 2:23). Page 201.

Index of Readings for Year B

*Based on the Lectionary prepared for trial use by
the North American Committee on
Calendar and Lectionary*

254